Three Myths of Internet Governance

Three Myths of Internet Governance

Making Sense of Networks, Governance and Regulation

Richard Collins

intellect Bristol, UK / Chicago, USA

First published in the UK in 2009 by
Intellect Books, The Mill, Parnall Road, Fishponds, Bristol, BS16 3JG, UK

First published in the USA in 2009 by Intellect Books, The University of Chicago Press, 1427 E. 60th Street, Chicago, IL 60637, USA

A catalogue record for this book is available from
the British Library.

Cover designer: Holly Rose
Copy-editor: Heather Owen
Typesetting: Mac Style, Beverley, E. Yorkshire

ISBN 978-1-84150-233-5

Printed and bound by Gutenberg Press, Malta.

Contents

Acknowledgements

Thanks to Manuel Alvarado, Danny Birchall, Carla Bodo, Les Budd, Matthew Collins, Tony Curzon-Price, Roger Darlington, Ian Jarvie, Tim Jordan, Johannes Piepenbrink, Celestino Spada, Angus Stewart, Grahame Thompson, John Tulloch and Howard Williams for information and/or discussions on these matters and to many interviewees for their generous cooperation and commitment of time. Chapter 8 draws on research made possible by financial support from the Department of Sociology at the Open University and the joint Open University/University of Manchester ESRC CRESC research centre. It was completed when the author was Senior Research Fellow at the Annenberg Center for Communication at the University of Southern California. The author expresses his gratitude and indebtedness to the Open University, CRESC and to the Annenberg Center (and to his colleagues there especially the Director Professor Jonathan Aronson) for the scholarly support and stimulation the Center provided.

Chapters were previously published as follows.

Chapters One and Two. Chapter One as 'Online and legacy media in the UK', in *Economia della Cultura* 4/2008 pp. 523–35. Chapter Two in *Economia della Cultura* 1/2009 pp. 53–68.

Chapter Three. 'Three Myths of Internet Governance considered in the Context of the UK', *Prometheus* 22.3 2004, pp. 267–91 and, revised, as 'Networks, Markets and Hierarchies. Governance and Regulation of the UK Internet', in *Parliamentary Affairs*. 59. 2006. pp. 314–30.

Chapter Four. 'Die BBC, das Internet und "Public Value"', *Aus Politik und Zeitgeschichte* 9–10. 2009, pp. 32–8. At http://www.bpb.de/files/ZXV87B.pdf

Chapter Five. 'Hierarchy to Homeostasis? Hierarchy, Markets and Networks in UK Media and Communications Governance', *Media Culture and Society* 30.3. 2008, pp. 295–317.

Chapter Six. 'Trust and trustworthiness in the fourth and fifth estates', *International Journal of Communication*. 2. 2009, pp. 1-20. At http://ijoc.org/ojs/index.php/ijoc/index

Chapter Seven. 'Associative or Communal Society. The Globalisation of Media and Communications and the Claim for Communality', in P. Askonas and A. Stewart (eds.) (2000), *Social Inclusion: Possibilities and Tensions,* Basingstoke: Macmillan, pp. 186–204.

Chapter Eight. 'Rawls, Fraser, Redistribution, Recognition and The World Summit on The Information Society', *International Journal of Communication* 1. 2007. pp. 1–23. At http://ijoc.org/ojs/index.php/ijoc/article/view/51/16.

Chapter Nine. 'Trilateralism, Legitimacy and The Working Group on Internet Government', *Information Polity* 2007 v 12. 1–2, pp. 15–28.

Chapter Ten. 'E-Governance and the Governance of the Global Internet', in L Budd and L-J Harris (eds.) (2009), *eGovernance: Managing or Governing?* New York: Routledge, pp. 53–70.

Introduction

These essays reflect my interest in problems arising in the world outside the academy and in particular those posed by the 'new' (if the Internet can still be called new) medium of the Internet. The Internet is not only an object of fascination in itself but demands attention because it is dramatically reshaping 'legacy' media – notably the long established mass media of newspapers and broadcasting. Unlike the 'legacy' media world which sharply divided private, one-to-one media (posts and telephony) from public one-to-many media (cinema, radio and television, newspapers) the Internet makes possible any communicative relationship from one-to-one to one-to-many. The Internet decouples price from time and distance and, because based on the infrastructure of the global any-to-any telecommunications system, makes communication to the far side of the globe as easy as that to the next room in the house: Skype, e-mail, file transfer and web browsing make the online world one of virtual co-presence. The Internet erodes the categorical distinction between producer and consumer that characterized one-to-many media and has called into existence the 'prosumer': one who originates, receives and interacts with Internet-based content. The Internet is, as Kevin Werbach (1997: 1) claimed, a substitute for any and all existing media and thus, potentially at least, can reconfigure any or all media markets. The Internet therefore makes a very big difference.

But most Internet scholarship takes the United States' experience as its focus. There are easily understandable historical reasons for this – not least that the Internet started in the United States (US) and the US remains the largest single Internet space (though not for much longer). Much work of real and enduring quality has come from US scholars but their focus on the idiosyncrasies of the US has, misleadingly, constructed a world of for-profit domain name registries, fretting about network neutrality and the like as a global experience. It is not. The World Summit on the Information Society (WSIS) provided a striking instance of a clash between US Internet-think and rival paradigms, as my Chapters 8–10 claim. The tense, and as yet unresolved, conflicts which figured through the WSIS exemplify a general truth: that the reciprocal shaping of the Internet and its surrounding contexts depends on the nature of those contexts – juridical, economic, political and media-cultural. The Internet is global – and that is one of the most important and wonderful things about it – but it is also local and national and that is not yet sufficiently acknowledged in scholarly engagement with it. Accordingly, my focus here is on the Internet as a global force situated in specific, largely United Kingdom (UK), contexts.

My object is, then, a particular one, but what of my style of engagement with it? All of the above might justify many sorts of scholarly engagement with the Internet by those of us in the media studies trade. Why my sort, distinguished as it is by both an empirical and sceptical turn of mind, framed by my engagement, from a university base, with concrete issues of media regulation and policy (and liberally sprinkled with arcane gleanings from those worlds – few, after all, think life long enough to get excited by news of the market share of narrowband unmetered Internet access in Hull) and informed by a methodology of hanging about with businessmen (and women), policy makers and politicians? The empirical and sceptical mindset just seems to be hardwired – some of us are just stonekickers in the Dr Johnson mode (though not all stonekickers necessarily embrace footbruising as the method most likely to change an idealist's mind). But why the engagement with the world outside the academy? In his *Seventh Letter* (Plato 360 B.C) Plato confesses his fear of being taken 'wholly and solely a mere man of words' when accounting for his entry into the public life of Syracuse. He then reversions this story, putting on it a more positive spin, describing it rather as an act of obedience 'to reason and justice'. This confession (whether or not actually written by Plato doesn't much matter) resonates with me. Despite Plato's intervention in the policy domain, having neither convinced Dionysius to become a Platonist nor prevented Carthage from invading Sicily, the siren call of a metaphorical Syracuse has been heard by not a few academics. But those of us seduced by Syracuse are embracing a notoriously uneasy relationship. For a paid intellectual, with ex-officio duties to the academy, to look to the world beyond the academy is hazardous: the scholarly norm is to look inward to the academy and to one's peers. Hence the difficulties research councils experience in securing dissemination to non-academic users, the low scores customarily attributed to extra-academic 'measures of esteem' in our regular academic pecking-order sessions such as the RAE (Research Assessment Exercise) and the well-reciprocated customary mutual disdain with which scholars, journalists and policy makers address each other.

It would be too much to claim that I have influenced public life but engagement with public life has exercised, and continues to exercise, a seductive attraction. I like my work to be tested against the public life criteria of accuracy, timeliness and usefulness. I find those engaged in the world to be good sources of data and often of well-founded and penetrating analyses. I have been fortunate that my skirmishes with Syracuse have not earned me Plato's reward of living 'outside the acropolis among the mercenaries' (though some might think that well characterizes the contemporary academic lot). Perhaps because I think the real world problems and issues, that almost invariably form my starting point, can be clarified through recourse to the concepts generated in the academy. I write 'concepts' for I think there is little that deserves the name 'theory' in the social science academy – though there are analytical concepts with genuine heuristic power. But what does a new 'thing' (and, in Chapter 3, I propose that the Internet is not a 'thing' – but this fallacious metaphor offers a useful economy here) do to an established corpus of social scientific concepts – globalization, civil society, network theory and so on? Does it confirm or qualify concepts such as these which inform and underpin dominant social scientific enquiries and heuristics? And how do these concepts (which, not to be too idealist about it, have a life of their own and inform and direct human actions and thereby shape the world including the Internet and 'legacy' media) help us understand the novel phenomena and practices which have drawn and maintained my attention over the last decade and more? Here are some of my answers.

There are four principal foci considered in these essays: the relationship between the Internet and 'legacy' media (notably in Chapters 1 and 2); the Internet in the UK (Chapters 1–5); the global governance of the Internet (Chapters 8–10) and the reciprocal impact of the Internet and established scholarly conceptual paradigms (notably in Chapters 5–8). All of these themes address the 'three myths' signalled in the title of this book. The three myths are identified in Chapter 3 as first, the myth dominant in the public policy domain that Internet governance is best when the market decides; second, the myth dominant in scholarly discussion of the Internet that network governance and self-regulation is both pervasive, effective and applicable to the Internet as a distinct, bounded and singular 'thing'; third, the myth that Internet governance is quite distinct from the governance of 'legacy media' (notably the established electronic communications media of broadcasting and telephony) and that the national is relatively unimportant in Internet governance.

The first and second myths, that the market should prevail and that network governance is pervasive, are challenged in accounts, notably in Chapters 3, 5 and 10, which show both that different governance regimes (market, network and hierarchy) actually do prevail and that their combination has resulted in, by and large, effective governance which serves public interest well (i.e. that they *should* prevail). The myth of the Internet as a distinct 'thing' is challenged in the accounts (notably in Chapters 1–4) which show that the Internet is both intimately interrelated with 'legacy' media and (in Chapter 3) a series of separate, interconnected, layers rather than a single entity. The Internet reconfigures the global and the national (almost all chapters but Chapters 3, 5, 7 and 10 in particular) but, despite the comparative lack of attention to the national that exists in much Internet scholarship – part of the third myth: both the global and the national are clearly relevant – the Internet articulates these relationships in new ways. The Internet has established new phenomena and relationships; its intrinsically interactive and dialogic character, notably in Web 2.0 applications, is considered in Chapter 6 and the new institutions and practices of global Internet governance are considered in Chapters 8–10.

Chapters 1 and 2 focus on the Internet's impact on 'legacy media', notably in the UK. The Internet constitutes a threat to legacy media in that time spent on the Internet tends to reduce time spent on 'legacy' media such as broadcasting and newspapers; advertising is migrating to the Internet from legacy media: much of the classified and recruitment advertising, that formerly sustained newspapers, is now on eBay and recruitment websites; display advertising, that formerly supported both broadcasting and newspapers, has migrated to search engines. To be sure, some advertising will remain with 'legacy' media but much seems to have gone for good. But the Internet also offers opportunities. There are lower barriers to entry, and the Internet thus offers some potential mitigation of the concentration of media ownership, despite the powerful advantages to online operation that offline incumbency offers, which has threatened media diversity and pluralism. Novel media hybrids, including 'bi-media' operations, have entered the market and, latterly, users have been able to access, and produce, inventive combinations of text, sounds and images via the Internet. Even more important, perhaps, the hard, categorical, distinctions between media producers and consumers have eroded as Web 2.0 has made possible another form of hybridity: the 'prosumer' who, at best, is able to collectively deliberate and collectively create authoritative forms of content via Web 2.0 platforms.

Web 2.0 offers opportunities to enhance trust and to mitigate a pervasive popular mistrust of the media. But it is important to recognize that mistrust is sometimes well founded – trust is not always a good thing. To restore and to sustain trust is laudable only when the object of trust is trustworthy. Otherwise those who trust are condemned to experience happiness of the kind Swift defined in section IX of *A Tale of a Tub*, (Swift 1704) that is 'the sublime and refined point of felicity, called, the possession of being well deceived; the serene peaceful state of being a fool among knaves'.

However, despite the perils of placing trust in those who do not deserve it, Web 2.0 applications do make possible a novel, trust-enhancing, dialogic relationship between media 'prosumers'. This relationship is based in a traditional communicative mode, delightfully characterized by Onora O'Neill (on whose arguments I draw) as a distinctive property of the time of the 'Kings of old' (O'Neill 2002a: Lecture 5).

I argue, principally in Chapter 6 but foreshadowed in Chapter 2, that Internet content may exemplify an O'Neillian dialogue-based trustworthiness and authoritativeness (a form of trustworthiness) deriving from collective deliberation, peer assessment and consensus building. Wikipedia and Slashdot provide outstanding cases in point. But, of course, dialogue and peer consensus are neither sufficient nor necessary for the creation of trusted and trustworthy content. Dialogue and peer consensus, whether based on Web 2.0 or the face-to-face encounters of the times of the kings of old, may facilitate and engender trust and facilitate provision of trustworthy content but they do not provide the only route towards the achievement of such objectives. O'Neill herself expresses her mistrust of what she calls 'new communication technologies' and counsels, sensibly and constructively, a different route to trust and trustworthiness through the use of stronger and more binding professional codes to govern journalistic practice. But, whether or not she is right about new media, her notion of trust based in dialogue provides a fruitful point of departure for understanding the basis of the success of (some) Web 2.0 content and also points towards powerful normative bases for action.

The intimate mutually-determining relationship between 'legacy' and new, internet-based, media means that it now makes less and less sense to consider either the Internet or broadcast and print mass media as distinct and separate entities. Convergence has taken place – imperfectly, unevenly and incompletely but the paradigm has changed and both scholarship and policy should acknowledge this fundamental structural change. In Chapter 3, I describe how the structure and governance of the Internet in the UK exemplifies a paradigmatic reconfiguration of the institutions of media and communications. These are changing from a characteristically vertically integrated to horizontally disaggregated form. Convergence is also making (and this is by now so firmly established a proposition as to be a truism) media governance, regulation and organization global – as I argue in Chapters 7–10. But globalization does not manifest itself identically everywhere – as I argue explicitly in Chapter 3, the national may still count for much.

But globalization means that hierarchical governance (at least when organized nationally – and there is no fully effective and comprehensive transnational global system of media and communication governance and regulation) can no longer be fully effective. Accordingly, other governance regimes, sometimes in conjunction with hierarchy, have provided for a remarkable system of coordination which sustains the strikingly effective international Internet system of electronic communication – though this integrated system of coordination, which largely evolved without systematic central planning and direction, has distinctive national and local modalities and mutations.

Strikingly effective? Does this Pollyannaish term really apply to Africa where only about 6 per cent of Africans have access to the Internet?[1] Perhaps so when African access rates are increasing by 1,100 per cent annually and even in one of Africa's most mature electronic communications markets, South Africa, access is increasing by more than 91 per cent annually. The metaphor of the half full and half empty glass, which I have used in respect of the UK, can be used to characterize the Internet internationally. The half-empty-glass-theory would point to the dramatic digital divide between Africa and, say, the Yellow Sea Asian tigers. Proponents of the half-full-glass-theory would point to the rapid catching up of under-Internetted localities as the ITU's ICT Development Index testifies. The International Telecommunication Union ICT index of 2007 (ITU 2009) shows striking, albeit unequally distributed, increases in global Internet access between 2002 and 2007: the number of French homes with Internet access grew from 23 per cent to 49 per cent; Albanian homes grew from 2.8 per cent to 7.8 per cent; Latvian homes from 8.5 per cent to 51 per cent; South African from 1.9 per cent to 4.8 per cent; UK homes from 50 per cent to 67 per cent and so on.

Governance is, of course, a major theme of all these essays. In Chapter 5, I consider explicitly the claims made by Castells and others that network governance is a newly salient modality of modern governance and enjoys an elective affinity with the Internet. Taylor (2001) has argued that the complexity of modern societies mandates network governance and Castells (1996: 469), more empirically, that networks constitute a 'new social morphology' which is based on information technology. What empirical basis is there for such claims? My examination of the Internet in the UK (Chapter 3) provides some support for them – as it does for the claims of Moran (2003) and others to the effect that governance in the UK, including media governance has shifted from hierarchical to market governance. But these claims are not readily fully reconciled. Rather I propose in Chapter 5, using the evidence of the UK, that there has been a shift (albeit incomplete) towards self-regulating, homeostatic, systems of governance – exemplified by both market and network governance – though hierarchy is far from absent. Repressed hierarchy returns because both market and network governance have distinctive forms of failure, each of which calls up a hierarchical response so that public policy objectives may be achieved. Moreover, the nature of each distinct form of governance is subject to change and transmutation: hierarchical governance in the UK has become, for example, more consultative and transparent but also, because more discretionary, somewhat less predictable.

In Chapter 5 I instance the BBC as a major institutional manifestation of hierarchical media governance in the UK, and in Chapter 3 refer to one of its most controversial impacts on the UK Internet content sector. Chapter 4 focuses specifically on the BBC's engagement with the Internet. It was an early adopter[2] and the BBC has played a leading role in UK Internet development and both the dark and light sides of its forceful online presence demand attention. It has facilitated access to an enormous range of content, projected a UK view of the world across the world, pioneered online access to broadcast content but has also been found to have damaged the potential of other providers and to have acted anti-competitively.

In Chapter 7 I propose that the Internet both exemplifies and accelerates the globalization of communications. It is claimed that one of the chief consequences of this process is, or will be, the dissolution of social cohesion. I argue however, that the globalization of communications is threatening only if cohesion is thought to depend on a shared culture, on what Max Weber called (and his term is borrowed in the title of the essay) communalism. If, alternatively, cohesion is thought to depend on (Weber's term again) associative relationships, then communications globalization may be less challenging than anticipated; both in respect of the pragmatic issue of social cohesion and the issue of principle – a putative right to collective identity. The empirical examples considered reflect the time at which the essay was written but time has not, I think, undermined either the plausibility of my arguments or the force of the evidence cited. I wrote, of media, language, social cohesion and rights that 'the nearest to which Europe has come to a shared contemporary symbolic culture is in the English language media – notably television and film' and supported my proposition by citing the proportions of English and non-English channels of European television. But I believe the same argument could be equally well sustained by citing the salience of English on the Internet where the current preponderance of English seems to be of a similar order of magnitude to that Moeglin (whose work I cited in aid of my argument) identified in respect of European television nearly 20 years earlier. English speakers are the largest single language group using the Internet (accounting for an estimated 29 per cent of Internet users – see Internet World Stats [nd]) and the proportion of English language Internet content, if Greffenstette and Nioche's (2000) inventive (albeit now dated) study is a reliable guide, is of the same order of magnitude. They found that the ratios of English to non-English content on the web in 7 European languages other than English was 1: 0.24 – though the proportion of non-English languages was growing (see also Crystal 2001). Wikipedia suggests that this 20–25 per cent share of English in a wider linguistic and cultural pool remains fairly constant – in 2009 Wikipedia claimed that around 20 per cent of Wikipedia articles are in the English language (derived from Wikipedia statistics [nd]).

Chapter 8 is a good example of my real world problem rather a than theoretically-generated approach to scholarly writing. This reflection, the first of three chapters stimulated by the same experience – the World Summit on the Information Society (WSIS) and its pendant Working Group on Internet Governance (WGIG), derives from my puzzlement, when participating in the event, as to why something, notably the Internet, that worked so well was fought over so intensely? And why, when practical problems of resource allocation, freighted with a heavy and obvious overburden of equity issues, were under consideration was so much time spent fretting about control of the Domain Name System (DNS) rather than squabbling about the allocation of resources to mitigate the digital divide? Concepts drawn from Nancy Fraser's (2000) work on recognition and John Rawls (1999) on redistribution and the 'difference principle' helped me resolve this puzzle – at least to my own satisfaction – and in the course of doing so I came to think that key aspects of networked communications, notably the network externality, which inherently incentivizes connectivity, and the pervasive economies of scale and scope in media and communications, provided a basis on which to critically engage with Rawls' arguments and to rethink the digital divide.

The WSIS was the first UN Summit on a communication topic. It was also notable for giving civil society a procedural, albeit controversial, legitimacy which enabled civil society representatives (including myself) to participate in the Summit (and the WGIG) along with longer-established constituencies, notably business and government. As I indicated above, the Summit focused on two issues – on the digital divide and on the management of the DNS, the Internet naming and addressing system. Each of these concerns raised, as I foreshadowed above, important politico-philosophical issues which I chiefly have considered in Chapter 8. The link of the first topic to classical problems in political philosophy is obvious: it involves issues of redistribution which have long been the object of philosophical enquiry and which figure powerfully in the work of one of the leading contemporary figures in political philosophy, John Rawls. But the second topic, the governance of the DNS, is also, and more surprisingly, linked to an issue of some contemporary philosophical salience: that of recognition. And recognition, one its major proponents has argued, has displaced distribution from its centrality as a problem of contemporary political philosophy and of practical politics. As Nancy Fraser (1997: 11) claims, 'Cultural domination supplants exploitation as the fundamental injustice'.

Redistribution and recognition were linked, in the specific context of the WSIS (and its pendant WGIG), to the question of legitimacy and this question of legitimacy and the conduct of the WSIS/WGIG are considered in Chapters 9 and 10. What legitimacy did the incumbent institution, the Internet Corporation for Assigned Names and Numbers (ICANN), controlling the DNS possess and what legitimacy did the institutions (governments, business and civil society) participating in the WSIS/WGIG enjoy? The formal legitimacy of ICANN and civil society, and thus their entitlement to 'recognition', was fiercely contested despite each institution being able to offer a plausible case (or at least a case no less intrinsically plausible than those of relevant alternative and related institutions such as the ITU, business and at least some governments) for their legitimate participation in proceedings and their discharge of their institutional roles. But their claims to legitimacy were rooted in output legitimacy – they more or less effectively contributed to the achievement of jobs in hand – rather than the formal, and exclusive, legitimacy claimed by governments (the chief locus of criticism of civil society and ICANN). Finally, as earlier foreshadowed, the WSIS saw a clash between an 'American' way of looking at and managing the Internet, a way embedded in the institutions and working practices of the Internet for obvious historical reasons, and a much more authoritarian 'top down' statist way. There were, and are, real issues represented in clashes such as these, for the good arguments are by no means the exclusive possession of one side of the debate. But though the WSIS/WGIG debates showed that there may be better alternatives to the status quo they also suggested that there may be very much worse things than the messy, imperfectly legitimized, Americanized, established dominant order.

The controversial doctrine of 'trilateralism', under the name of which civil society was 'recognized' in the WSIS/WGIG, forms the focus of Chapter 9 which also describes the institutional configuration in which the trilateralism controversy was enacted. Here, I also consider the status and conduct of ICANN, the institution at the centre of the WSIS controversy, which continues to coordinate a central and indispensible Internet resource – the DNS. These controversies were enacted through institutional conflicts of a representative character: they exemplified enduring contemporary mismatches between global relationships and institutions on the one hand and national mentalities and power structures on the other. Moreover, they (not necessarily congruently) also exemplified in an international context some of the discontinuities and conflicts between different forms and practices of governance – notably network and hierarchical governance – considered in Chapters 3 and 5.

The discontinuities between governance practices and mentalities are further explored in Chapter 10 where a metaphorical distinction between hierarchical communications governance (exemplified in the coordination and conduct of telephony) and network governance (exemplified in the coordination and conduct of the Internet) is made by contrasting 'Bellheads' and 'Netheads'. How do the Internet 'Netheads' conduct their business? Here I consider the case of ICANN describing its contested, and evolving, governance arrangements and situating them in a general contemporary context – that of the disjunctions between the existence of what Held (2004: 20) calls 'communities of fate' and the robustness and legitimacy of their governance.

These essays were first published between 2000 and 2009. By and large, I have not updated them. Readers can thus see how, if at all, events have confirmed or qualified my analysis without me falsifying the record. But I have made some additions and excisions to reduce redundancy, improve the prose, harmonize the referencing and add material that was present in unpublished drafts but which was lost when edited to length for final publication. Moreover, some remaining elements in individual chapters may reflect the specific context for which particular essays were originally written. For example, the first two chapters: 'Online and legacy media in the UK: a half empty glass?' and 'Online and legacy media in the UK: a half full glass?' were written for an Italian journal (and so Italy is foregrounded as a point of comparison with the UK). The fourth, 'The BBC, the Internet and Public Value', was written for a German journal (hence the particular references to Germany). However, at least one chapter appears in a form different from that in which it was published. Chapter 3 is the major case in point, the core argument has been published in more than one successively reworked versions and what is published here is a further version – an amalgam (refinement?) of previous published instances. Preparing this material for publication as a book has provided powerful reminders of the Protean character of the Internet – uncomfortably often urls have changed and material cited has disappeared from the web. Heather Owen, the copy editor, has laboured mightily to identify such areas of difficulty. For the most part, I've been able to respond to her discoveries that an url has ceased to work by tracking down a new location for the material cited. But sometimes this hasn't been possible (e.g. in Chapters 9 and 10) but for other sites which have apparently been extinguished by their hosts the wonderful Internet Archive Wayback Machine (see http://www.archive.org/web/web.php accessed on 26.6.2009) has enabled me to retrieve and re-reference sources. I am enormously indebted to Heather for her thoroughness in working through my copy and identifying difficulties. She has made a considerable contribution to whatever authority and clarity this book may possess and I'm happy to testify here to my debt to her.

Finally, no book ever has a single author – despite the claims of cover and title page. I owe a great deal to colleagues and other interlocutors who have helped refine my arguments, direct me to information that would otherwise have escaped me and save me from claims that I would otherwise have had cause to regret. It would be otiose to name names but an anonymous interlocutor does deserve acknowledgement – the publisher's peer reviewer of my typescript: many thanks to him or her for their encouraging and salutary commentary. My thanks to all concerned. This work has been much improved through the help of others – any blame is certainly mine.

Notes

1. See Internet Usage Statistics for Africa at http://www.internetworldstats.com/stats1.htm accessed on 10.4.2009.
2. see the informal history of BBC Online at http://www.bbc.co.uk/blogs/bbcinternet/2007/12/brandons_history_of_bbc_on_the_2.html accessed on 26.6.2009.

Chapter 1

Online and Legacy Media in the UK: A Half Empty Glass?

In 2002, 12.8m national newspapers were sold on an average day. This year, it was fewer than 11m and in 2013 it will be slightly above 9m, according to Enders Analysis, the media research specialist. Advertising revenue across national titles is predicted to fall from £1.9bn last year – a figure broadly flat over the previous five years – to £1.2bn within five years... A former British newspaper owner, who asked not to be named, said: 'The plain truth is that there is an oversupply of newspapers and an undersupply of advertising revenue'...Douglas McCabe, one of the Enders analysts, said a catastrophic decline in national newspaper display advertising has combined with a structural change that has seen the internet emerge as a key rival. (Fenton 2008b)

Introduction

The citation above from recent coverage of the media sector in UK newspapers tells a simple and unequivocal story of a crisis in 'legacy' media. Although the story focuses on UK newspapers, similar stories abound about broadcasting and about the media elsewhere.[1] Legacy media are experiencing a structural change that has seen the internet emerge as a key rival. Technological determinism, which this story perfectly exemplifies, is the leading contemporary story of this kind and is loved by journalists, politicians and social scientists. Journalists love such stories because they provide marketable heuristics to understand the world; politicians because a clear narrative enables them to market themselves, sometimes successfully, to electors as the bearers of solutions; and social scientists love them because simple stories provide something for them to scoff at.

There is no shortage of utopian claims by journalists and politicians for social scientists to scoff at. Kenneth Baker (now Lord Baker), when UK Minister for Industry and Information Technology, in 1982 claimed (of information and communication technologies) 'In the long run, I believe that the revolution that they will bring about will have more far-reaching effects on our society than the Industrial Revolution 200 years ago'.[2] Al Gore likewise proposed that 'the information infrastructure is to the US economy what transport infrastructure was to the economy of the mid-20th century' (Gore 1994: 22) and Nicholas Negroponte foresaw (in 1995) that 'Early in the next millennium your right and left cuff links or earrings may communicate with each other by low orbiting satellites and have more computer power than your present PC' (Negroponte 1995: 6).

Ecstatic professions such as these are exemplary targets for scoffers. Why, one might speculate, would one want one's cufflinks and earrings to communicate with each other? One might also, once a Negropontian ecstatic flush had passed, reflect that though Negroponte's prediction sounds bold, in fact 'early in the next millennium' might reasonably be taken to mean 'sometime in the next three to four hundred years'. Curious to find a claim that is both ecstatic and bathetic. But to so scoff is to commit a category error – these are hyperbolic claims of the kind that (almost) all of us make from time to time ('I love you to bits', 'I'll never travel on United/Alitalia/British Airways again', 'I thought your article/lecture/performance was fantastic') and to judge them by the criteria of sober science (or even of social science) is to mistake the kind of claim being made.

Despite their extravagant rhetoric (as sober social scientists habitually point out – see Curran, forthcoming, for a notable recent instance) such claims point to important truths. Notably that technology has made a difference and that no plausible explanation of change to the contemporary media can leave out technology as a decisive factor – though not the only factor. The difficulties of prediction, that make technological determinists' claims easy to parody – even when they are not misrepresented – are confirmed by instances of reverse technological determinism where technology's importance is underestimated. I can cite several such misrecognitions from my own work;[3] another, perhaps more convincing because by more distinguished a writer, is Anthony Smith's measured, but misleading, prediction in 1980 that 'breaking into their [i.e. television's and newspapers'] highly organised audiences will be the task of many decades… A transformation with real social and political consequences will be possible only when the existing holders of the major blocs of audiences are ready to loosen their grip' (Smith 1980: 302).

There is growing evidence to suggest that a transformation of the kind signalled by Smith has emphatically come to pass and that changes in media technology have been decisive in effecting this transformation both earlier than Smith anticipated and well before incumbents were willing to 'loosen their grip'. In their former heartlands of Western Europe and North America, 'legacy' media are in rapid decline. The existing holders of the major audience blocs are having their grips involuntarily loosened as a flood of recent reports of job losses in the UK newspaper and television sectors suggest (Fenton 2008a, 2008b; Sabbagh 2008). True, in 'tiger' economies such as China[4] and India the number of newspaper titles and reputed consumption is growing. But elsewhere there is a general absolute decline in newspaper consumption and often a fall in television consumption. And even when television consumption has not fallen in absolute terms, it has customarily fragmented. At best, a stable quantum of broadcasting consumption time has been divided between an increasing number of channels, thus driving down consumption of any individual channel with a consequential fall in advertising revenue per minute of broadcast time. These declines in legacy media contrast with growth in 'new', digital and particularly online, media.

Essentially, what we are seeing is the effect of the long-anticipated (and the subject of many premature sightings) convergence of electronic communication media. The UK regulator, Ofcom, exemplifies convergence by claiming 'operators are providing services which cross the traditional boundaries of communications; for example telecommunications operators are offering content over their infrastructure, and broadcasters are using the internet and mobile platforms for distribution' (Ofcom 2008c: 13). But the metaphor 'convergence' conceals more than it reveals. It suggests everything becoming similar. Although technology and markets may be converging (a single platform may provide voice telephony, television and radio, e-mail and instant messaging and thus enable firms in hitherto separate markets to compete) products and services are becoming highly differentiated. New entrants abound, 'legacy' services hybridize and proliferate and consumers and providers metamorphose into 'prosumers'.

Technological (and regulatory) change has enabled firms to break out of hitherto separate sectors and thus both compete against each other and to develop novel syntheses of products and services. Long-established media forms and business models are co-present with a febrile flow of innovative goods and services. As Kevin Werbach claimed in his prophetic paper *Digital Tornado,* 'The Internet is substitutable for all existing media' (Werbach 1997: 1). Rather than convergence as everything becoming the same, the concept of convergence as substitutability best enables us to account for the striking contemporary changes to mass communications experienced where there are high levels of Internet penetration and use. The UK is one such locality and 'legacy' media, notably newspapers (the principal sector considered below) and broadcasting, have experienced intensive and extensive change resulting in a crisis for a long-settled media order and for the established firms and user relationships which characterized it.

Data and doubt

These generalizations, though I make them confidently, are subject to several health warnings. They are based on the incomplete authoritative data sets currently in the public domain. Moreover, what follows focuses on the newspaper sector and on the UK and is heavily dependent on information supplied by a leading trade association, IFRA and the UK Association of Online Publications (UKAOP).[5] This data may be tainted by the difficulties of allocating costs and revenues in firms which provide both online and offline media services and by competing online papers using different methodologies to identify patterns of usage.[6] Moreover, the structure of the UK's media industries is different from that in many other European Union member states (there is, for example, very pronounced metropolitanization notably in the newspaper sector) and the impact of the Internet on legacy media appears particularly strong in the UK – trade associations claim, for example, that the UK has a higher proportion of advertising spend online than any other country. But if the UK is an exceptional case, its exceptionality may foreshadow developments elsewhere. Although the extent to which the UK can be seen as a precursor of international trends is subject to the limitations of authoritative international comparative data available in the public domain.

UNESCO's comprehensive *World Communication Report. The Challenge of the New Technologies* (authored and compiled by Lotfi Maherzi – UNESCO 1998) dates from 1997 and draws on data from the early 1990s. It was followed by the *World Communication and Information Report 1999–2000* (UNESCO 1999) which appears to be the most recent study sponsored by UNESCO. The best source of comparative newspaper circulation statistics is the annual *World Press Trends* published by the World Association of Newspapers (WAN) but the latest, 2008, edition was not publicly available in any UK library (including the British Library where the latest annual held dates from 2001).[7] However, even this source, albeit likely to be the most accurate, comprehensive and current data available, does not present fully comparable data as the WAN (2008) specimen country studies (e.g. Germany and Ireland) make clear.

UK newspapers themselves also provide fragmentary, but generally authoritative and current UK data. For example, the *Financial Times* published (in its hard copy but not online version) tables showing recent job cuts in UK national newspapers,[8] newspapers' declining (and the Internet's increasing) share of UK advertising revenue[9] and falling national newspaper circulations[10] (see Fenton 2009: 17). The best available source of comparative (albeit incomplete) data seems to be Ofcom's annual *International Communications Market Report* (Ofcom 2008a) which presents data to the end of 2007 and provides an authoritative up-to-date (though not comprehensive) account of electronic (but not print) media in the UK, France, Germany, Italy, the United States, Canada and Japan complemented by less complete data for Ireland, Poland, Spain, the Netherlands,[11] Brazil, Russia, India and China (see also Anheier & Isar 2008; UNCTAD 2008).

All six countries (France, Germany, Italy, Spain, UK, US) on which Ofcom reported extensively (Ofcom 2008a: 126) saw a significant increase in time spent on the Internet in the period 2004–2008. Increases ranged from an annual, year-on-year cumulative increase of 6 per cent in the US (which, though the lowest level of increase, had the highest absolute average level of time spent on the Internet) to 21 per cent in the UK (the highest level of growth and second only to the US in absolute terms). Comparing the proportion of advertising expenditure on the Internet in twelve countries, Ofcom (2008a: 108, drawing on data from the World Advertising Research Center) found that migration of advertising online had also been faster in the UK than anywhere else and that in the UK, the Internet's share of total advertising expenditure was, at 19 per cent, higher than elsewhere.[12]

Italy and the UK

Ofcom's data made it clear that there are significant national variations in media use. A comparison between Italy and the UK provides some interesting cases in point.[13]

Italy is the biggest broadcast mobile television market in Europe with nearly 1 million DVB-H subscribers (Ofcom 2008a: 3) but has relatively low pay-TV penetration of only 22 per cent whereas 47 per cent of households in the UK subscribed to pay-TV (Ofcom 2008a: 4). However,

	UK 2007 (£m)	*Italy 2007 (£m)*
Total TV revenue	10447	6326
Subscription	4288	2049
Advertising financed	3544	3183
Public finance	2615	1114
Total radio revenue	1262	961
Advertising financed	613	480
Public finance	570	480
Internet revenues	2560	2298
GDP per head	22431	18114

Source: Ofcom 2008a: 287, 288, 293, 294.

since 2002, the Italian TV sector grew faster than elsewhere at an average yearly rate of 9.4 per cent whereas the UK grew at only 4.8 per cent annually and the radio sector in Italy similarly grew faster than in the UK (at 4.4 per cent p.a.) whereas the UK radio market rose by only 1.8 per cent (Ofcom 2008a: 23).

Among the countries considered by Ofcom, the Internet's share of total advertising expenditure was highest in the UK at 19 per cent (followed by Sweden at 17 per cent) whereas Italian growth was second lowest among countries considered at 3 per cent (Ireland was lowest at 1 per cent) (Ofcom 2008a: 107). In the UK, television and radio accounted for nearly one-third of advertising spend in 2007 (90 per cent of which was taken by television and 10 per cent by radio). But in Italy radio and television accounted for a majority of all advertising spend in 2007 (Ofcom 2008a: 27). Television's share of UK advertising spend was 27 per cent but in Italy was 52 per cent (Ofcom 2008a: 153).

Italy has relatively low broadband penetration and growth slowed in 2007 at 41% compared with the UK's 60 per cent in 2007 (Ofcom 2008a). Ofcom attributed this to a relatively low level of PC ownership at 48 per cent in Italy whereas about 65 per cent of UK homes have a PC (see Eurobarometer 2008: 55) compared to 90 per cent of households in the Netherlands and 82 per cent of households in Sweden which have PCs (Ofcom 2008a: 194). In Italy, 58 per cent of internet users used broadband in 2007 whereas in the UK 85 per cent did (Ofcom 2008a: 241).

Ofcom found that national newspapers were the offline media which suffered most as Internet use grew: in all countries over a quarter of respondents claimed they read national newspapers less and it was only in Italy that the number of people who believed they read national newspapers *more* than they had done before going online exceeded 10 per cent (at 14 per cent) (Ofcom 2008a: 133).

In the UK, more than a fifth of respondents nominated the Internet as their main source of information for 'sport', 'entertainment' and 'news about your country'. This was fewer than in either Japan or the US and was comparable to Canada, France, Germany and Italy. However, strikingly, more Italians nominated the Internet as their main source of information about their country than did respondents elsewhere in Europe (Ofcom 2008a: 129). Not surprisingly, increases in Internet use have impacted on respondents' use of legacy media (though available data is open to differing interpretations).

Ofcom's findings, derived from responses to the question 'Since starting to use the internet, which if any of the following activities do you believe you undertake more or less offline?', can be interpreted either (or both) to suggest a substitution of new media for legacy media or as evidence of the durability of established patterns of consumption. Data which suggests substitution includes the finding that in all seven countries, cited by Ofcom, some respondents stated that, on average, their consumption of television had declined. However, in all countries most respondents claimed that their Internet use had not reduced their use of television and everywhere *some* respondents stated that their use of television had *increased*. However, everywhere *more* respondents stated that their television use had *fallen* in comparison to the number who claimed it had increased. The net fall in television consumption ranged from 21 per cent in Japan to 7 per cent in the US with European respondents (in France, Germany, Italy and the UK) clustering in the 15 per cent–19 per cent range (Ofcom 2008a: 132).

In respect of radio, 23 per cent of respondents claimed they listened to less radio since beginning to use the Internet, but 13 per cent claimed they listened to more radio (Ofcom 2008a: 246). Again there were national differences: in Italy only 25 per cent of respondents claimed that their radio use had fallen whereas in Japan 27 per cent claimed a fall (Ofcom 2008a: 250). A more striking effect of the Internet was evident when respondents referred to their use of national newspapers: fewer claimed that their use of newspapers had increased, more claimed that it had diminished and in France more claimed that their use of newspapers had fallen than claimed that there had been no effect. The reported decline in newspaper consumption ranged from 47 per cent of users in France to 26 per cent in Japan but everywhere more than a quarter of respondents stated that their consumption of newspapers had fallen since they started to use the Internet (Ofcom 2008a: 133).

Overall, there seems thus to be strong evidence to suggest that the Internet has reduced consumption of legacy media, though its effect varies significantly from country to country and from medium to medium.[14] Of course, none of this data is decisive evidence of causality – correlation does not necessarily indicate causation. But the weight of evidence surely suggests that it is likely that new media are displacing legacy media in both of legacy media's principal client groups – advertisers and readers/viewers – and that these effects are most marked in respect of, first, newspapers and, second, television (whereas the impact on radio is less marked). Data also suggests that context matters a lot – there are significant national differences in response to a shared experience of technological change. There is much to suggest that the UK may be an exceptional case for, there, the migration of advertising from legacy media to the web has been more rapid and comprehensive than elsewhere. This may be due to the distinctive structure of its legacy media or (see Elstein 2008) to quirks of the UK's regulatory regime.[15]

UK online and offline media

Ofcom's comprehensive annual account of the electronic communications sector (Ofcom 2008a) is complemented by the UK Film Council's annual review of the film sector (see UK Film Council 2008). Current consumption data is available at BARB (Broadcast Audience Research Board) (www.barb.co.uk) and RAJAR (Radio Joint Audience Reseach) (www.rajar.co.uk) No comparable compendium exists for the newspaper sector although combining data from the Newspaper Society, which provides data on local and regional newspapers (see Newspaper Society nd), the House of Lords Select Committee on Communications' Report *The Ownership of the News* (House of Lords 2008a and 2008b), with current circulation statistics from the Audit Bureau of Circulation (ABC 2009), fills most gaps.

Radio and television

The UK broadcasting sector has three major elements: advertising-funded free-to-air services (in television the three main terrestrial analogue/digital channels are ITV, Channel 4 and Channel 5 [*five*][16] and a host of national and local commercial radio stations), subscription-funded services (dominated by BSkyB and transmitted by satellite) and the licence fee-funded (public finance) BBC (providing television and radio). People in the UK listen to the radio for 22.3 hours a week and the BBC's stations account for nearly 55 per cent of this consumption. In respect of television, people watch for around 27 hours a week, with the BBC accounting for about 30 per cent of this total, advertising-financed television for about another 30 per cent, and other channels the remainder. BSkyB has approximately nine million households subscribing and an ARPU (average revenue per user) of £430pa translating to annual revenues of about £4.9bn (BSkyB 2008). The BBC's income for 2007–8 was £4.4bn, of which approximately £3.7bn derived from public funds (see BBC 2008a). The advertising-funded channels (notably ITV/Channel 3, Channel 4 and *five*) accrued revenues of around £3.5bn in 2006 (source Ofcom 2008a). The BBC's radio spend in 2006 was approximately £637m and commercial radio's £512m (Ofcom 2008a). Comparable data for the Internet/online sector is not available, however Ofcom estimates an average monthly expenditure per UK household[17] on Internet and broadband services in 2006 of £10.20 (compared to an average monthly spend on television of £25.42 and on radio of £2.60, most of which is on connectivity (see Ofcom 2008a: 18). In broad terms, the UK broadcasting sector has a very large public broadcaster and a very successful dominant pay-TV operator and (rapidly) declining advertising-financed broadcasters.

Newspapers

The UK newspaper sector is notable for the absence of explicit public subsidy (though zero-rating for VAT constitutes a significant measure of public support for the sector –

but this concession does not apply to online versions of newspapers); for its pronounced metrocentric structure (the most widely-read morning newspapers are produced in London); and for its domination by a few large corporations. News International accounts for 36 per cent of national newspaper circulation, Trinity Mirror group for 20 per cent, the Daily Mail and General Trust for 19 per cent, Northern and Shell for 12 per cent and the Daily Telegraph group for 6 per cent. The Guardian Group accounts for a further 3 per cent and the Independent and the Financial Times each for a further 2 per cent (House of Lords 2008a: 42–45). Local and regional newspaper publishing is similarly concentrated with four groups: Trinity Mirror, the Daily Mail and General Trust, Johnston Press and Newsquest Media Group accounting for around 70 per cent of the market (House of Lords 2008a: 46).

Film

Finally, in the UK film sector, in 2006, cinema attendances were around 165 million and DVD/video sales and rentals totalled about 240 million units. These figures indicate a plateau in cinema attendances and some degree of decline in video sales in the UK. Expenditure and time-use surveys suggest that there has been some substitution of Internet for DVD/video use and that this seems to have been particularly strong amongst 15–24-year-olds. However, it is hard to find clear evidence of substitution effects away from cinema attendance (Bakhshi 2006).

News and evolving markets

Survey research suggests that UK citizens are, despite comparatively high levels of newspaper readership, particularly reliant on television as their primary source of news: as Ofcom states 'television remains by far the most used source of news for UK citizens' (Ofcom 2007). In consequence, the fall in advertising revenues accruing to legacy media, particularly to television, has put in question the quality and plurality of news provision in the UK. Although many users nominate the Internet as a source of news, the Internet's most important source of news (e.g. Wikinews and news aggregators such as Google and Yahoo) is legacy media (see Paterson 2005). The declining ability of legacy media to fund a plurality of independent quality sources of news, and the absence of comparable new entrants, has increasingly become a focus of public concern (see, among others, Ofcom 2007 and House of Lords 2008a).

But despite some uncertainties arising from incomplete data, there is no doubt that revenues have fallen and costs risen for both the UK newspaper and broadcasting sectors. For example, the cost of important inputs such as newsprint has risen,[18] as has the price of radio frequency spectrum (which, formerly, broadcasters usually enjoyed at below market prices and often at no cost). Moreover both newspaper readership and incumbent broadcasters' share of television viewing have fallen. Whereas in 1992, 59 per cent of UK adults read a national daily, by 2006 the total had fallen to 45 per cent (source: National Readership Survey in House of Lords 2008b: 582). Despite these falls in consumption, UK national newspapers succeeded in raising prices in 2007/8 and Chris Marshall, an official in the Department for Business, Enterprise and Regulatory Reform (BERR) with responsibilities for the newspaper sector, stated that they still enjoy 'high margins' though he stressed that circulation was falling around 3–5 per cent annually and that this decline in circulation, as well as competition from the Internet for advertising revenue, threatened the 60–70 per cent of newspaper revenues which accrued from advertising. He estimated that newspapers' advertising take was split 10 per cent/90 per cent between online and offline revenues (Marshall 2008).

In broadcasting there have been analogous changes: in 1992 the BBC had a share of viewing of 42 per cent, ITV 41 per cent, Channel 4, 10 per cent and other channels 5 per cent whereas in 2007 the BBC had a share of viewing of 30.5 per cent, ITV, 19.2 per cent, Channel 4, 8.6 per cent and other channels, 41.6 per cent (source BARB 2006).

Internet

The impact of the Internet on legacy UK media has been twofold: Internet users consume less television and radio and read fewer newspapers than do non-users (Dutton and Helsper 2007: 24) and the Internet has attracted a considerable volume of advertising revenue from legacy media. Moreover, the Internet reduces entry barriers and thus exposes incumbents to intensified competition (or the threat of competition). These factors have stimulated an abundance of fulsome testimony to the power of the Internet. For example:

> 50 web publishers who replied to the Association of Online Publishers' sixth annual census – published today – were emphatic about the growth of their businesses. AOP members, including BSkyB, Guardian Media Group, the Financial Times and CondéNet UK, reported total digital revenue up 52% for the year – and forecast further growth of 31%. That compares with overall growth of 9% across the traditional businesses'. (Kiss 2007)

As Internet penetration and use have grown, these substitution effects have become increasingly important. At the end of 2006 around 17 million UK homes (and SMEs) had Internet connectivity of which around 13 million (approximately 78 per cent) were broadband connections (Ofcom 2007: 287). Moreover, there has been a striking migration of UK advertising revenue to the Internet. Sites such as eBay have severely reduced the volume of classified advertising ('small ads') placed in newspapers and magazines; primelocation.com and others have done the same for advertisements of houses for sale; jobs.ac.uk for academic jobs, and so on. Google (and other search engines) have similarly reduced the volume of display advertising spend in legacy media. The UK is estimated to have twice the global average proportion of its total advertising spend online and the shift from offline to online seems to be accelerating. Of the 2007 UK advertising market of around £18.4bn, Internet advertising accounted for about 15.3 per cent (whereas television accounted for about 21 per cent, newspaper display advertising about 19.9 per cent and newspaper classified about 15.1 per cent). Online advertising in the UK grew by 41 per cent between 2005 and 2007 and in 2006/2007 online advertising overtook national press advertising, i.e. not including regional and local papers (IAB/PWC 2008; see also Ofcom 2008a). These changes mean that:

> nearly 80% of publishers remain confident that the online advertising model is sustainable – with display the most common form of ad revenue for 82% of publishers, and sponsorship employed by 50%. Forty-four per cent publish classified recruitment ads, with classified property, motors and dating published by 16%, 14% and 12% respectively. (Kiss 2007)

Conclusion

For advertising-funded legacy incumbents, survival is becoming harder. The structural trends considered above have been amplified by the impact of the 'credit crunch' and the global economic recession which has accompanied it. The Internet has provided both an alternative to, and, for some purposes, a more effective advertising medium than legacy media provides. The Internet's impact has been amplified by the absolute fall in advertising expenditure that the recession has triggered and the effects on advertising-funded media have also been transmitted to media funded in other ways – and notably to those which have enjoyed public finance: notably the BBC. The BBC has grown in relative power and this has stimulated demands for its funding to be more widely shared. The threat to pluralism in legacy media, as advertising finance falls, is, however, matched by opportunities to sustain and extend pluralism by supporting emerging Internet-based media.

Notes

1. See, for example, the testimony to spilled blood in the US media sector at http://www.latimes.com/business/la-fi-tribune9-2008dec09,0,5273854. Story accessed on 12.12.2008.
2. I was reminded of this classic utterance by James Curran's (see Curran 2009) use of it – though by omitting Baker's prefatory 'In the long run' he may be thought to have put his thumb on the scale to make Baker's statement appear more credulous and ignorant than it was. For the full text original see *House of Commons Hansard* 20.4.1982: 230 at http://hansard.millbanksystems.com/commons/1982/apr/20/satellite-and-cable-broadcasting accessed on 7.12.2008.
3. I am guilty of having claimed that 'the prognosis for satellite television is poor' and that 'The UK television market is too small' to sustain new television services (see Collins 1990: 89–90). And, further, that 'the evidence is that the 64 kilobit/second infrastructure of the British Telecommunications system is adequate for all foreseeable "needs pulled" services' (see Collins 1990: 144). I will not rehearse further painful cases in point.

4. Wikipedia claims the number of newspaper titles in mainland China rose from 42 in 1968 to more than 2200 in 2008. http://en.wikipedia.org/wiki/Newspapers_of_China accessed on 26.11.2008. In India, the Registrar of Newspapers for India claims an extraordinary 62,483 registered newspaper titles in 2006 with more than 2000 new titles registered in 2005-6 (the most recent period of report). https://rni.nic.in/ accessed on 26.11.2008.
5. See www.ifra.com and www.ukaop.org.uk. My thanks to Ruth Brownlee and Melanie Shah for their assistance. For an impressive and comprehensive treatment of a single national case see Marc Tessier's *La presse au défi du numérique* (2007) for the Ministre de la Culture et de la Communication, France.
6. The latter problem may soon be mitigated, Jicwebs (Joint Industry Committee for Web Standards) said the committee is 'implementing a strategic review of the analytics methodologies for national newspapers' (cited from ABCe: Web traffic standards to be reviewed Jemima Kiss in guardian.co.uk on Thursday May 22, 2008. At http://www.guardian.co.uk/media/2008/may/22/abcs.telegraphmediagroup accessed on 1.12.2008). Nonetheless, reliance on high level industry standards, such as those provided by ABCe, may discriminate against new entrants and small companies because of the high cost of data provided by such organisations. See http://www.asa.org.uk/asa/adjudications/Public/TF_ADJ_45583.htm and http://www.contractoruk.com/004150.html both accessed on 15.1.2009.
7. British Library system number 006578971.
8. 90 at *The Independent,* 50 at *The Telegraph,* 400 employed by the *Daily Mail and General Trust,* 58 at the *Financial Times* and 86 at the *Daily Express.* The FT did not specify the time period in which these cuts had taken/would take place.
9. From 2002 to 2013 actual and forecast spends fell (for national newspapers) from c12% to c7% and (for regional newspapers) from 20% to c 8% and grew (for the Internet) from 0% to 34%.
10. Ranging from 8.5% for the *Daily Star* to 0.1% for *The Sun.*
11. For data on the Netherlands see also TNO's *Marktrapportage Elektronische Communicatie December 2006* at http://www.tno.nl/content.cfm?context=markten&content=publicatie&laag1=182&laag2=1&item_id=57 accessed on 12.12.2008.
12. It's not clear from Ofcom's account whether eBay is included as an element of Internet advertising: there is no indication to suggest that it is. If eBay is excluded from these statistics then they are likely to understate the impact of the Internet on the revenue base of legacy media, for much of what was formerly marketed through newspaper classified advertising ('small ads') is now marketed through eBay and equivalent auction sites.
13. Ofcom's data covers only electronic media and not newspapers. However, the striking differences in the structure of the UK and Italian press (one highly metropolitanized and the other regionalized) makes meaningful comparisons of these countries' press sectors difficult.
14. The annual German ARD/ZDF Online Study (see www.ard-zdf-onlinestudie.de accessed on 28.5.2009) provides illuminating data and reinforces my contention that effects vary significantly from country to country and medium to medium. As I argue in Chapter 3, the Internet is not a single 'thing' and the national factor is very important – generalizations from one country's experience must be made with great caution. A number of useful, though because of their length, indicative national surveys may be found at the LSE kidsonline reports site: e.g. http://www.lse.ac.uk/collections/EUKidsOnline/Reports/WP2Germany.pdf accessed 28.5.2009. Other national studies are accessible through the LSE repository at http://www.lse.ac.uk/collections/EUKidsOnline/repository.htm accessed on 28.5.2009.
15. A different, but nonetheless significant, regulatory decision has inhibited the main UK advertising financed broadcasters (in collaboration with the BBC) from fully exploiting their content online.

The Competition Commission has provisionally found the broadcasters' proposal (Project Kangaroo) 'would be likely to lead to a loss of rivalry between the parties, amounting to a substantial lessening of competition'. See http://www.competition-commission.org.uk/inquiries/ref2008/kangaroo/pdf/notice_provisional_findings.pdf accessed on 4.12.2008.

16. ITV is the name usually attributed to Channel 3, programmes on Channel 3 are provided by ITV plc, which holds licences for the whole of England and Wales, and by STV and UTV which hold the remaining licences for the Channel Islands, Northern Ireland and Scotland. ITV plc also provides digital channels notably ITV2, 3 and 4 and Men and Motors. Channel 4 is both a channel and the name of the public sector, non-profit, organization which provides services on this channel. The organization, Channel 4, also provides a series of digital channels notably E4, More4 and Film4. *five* is a firm owned by RTL which is licensed to provide television services on Channel 5. It too provides digital channels such as *fiver* and 5US.
17. The Office of National Statistics estimates a total of 25.3m UK households in 2006. See http://www.statistics.gov.uk/STATBASE/Expodata/Spreadsheets/D7678.xls accessed on 2.12.2008.
18. On October 17th 2008, Reuters reported a 15–20% price rise for Norwegian newsprint in 2008, see http://uk.reuters.com/article/tnBasicIndustries-SP/idUKLH33688320081017 accessed on 12.12.2008.

Chapter 2

Online and Legacy Media in the UK: A Half Full Glass?

> Job cuts are expected to be announced later this week at The Daily Telegraph[1] and Sunday Telegraph, which becomes the latest national newspaper group to respond to the deteriorating economy by saving money…The quality newspaper market is down by around 10 per cent since the summer, in what is traditionally the most important season for advertising. Last week The Independent, fourth in the market, announced 90 job cuts, out of a workforce of 425. (Sabbagh 2008)

> 'These are extraordinary times for ITV. The economic outlook has worsened significantly since the summer and businesses right across the UK, including most of our customers, are facing considerable uncertainty,' John Cresswell, chief operating officer, wrote to his staff. 'Analysts' current consensus is that total television advertising is expected to be down by around 5 per cent in 2008, and by 6 to 7 per cent in 2009. The need for action is therefore urgent. We need to accelerate our plans to improve the efficiency of all our operations now'. (Fenton 2008a)

Legacy media and online strategies

The Internet is not the only significant form of competition undermining established media business models[2] (free sheets provide another obvious case in point) but its impact exceeds other factors. And, despite some evidence in the third quarter of 2008 that growth in UK Internet advertising is slackening, the impact of the Internet has been sufficient for offline 'legacy' media to have responded by moving online themselves. Their 'bi-media' strategy makes the impact of the Internet on 'legacy' media difficult to assess with precision (on and offline advertising is sold in bundles, making it difficult to attribute revenues to on and offline products – there are significant common costs in bi-media firms, for example newsrooms tend to be integrated, supplying both on and offline media and so on). The move to bi-media has both engendered innovative 'hybridized' online media products/services (characteristically online 'newspapers' offer television- and radio-like services from their sites) and has also put in question the traditional 'montage of attractions' content models of legacy media. When there are specialist sport, finance, fashion and news sites why use a newspaper (whether on or offline) which provides a bit of everything but does not, and cannot, provide the depth and comprehensiveness of specialized sites? Similarly, the traditional integrated broadcast schedule with 'inheritance', 'hammocking', etc., has been displaced by themed channels.

Nonetheless, legacy media and their established marketing strategies and business models, continue to dominate the UK media landscape for, despite the growing salience of online media, legacy media still enjoy significant advantages. And although these advantages may not be sufficient to compensate for the decline in offline 'legacy' businesses (e.g. linear terrestrial broadcasting or hard copy newspapers) they significantly advantage legacy media's online businesses and inhibit the growth of new online entrants. Legacy media firms have established brands, which have proven to be fungible across platforms, established systems and institutions of content production (such as newsrooms and advertising sales departments) which can be re-versioned and thus have pools of assets which enable them to provide services online cheaper than a stand alone operation. Established brands can be shared with (for example) dating and travel services provided online with a consequential flow of revenue to the brand owner. And legacy assets, such as an archive, can often be better exploited online than offline.

Marshall (2008) claimed that 'UK papers have been slow to see the value of their archives'. Some papers, such as *The Scotsman*, have digitized and exploited their archives (see also *Guardian* 2009):

> *The Scotsman* offers a fully digitized contextual archive from 1817 to 1950 containing over a half million pages and over 8.5 million articles. Since its 2004 launch, traffic has grown to 3.4 million monthly users (as of July 2006) and it now generates a profit by selling archive passes to patrons across the world...This is the first time a UK newspaper publisher has offered its entire archive in a fully searchable format to the general public and realized a quick return on their investment. *The Scotsman* offers a wide range of individual subscription options as well as corporate and educational packages. (Scotsman Archive nd)

Significant claims have been made for such initiatives although Marshall (2008), again, claimed that there are only 'very, very low revenues from archives'.

But these residual advantages and assets have not always proven sufficient to meet new challenges. Legacy media's attempts to develop and sustain new business models have enjoyed mixed success – subscription access to online services is a case in point where there is considerable consumer resistance to paying for web-based content and the number of newspapers providing subscription services online has declined (although subscription finance has been considerably more successful in television):

> As confirmed by the FT's[3] recent switch to a model less reliant on subscription, the industry is continuing to move away from paid access to content. Many publishers said they had dropped or planned to drop charges; 60% of surviving paid-for content is comprised of archives and special reports. (Kiss 2007)

The *Financial Times* (FT) is exceptional in English language media (though subscription finance may remain a viable business model in other national contexts as the case of *Le*

Monde suggests) in adhering, even in the qualified way indicated above, to a subscription-based business model. Other titles, such as the *Wall Street Journal* (WSJ), the *Irish Times* and the *New York Times,* have retreated from a subscription model (see also Herbert and Thurman 2007) which, it is claimed, has weakened the power and value of legacy brands:

> Because you have to subscribe to access both current news articles and the archive, the *Journal* is leaving only a faint footprint in cyberspace…Since most people refuse to pay for WSJ stories, most bloggers are reluctant to link to them…the next generation of readers is growing up by accessing news over the internet, and one place they are not surfing to is WSJ.com. (Peneneberg 2005)

It is important to acknowledge that the newspaper sector's difficulties antedated the Internet in the UK and elsewhere. In the US a great deal of scholarly and professional attention has long been focused on a declining newspaper sector. However, competition from the Internet is particularly hard for legacy newspapers to combat successfully because the strategic remedies that have been advocated for the newspaper play to particular strengths of the Internet. Marshall (2008) referred to UK online newspapers' strategy of attempting to 'draw reader in, leave comments behind, get them engaged' but these, of course, are strategies at which online (rather than hybrid on/offline) media excel. A similar point emerges from discussion of challenges experienced by the newspaper sector on Slate, (one of the USA's leading 'e-zines'): the standard remedies proposed for the newspaper sector are precisely those where the Internet has enormous comparative advantage.

> The solutions proposed by *Preserving the Press* [Bogart 1991] and Shaw's [1976] article read like the standard prescriptions written today: Make an attempt to 'reconnect' with readers, who feel alienated from newspapers. Make coverage more local. Hook kids when they're young. Let readers 'sound off' about issues on special pages of the paper. Connect with and hire minorities. Expand the weather report. Introduce or expand op-ed pages. Spice up the design and print more color. Run more lifestyle, consumer, and personal-finance articles. Chase potential readers—and advertisers—into the deep suburbs. (Shafer 2006)

As Marshall (2008) further observed, 'publishing in general is backward looking, it's still trying to shake off the Fleet Street image'.

The half empty glass

Despite legacy media companies' attempts to develop new business models and to innovate in the form of their products, online developments have placed intense financial pressure on legacy media sectors including newspapers and broadcasting. This pressure is reflected in changes in the market values of leading companies (which have, of course, also been affected by macro market trends such as the 'credit crunch'). Leading cases in point include the leading UK commercial television broadcaster, ITV, the share price of which fell from 105p per share in January 2007 to 83p in January 2008 and to 32p per share in mid-October 2008. In the newspaper sector, the share price of a leading newspaper company, with interests in both local and national newspaper publishing, Trinity Mirror, fell from 477p per share in January 2007 to 345p per share in January 2008 and to 42p per share in mid-October 2008. Not surprisingly, a financial analyst (ABN Amro limited circulation research note on 1.7.2008, in a pdf sent to clients), commenting on the prospects and valuation of Trinity Mirror, stated that 'These are desperate times and they call for desperate measures'. ABN Amro urged a merger between Trinity Mirror and another large newspaper publisher, Johnston Press – a union which has, at the time of writing, yet to be consummated.

Developments such as these have led to acute pessimism over the future of established news media, with an anticipated consequential adverse impact on pluralism, journalistic and editorial standards and on the range, authority and credibility of news (see, for example, Gillin 2009 and Schonfeld 2008).

And Ofcom's exemplary study *New News, Future News. The challenges for television news after Digital Switch-over* (Ofcom 2007) found that 'Economic circumstances make it much less likely that commercial broadcasters would choose to carry news for the UK nations and regions at anything like its current level, in the absence of effective regulatory intervention'. Roy Greenslade, formerly editor of the *Daily Mirror* and latterly a highly-reputed media expert, has claimed: 'media outlets will never generate the kind of income enjoyed by printed newspapers: circulation revenue will vanish and advertising revenue will be much smaller than today. There just won't be the money to afford a large staff' (Greenslade 2007).

Facts on the ground bear out such contentions. For example, in August 2008, an anticipated 65 job losses among Trinity Mirror journalists was reported (Ponsford 2009) and 45 at Johnston Press (Olivier 2009). Indeed, even before the staff-shedding envisaged by Greenslade and others, serious doubts have been raised about the quality, range and character of news in the UK. In 2005, Paterson (2005) found that news websites were heavily dependent on a few sources, notably the international news agencies Reuters, AP, AFP and the BBC and Davies' (2008) account of a content analysis of more than 2207 stories drawn from five top UK national daily newspapers argued that more than 70 per cent[4] of stories are derived from press releases or news agency sources and, at most, 20 per cent (and possibly as few as 12 per cent) were originated by journalists. Newspapers are certainly shedding staff but it is not only newspapers that are doing so: in September/October 2008 the UK's largest commercial terrestrial television broadcaster, ITV, cut 430 regional news jobs, making a total for the first 9 months of 2008 of around 1000 ITV jobs lost.

The half full glass

Thus far I have presented the impact of the Internet on the UK media as largely negative: as a glass at least half empty and with its contents rapidly draining away. But the glass can also be seen as half full if positive aspects to media convergence and change are acknowledged: these include enhancement of the reach of established media; new entrants providing services; positive aspects to the changes in the character of journalism (as 'citizen' or 'distributed' journalism grows more salient); the emergence of Internet information and comment fora as a 'fifth estate'[5] and the availability of innovative 'hybridized' media forms. Ofcom's *Communication Market Report* (2008c: see around p 97), for example, reports a continuing growth in the number of unique monthly users to UK newspapers' websites (annual growth rates range from 143 per cent for the *Financial Times* site, which has around 0.4m unique monthly users, to 4.4 per cent for the market leading *Guardian* site, which has around 1.7m unique monthly users). Dutton and Helsper (2007: 69) found that 49 per cent of those reading an online newspaper did not read the offline homonym – online publication thus extends newspapers' reach: the *Guardian* is a major case in point, marketing itself as 'the world's leading liberal voice'.[6]

The home pages of online newspapers, such as the *Guardian* and the *Daily Telegraph* testify both to their adherence to long cherished journalistic values (e.g. timeliness – the *Guardian* site features a header stating how recently it has been updated – often claiming 'Last updated less than one minute ago') and to their embrace of the new through hybridization and innovation. RSS feeds enable users to 'pull' self-selected content, assisting those who want a news and information diet that fits their own pre-determined criteria (rather than the editorial priorities of the 'paper') and enables them to construct a kind of *Daily Me* echoing their 'prosumer' choices; video inserts are embedded in the page and activated by clicking; click-throughs also provide access to downloadable podcasts and audio snippets. The printed newspaper has become an interactive multimedia product with a scalable balance of 'pushed' and 'pulled' material. It has also, of course, become de-territorialized – the *Telegraph* online can be accessed from anywhere (and at any time) in the world with Internet connectivity.

These hybrid entities dispose, at least in theory, of significant potential economies of scope and scale not least through the integration of on and offline newsrooms and the replanning of the architecture and consequential re-engineering of the day-to-day operation of newsrooms. Marshall referred to the possibility of using hitherto lightly-used, under an exclusively print business model, sub-editors' time (e.g. in the mornings) for on-line media activities. The *Daily Telegraph/Telegraph Online* has been a pioneer in this and other respects. Its re-engineering of newsroom architecture, as a hub and spoke operation with a central hub where editors sit and where bi-media editorial decisions are taken, has become a bi-media industry norm. But the extent to which potential economies are actually realized is difficult to assess. Advertising is customarily sold in on- and offline bundles, so revenues cannot be disaggregated and allocated to on- and offline versions, and when operations are integrated (as in a *Telegraph* style newsroom) costs are similarly difficult to disaggregate. Moreover, under some business models there are significant cost increases when online versions of a newspaper are produced. Anne Spackman, Comment Editor of *The Times* (formerly *Times On-line* editor-in-chief), stated at a meeting organized by Goldsmiths' College, University of London, that *The Times* spends 'hundreds of thousands of pounds a year to moderate comments online' (author's contemporary note 19.11.2008). Moreover, as Marshall (2008) claimed, as local newspapers consolidate and centralize news rooms and reduce journalistic and editorial headcounts (processes which customarily go together but which are not necessarily connected) quality often falls and litigation rises as the checking which sub-editors formerly provided falls away as they are spread more thinly. However, though quality (and plurality) has clearly suffered in offline newspaper journalism, the barriers to entry inherent in the high fixed costs of both broadcasting and newspapers are no longer so significant for Internet-based enterprises. The collaborative, 'open source', Web 2.0 model which underpins web-based institutions such as Wikipedia has, at best, made it possible for large-scale and high-quality public goods to be produced and disseminated at low cost. This model has provided a basis for some, albeit fragile, new entrants to the UK's public media sectors of real quality.

New entrants

New entrants range from sites such as openDemocracy (which started in 2000/2001) and has acquired a high reputation for its range of dialogic/debate-based international citizen journalism, embodying the attributes of Dutton's 'fifth estate', to Rick Waghorn's Norwich City soccer club-focused site. openDemocracy.net combines user generated content with expert editorial origination and amendment of content whereas Waghorn's site (norwichcity.myfootballwriter.com) is much more rooted in the established idiom and practices of 'legacy' journalism. Waghorn claims his site has 'the standards and commitments to quality you would expect from a trained and experienced, professional journalist – just a journalist that's now free from the space and time constraints traditionally imposed by a print press'. He asserts that the core competence which sustains the site is his own local, expert, knowledge: 'There are lots of journalists who may know more about national football or about England, but nobody will know more about Norwich football than me. Punters know I have a personal relation with a team' (POLISMedia 2009). Waghorn was formerly a sports writer on the Norwich *Evening News* and, after losing his job there, set up his Norwich City FC-centred site: lower costs, Waghorn's expert knowledge and informed judgment, and specialization, attracting local advertising and low threshold subscription revenues have established what seems to be a durable service.

openDemocracy is on a bigger scale with four full time workers and costs around £250,000 a year. It is distinguished by its use of writers from the localities under consideration, according to Isabel Hilton, editor-in-chief: 'we use African writers when an African issue is under consideration'; by its commitment to 'non-metropolitan voices' – 'we don't publish on the basis of a metropolitan outlook'; and by its dialogic and debate format – 'we typically commission more than one piece' – and 'we still regard ourselves as a debate site' (Hilton 2007). SEOmoz ranked openDemocracy 9/10 and Alexa ranked the site 3,071 among UK users.

However, despite the growth of news and comment internet sites/media and a host of blogs (e.g. ekklesia.co.uk, indymedia.org.uk, openDemocracy.net, iandale.blogspot.com, 18doughtystreet.com, pickledpolitics.com, liberalconspiracy.org, thefirstpost.co.uk) many sites have a mayfly life and survivors are often extremely fragile. openDemocracy owes its existence to support from foundations. It launched with $5m of support from foundations, among which the US-based Ford Foundation was the biggest contributor. In the last two years, in spite of a growing celebrity and reputation, openDemocracy has been in decline. Staffing has fallen from 15 to only 4 full-time staff (further supported by interns and contributions from associated projects) and the range and quality of content has changed accordingly. Although openDemocracy secured approximately 1,000 donations in 2007 (around 10 per cent of revenues, a further 5 per cent being earned from sale and syndication of content and the remainder being met by donations from foundations) its expenditure on core activities amounts to about £150k per annum. Of this very modest sum, its editor-in-chief, Tony Curzon-Price (2008), stated that only about 10 per cent can be devoted to commissioning and paying for contributions whereas premises, connectivity and webhosting account for about a further 10 per cent and core staff salaries the remaining 80 per cent.

openDemocracy displays some of the characteristics of the nascent, but fashionable, distributed, network or citizen journalism which Roy Greenslade characterized as 'a situation in which relatively small core staffs will process material from freelances and/or citizen journalists, bloggers, whatever (and there are many who think this business of "processing" will itself gradually disappear too in an era of what we might call an unmediated media)' (Greenslade 2007, discussed in Beckett 2008a and Bradshaw 2007). Distributed journalism has, at best, the authority and immediacy of direct experience and the trustworthiness that the dialogic and inherently self-correcting capacity of Web 2.0 deliberation potentially endows.

Web 2.0 and trust

Web 2.0[7] applications, including user generated content, were well characterized by Tim O'Reilly, sometimes credited with first using the term 'Web 2.0', as 'applications that harness network effects to get better the more people use them' (O'Reilly 2006). Interactive, Web 2.0, media thus potentially satisfy the normative criteria implicit in the leading UK philosopher, Onora O'Neill's claim that:

> Well-placed trust grows out of active inquiry rather than blind acceptance. In traditional relations of trust, active inquiry was usually extended over time by talking and asking questions, by listening and seeing how well claims to know and undertakings to act held up. That was the world in which Socrates placed his trust – and his reservations about publishing. Where we can check the information we receive, and when we can go back to those who put it into circulation, we may gain confidence about placing or refusing trust. (O'Neill 2002a)

Web 2.0 applications, such as Wikipedia and the 'citizen' journalism to which Beckett and Bradshaw refer (and which openDemocracy enacts), employ and foster collaboration and dialogue and thus, if O'Neill is right about the trust fostering attributes of dialogue, enhance trustworthiness and potentially establish Web 2.0 online media as no less, and perhaps more, trustworthy than its offline equivalent. At its best Wikipedia accelerates and makes more extensive and inclusive the collaborative processes of peer review, critique, factual correction and consensus-building that underpin offline scholarship. It has at its best an intrinsic self-correcting capacity. But at its worst (though this worst seems scarcely different to similarly abusive behaviour offline) Wikipedia is prey to systematic falsification and bias. Not surprisingly, controversy over how far Wikipedia (and user generated content in general) can be trusted is rife (Kleeman 2007).[8] However, others have embraced the networked, dialogic, Web 2.0 model.

The dialogic model can claim authority through its similarity to other forms of authentification based on peer consensus such as that which (albeit operating more slowly) obtains in the scholarly community: peer review and correction establishes authoritativeness and trustworthiness. And also through its empirical record. Beckett cites an exemplary case whereby a 'wiki'-like fact-checking and dialogic verification of the output of professional journalists helps 'the news media address the crisis of trust in journalism as a way of re-building its relevance and authority' (Beckett 2008a: 62). Beckett gives a powerful instance of this process, referring to Reuters' response to the revelation, on the political blog Little Green Footballs (styled by Wikipedia as the 'headquarters of the lizardoid army') that a Reuters' news photograph had been faked (see Beckett 2008a: 63). Reuters' own internal verification processes had not identified the falsification but once Little Green Footballs had done so Reuters rectified the error and revised its own operating procedures. However, the case of Wikinews demonstrates that a Web 2.0 model is not sufficient to ensure comprehensiveness or authoritativeness in news coverage. Wikinews is parasitic on legacy media and seldom consists of more than cut-and-paste compilations from established and authoritative legacy media sources. A quantum of professional journalists and editors seem to be required if the virtues, timeliness, authoritativeness and comprehensiveness, of legacy media's news reporting at its best are to be secured consistently online. And thus-far sufficient resources are at the disposal only of legacy media and consistently manifested online only in hybrid operations such as legacy media's online versions. Crowdsourcing (see Wikipedia definition) may come to provide Web 2.0 online media with sufficient resources to match, and perhaps surpass, those of legacy media.

Media have built legitimacy through adoption of one of two potential paths to authority and trustworthiness. The first, which is characteristic of new rather than legacy media, employs user review to establish authority (with a corresponding expectation that authors will revise and amend in the light of convincing peer commentary) and is characteristic of Web 2.0 media (such as Wikipedia). The second, characteristic of legacy media, derives from authors' (both individual journalists and editors and the collective authorship, embodied in an institution such as the *Financial Times* or *Wall Street Journal,* which includes journalists' and editors' work but also the work of sub-editors, fact checkers, proven and trusted sources and so on) status as experts: an expert status based on adherence to proven procedures and practices which have been found to ensure a high level of correspondence between the real world and its representation.

However, both methods potentially endow their exponents with legitimacy. Neither does so necessarily, as the compromised trustworthiness of the most highly legitimized of the UK's legacy media testifies.[9] In fact, there are seldom pure instances of either form of authentication – most public information is authenticated through a combination, in varying degrees, of both methods. They are non-exclusive and potentially mutually sustaining but online media are well fitted to draw on both whereas offline media are more strongly, and necessarily, wedded to the second.

Public finance

Generalization is often dangerous and, in this instance, especially so for important data is missing. It seems, however, that established media enterprises are, in varying degrees, in a crisis which arises from the erosion of the two supports on which their established business models depend: advertising and circulation/subscription revenues, In consequence, their provision (albeit imperfect) of a range and depth of authoritative news and information at affordable prices to all who wished to use it is under threat. New entrants may fill this gap but they may not, for legacy media incumbents have significant assets in their established brands and market positions and new entrants are, almost without exception, very fragile. The question arises: is there market failure in the provision of news and information and, if so, is failure on the scale and for a sufficient likely duration as to make public finance desirable?

The UK has, with the (significant) exception of exemption from VAT and (less significant) award of postal-pricing privileges, confined public support to the broadcasting sector. Unlike many other European Union Member States, the UK does not subsidize its newspaper press. However, the breakdown of the long-standing system of support for public service broadcasting has posed, and broadened, the question of the future extent and character of public service broadcasting finance beyond conventional radio and television.

Heretofore, public service broadcasting in the UK has been provided by four[10] free to air broadcasters: ITV and Channel 5 (*five*) (advertising-financed, for-profit commercial limited television companies), Channel 4 (a public sector non-profit advertising-financed radio and television broadcaster) and the BBC (a public sector not-for-profit corporation funded by an annual licence fee). The rapid decline in television advertising revenue (not least that occasioned by the migration of advertising online) has, it is generally but not universally agreed, fatally compromised the ability of the advertising-funded public service broadcasters to discharge their public service mandates. Ofcom estimates that around an additional £200m pa will be required to maintain a satisfactory quantum of public service broadcasting from providers other than the BBC. This estimate does not include any element for any decline in the capacity of newspapers to provide authoritative news and information services.

In its most recent, 2008, consultation on the future of public service broadcasting Ofcom invited comment on three possible future funding models: '*extended evolution*' (which reduces the public service duties of ITV and *five* and requires additional funding to sustain the public service mandates of the advertising funded broadcasters); a '*refined BBC/Channel 4 model*' (whereby only these two broadcasters would be charged with public service obligations in respect of which Channel 4 would require additional funding to discharge); and a '*refined competitive funding*' regime in which 'additional funding would be opened up to a wider pool of providers. Channel 4 could retain its PSB status along with its existing regulatory assets, but be required to bid for any additional funds alongside other providers. Current Channel 3 licensees and *five* could also bid for funding, alongside others, if they wished to continue to contribute' (Ofcom 2008c: 65). Ofcom identified different options (including reducing the BBC's licence fee revenues) for funding the public services associated with each option.

The third, competitive funding, option has its origins in an earlier tentative Ofcom proposal to establish a Public Service Publisher (PSP) at the heart of which was a vision of 'content for all distribution channels – broadband and mobile, together with a broadcast element' (see Ofcom 2005).

The Netherlands has implemented a scheme of public support for online providers of public service content analogous to that Ofcom anticipated in its PSP proposal. 26 Dutch public service Internet content providers have received public support of around 2.5m euros between 2003–2007 (see the 2008 study by TNO for the Stimuleringsfonds voor de Pers – TNO forthcoming). The PSP/third option has been fiercely resisted by the broadcasting incumbents, and hardly supported by the fragile new entrants that stand to gain by it because they, for the most part, lack the capacity to intervene effectively in the lobbying and politicking which has attended such policy initiatives. Nonetheless, the PSP/third option puts into discussion for the first time the possibility of public support for nascent online media operations which could and would supply public service content. It is too soon to tell what the outcome of Ofcom's consultation is likely to be. But the very existence of the consultation testifies both to the depth and intensity of the threats to incumbents posed by online media and to the opportunities online provision offers to extend, deepen and diversify public service and public interest media online.

Chief among the threats, perhaps, is the erosion of the resource base that has sustained pluralism in serious journalism and news dissemination. The core of this problem is the migration of sufficient of the advertising finance that, hitherto, has sustained news production and dissemination through legacy media (newspapers, radio and television) to the Internet. The biggest shift has been to search media such as Google and Yahoo which, though important aggregators and disseminators of pre-existing news, do not fund journalism and the production of original news copy. Pluralism in news supply may sometimes have been more apparent than real (newspapers rely on news agencies, seemingly separate broadcast news outlets relay news from the same newsrooms) but there can be little doubt that the economic base for pluralism in serious, original news journalism has diminished and seems likely to continue to do so (see, among others, Ofcom 2007).

Conclusion

Convergence has begun to transform the UK media landscape. From the perspective of the half full glass, it has made it possible for new entrants to improve the diversity, pluralism and quality of information services available in the UK: these new institutions may constitute the first fragile manifestations of a 'fifth estate'. Fourth estate incumbents have, in varying degrees and with mixed success, also begun to innovate and adapt and provide a fascinating miscellany of hybridized media products and services to UK (and extra-territorial) users. And the remarkable potential of Web 2.0, dialogic, types of deliberation and authentification has become apparent, giving rise to hopes for a new kind of dispersed, networked or citizen journalism. The difficulties of financing new entrants have been recognized and the consequential importance of reconsidering historic practices in allocating public finance to mitigate market failure and improve the range, quality and diversity of UK public media has been acknowledged by Ofcom, the chief relevant public authority.

But from the perspective of the half empty glass, incumbent newspapers and broadcasters are experiencing a rapid erosion of the viability of a long-established business model based on advertising finance. This trend has put in question the continued existence of a plurality of authoritative news sources as revenue streams, which formerly enabled newspapers to fund their own journalists and advertising-funded broadcasters to maintain a comprehensive news service, decline. In consequence, news in legacy media has become more reliant on news agencies and on press releases and the news feeds provided by Public Relations (see Davies 2008). More and more, the UK media display a consensus on news values with different media brands and products distinguished by variations in 'spin' and commentary. Of course, it is a moot point how far this is new. The mirror image of modernist technological utopianism is a sentimental attachment to a lost Golden Age of the media – a Golden Age apparent only to those wearing rosy backward-vision spectacles. But there can be little doubt (as Ofcom's 2007 *New News Future News* and the House of Lords' *The Ownership of the News,* 2008a, testify) that there is a major decline in the profitability of major media incumbents that has compromised, and is likely to continue to compromise, the quality and character of news services in the UK. The fragile economies of new entrants do not, yet, permit them to fill this gap.

For incumbents, life is becoming harder. For new entrants, life is nasty, brutish and usually short. The decline in public trust in the mass media, a decline rooted in a well-founded presumption that the media have become less trustworthy, makes public intervention, for example in the form of press subsidies or support for new web-based entrants (as Ofcom tentatively suggested in its proposition of a Public Service Publisher), likely to be unpopular and difficult to achieve. Nonetheless, despite the obvious, and credible, concerns to which public support for the media gives rise (government pressure on recipients of support, subsidizing inefficiency and tardy adaptation to changed circumstances, increasing moral hazard by rewarding failure etc., etc.), some form(s) of public support for the UK media (extending beyond, or possibly re-distributing portions of, the substantial sums – exceeding £3bn annually, devoted to the BBC) seems unavoidable. The question is whether such support will, to re-version Brecht[11], be directed to the sparky allure of the bad new things or the fading glory of the good old ones.

Notes

1. The *Daily Telegraph* is the UK's highest circulation 'broadsheet' (ie quality) national newspaper which achieved an average daily circulation of 843, 196 copies in October 2008. This compares with *The Times*' circulation of 629, 561 and the *Financial Times*' circulation of 451,676. *The Independent* achieved 201, 019 (see http://www.guardian.co.uk/media/table/2008/nov/07/abcs-pressandpublishing accessed on 27.11.2008).
2. See Picard (2003) which, though dated, suggests that newspaper publishers enjoy above average profitability. A judgement echoed by Marshall (interview 4.8.2008).
3. That is the daily newspaper *The Financial Times*.
4. For a sceptical review of Davies' book see http://www.channel4.com/news/articles/arts_entertainment/books/why+flat+earth+news+falls+flat/2038147 accessed on 20.1.2009.
5. A nice neologism of Bill Dutton's – see Dutton (2007). UK sites such as Ofcomwatch and Mayorwatch (www.ofcomwatch.co.uk and www.mayorwatch.co.uk) exemplify the emergence of effective, expert sources of focused commentary on public institutions and affairs.
6. See the descriptor preceding the www.guardian.co.uk url in the Google search result for 'Guardian'.
7. See http://en.wikipedia.org/wiki/Web_2 accessed 6.3.2007.
8. Cited in '*You couldn't make it up*' by Jenny Kleeman, first published in hard copy in '*times2*' on March 2nd 2007. At http://women.timesonline.co.uk/tol/life_and_style/women/the_way_we_live/article1457697.ece accessed 7.3.2007. See also the BBC's report of Jaron Lanier's charge that contributors to 'Web 2.0' sites adopt a 'mob mentality' at http://news.bbc.co.uk/1/hi/technology/6379621.stm accessed 15.3.2007.
9. In December 2008, Ofcom fined the BBC £95,000 for conducting radio competitions unfairly (see http://www.ofcom.org.uk/tv/obb/prog_cb/obb124/issue124.pdf accessed 4.1.2009). In July 2008, it had fined the BBC £400,000 in respect of eight separate breaches of the Ofcom programme codes.

Ofcom commented 'In each of these cases the BBC deceived its audience by faking winners of competitions and deliberately conducting competitions unfairly' (see http://www.ofcom.org.uk/media/news/2008/07/nr_20080730 accessed 4.1.2009). A year earlier, Ofcom had fined the BBC £50,000 for falsifying the results of a competition on the iconic children's programme *Blue Peter*. The BBC Trust stated that these 'were particularly serious as they resulted in children being misled to participate in a competition they had no chance of winning and in a child in the studio being involved in deceiving the audience' (see http://www.bbc.co.uk/bbctrust/news/press_releases/2007/ofcom_blue_peter.html accessed 4.1.2009). The BBC was not alone: in December 2007, Ofcom fined Channel 4 £1.5m and had previously fined *five* £300,000 and had also fined GMTV, the advertising financed but formally public service broadcaster, £2m. And the largest advertising funded, for profit, but formally public service broadcaster, ITV, was fined £5.68m by Ofcom for misconduct in conducting 'phone in competitions (see http://www.ofcom.org.uk/media/news/2008/05/nr_20080508 accessed 4.1.2009). Each and everyone (the tiny S4C excepted) of the UK's public service broadcasters were thus found deficient in trustworthiness by Ofcom in the period 2007–8.

10. There are also the publicly-owned not-for-profit S4C which provides Welsh language television programmes and is financed by government grant and advertising (the BBC is required to provide some programmes in the Welsh language to S4C) and the Gaelic Media Service which uses a government grant to fund provision of high quality programmes in Gaelic using both conventional broadcast and new media services.
11. Nicht an das gute Alte anknüpfen, sondern an das schlechte Neue (Don't hang on to the good old things but to the bad new ones). Attributed to Brecht by Walter Benjamin – see Walter Benjamin, *Fragmente. Autobiographische Schriften. Gesammelte Schriften* VI, Frankfurt/M.: Suhrkamp tabu wiss., 1991, S.537 ff. Cited by Gerd Peter at http://www.forum-neue-politik-der-arbeit.de/content/workshop/2006/Nicht%20an%20das%20gute%20Alte_Peter.pdf accessed on 4.7.2009.

Chapter 3

Three Myths of Internet Governance and the Internet in the UK

> It is through the complexity of the empirical that one gets a sense of the irreducibility and contestability of the social, the disjunctures between the programmatic statements of policy and the messiness of actuality…Empiricism is, in this sense, opposed to 'social theory' in so far as what is called social theory can too often over-determine what is and what can be said about empirical investigations. (Barry 2001: 22)

Introduction

The Internet is now indispensable. About 56 per cent of the 24m UK households are connected to the Internet (ONS 2006: 191) and, of these homes, more now have broadband access than have narrowband, dial up, access, though about a third of the UK's population has never used the Internet (Dutton et al. 2005: 10). The Internet exemplifies a shift in UK communication consumption patterns whereby, between 1991 and 2003, UK household expenditure on communications has almost trebled (ONS 2005: 2) – mobile telephony, subscription television and the Internet have all become familiar elements in daily life. The UK government has recognized its importance for the UK's economic, social and political future, for example, in the White Paper on Competitiveness (which stressed the importance of ICTs and the Internet for improving the UK's competitiveness and economic performance [DTI 1998]) and in aiming both to have all Government services available online and universal Internet access for all who want it by 2005. Yet, in spite of the Internet's importance and the challenges posed by an overstretched Internet infrastructure having to cope with the increasing demand of millions of new users for faster connections and new wireless applications, Internet governance, in contrast to earlier wired and wireless communication systems, is informal, uncodified and dispersed. Rather than the vertically-integrated end-to-end systems adopted for wired voice telephony and wireless broadcasting, the Internet is dis-integrated with different firms handing on traffic to each other, operating in separate layers and under different governance regimes.

Three myths of Internet governance prevail – none is well founded. First, the myth dominant in the public policy domain, that Internet governance is best when the market decides. Second, the myth dominant in scholarly discussion of the Internet that network governance and self-regulation is both pervasive and effective. Third, the myth that Internet governance is quite distinct from the governance of 'legacy media' (notably the established electronic communications media of broadcasting and telephony). The third myth has led

Internet scholarship to focus on the DNS (Domain Name System) and ICANN (Internet Corporation of Assigned Names and Numbers) with, as Wilson (2005: 31) has observed, a consequential neglect of national governance of the Internet. In this chapter I will explore these issues in the context of the Internet in the UK.

The UK Communication Act 2003 came into effect on 29 December 2003 and for the first time the governance of UK telecommunications and broadcasting has been brought together under a single statutory regime. The act was drafted to 'establish a new policy framework' and to 'simplify the regulatory framework' (DTI/DCMS 2002: 3), however, the Act is possibly the longest act ever to appear on the Statute Book with 411 clauses and 19 schedules! Moreover, sections of its predecessors, the Broadcasting Acts 1990 and 1996, the Telecommunications Act 1984 and the Wireless Telegraphy Act 1949, remain in force. But, in spite of the Act's length, the new policy framework it established seems poorly endowed with the 'resilience and adaptability for the future' (DTI/DCMS 2002: 3) which the sponsoring Secretaries of State sought to achieve; not least because the Act excludes the Internet. This exclusion may seem to betoken a surprising view of the future but is not accidental: the sponsoring Secretaries of State stated explicitly that 'it is not the intention… to extend regulation into the Internet' (DTI/DCMS 2002: 48).

The UK's policy stance of 'hands off the Internet' is widely representative of the stance taken by other states. The European Union Framework Directive (European Parliament and the Council of the European Union 2002c), in Recital 20, explicitly excludes a key element of the Internet's control infrastructure, Internet naming and numbering, from national regulatory bodies' responsibilities. Moreover, in contrast to the long standing treaty-based governance regimes for other forms of international communication, notably the post, telegraphy and telephony which are governed by international organizations affiliated to the United Nations (the Universal Postal Union and International Telecommunications Union), international governance of the Internet is divided between different institutions whose remits and authority are contested and uncertain. ICANN, the overall authority for Internet addressing, is the outstanding case in point. But the absence of explicit, hierarchical, mechanisms of governance does not mean governance is absent. Instead, self-governance seems to fill the gap – ICANN for addressing; the Internet Watch Foundation (IWF) for content control; setting of standards through requests for comment (RFCs) and so on. Mueller (1999: 498) described 'self-governance as a 'term commonly applied to the Internet itself' and identified 'self-regulation' as characteristic of the Clinton administration's approach to Internet – an approach also followed by the Bush administration. The Internet thus seems to exemplify what Taylor (2001) has argued is a general shift in governance in contemporary societies from hierarchy and markets to networks (Thompson 2003). Instead of hierarchy, Taylor argues that 'What is emerging at the moment is a new *network culture*' (Taylor 2001: 5) – a network culture that is characterized by self-regulation (Thompson 2003: 30).

Network governance is required, Taylor argues, because of modern societies' complexity. 'The moment of complexity', for Taylor, constitutes a 'tipping point where more is different' and engenders a shift to network, rather than hierarchical or/and market governance. In turn, Taylor (2001: 4) identifies the 'explosive development of cybernetic, information and telematic technologies since the Second World War' as triggering this 'tip' to network culture (see also Barabasi 2002, Castells 2001, Keohane and Nye 1998). From this perspective, the Internet is but the most recent, and arguably the most influential, of these technologies and is representative of network organization. And, Castells contends, network organization 'constitute[s] the new social morphology of our societies' (Castells 1996: 469). If network organization is displacing both hierarchy and markets as the dominant contemporary forms of governance then 'the 'new information technology paradigm provides the material basis for its pervasive expansion throughout the entire social structure' (Castells 1996: 469). Barry (2001) has made a similar observation: 'the network has come to be seen by many to be the basis for a "third way" beyond the opposition between statist social democracy and free-market capitalism' (Barry 2001: 86). The Internet thus has, if we follow this line of argument, both a crucial constitutive role in network culture and is also an exemplar of network culture.

But all these formulations imply that the Internet is a distinct medium; something we understand in the same way that we understand television, radio or voice telephony; something distinct, bounded and different from all other electronic media. There is an important truth here. The Internet has its own history (see, for example, Zakon 2003) and institutions (e.g. ICANN, national registries, Internet Service Providers [ISPs]). Such scholarly work as there is on Internet governance has focused on such distinctive Internet institutions and has constructed Internet governance as constituted of solely Internet issues – notably the DNS (see, among others, Geist 2001, Lessig 1999 and 2001, Marlin-Bennett 2001, Mueller 1999, Verhulst 2001, Vixie 2003). But there is also an important misconception in such a formulation. For the Internet and legacy media are intimately interdependent.

Internet services are carried on infrastructures established and used for voice telephony; new, hybridized services span both legacy and Internet media (e.g. the interdependence of television programmes and websites); the Internet and legacy media are, in some areas, substitutable (e.g. Voice over IP and conventional voice telephony). However, more important than such intimate interdependencies between Internet and legacy media is the way the Internet foreshadows a new form of electronic network architecture. From this point of view, the Internet is not a distinct new medium but rather is a stage in a continuing process of transformation from established technologically distinct media of communication to an integrated digital topology of interconnecting networks. We see this transition, often called convergence, in the transformation of the architecture of telecommunication systems from the vertically integrated structures characteristic of circuit switched systems to the layered structure characteristic of packet switched systems; in use of Internet Protocol (IP) standards in telephony (particularly mobile telephony) transmission paths; in hybridized multi-media and in the increasing extent to which the Internet substitutes for existing media (Werbach 1997).

The UK Communications Act 2003

Although the UK Communications Act 2003 was drafted to exclude the Internet, many of its provisions, particularly those that arise from the transposition of EU Directives,[1] mean that the provisions of the Act *do* extend to the Internet. For example, Internet transport is regulated in the same way as is transport of other telecommunication services. Article 1 of the European Union's Network and Services Directive (CEC 2002) provides that:

> 'electronic communications network' shall mean transmission systems and, where applicable, switching or routing equipment and other resources which permit the conveyance of signals by wire, by radio, by optical or by other electromagnetic means, including satellite networks, fixed (circuit – and packet – switched, including Internet) and mobile terrestrial networks.

This is clearly a formulation sufficiently wide to include the Internet. And though Clause 32 (1) of the UK Communications Act 2003 defines 'electronic communications network' differently from the Network and Services Directive (and without explicitly specifying the Internet) it does so in such a way that the Internet is included. Clause 32 (1) (a) provides that an electronic communications network is 'a transmission system for the conveyance, by the means of electrical, magnetic or electro-magnetic energy, of signals of any description'.

However, in other instances we can see a truth to the Secretaries of State's belief that the Act does not extend to the Internet. Clause 32 (2) excludes Internet content services[2] from the ambit of provisions for electronic communications services. Section 2 states:

> In this Act 'electronic communications service' means a service consisting in, or having as its principal feature, the conveyance by means of an electronic communications network of signals, except in so far as it is a content service.

The Act does not, therefore, provide powers for regulation of radio or television-like services distributed over the Internet. As Richard Hooper, the Chair of Ofcom's Content Board, stated: 'Ofcom has clear statutory duties over broadcast content, it would appear to have no statutory powers over content distributed via the internet or 3G mobile phones' (Hooper 2005: np). In consequence, there are recurrent demands for more comprehensive and effective regulation (hierarchical governance) of Internet content although the 2005 Oxford Internet Survey found no evidence of general public concern and stated rather that 'the public is undecided and of two minds about Internet [i.e. content RC] regulation' (Dutton et al. 2005: 48). The drafting of the Act thus means that far from being technologically neutral the Act applies different regulatory regimes to similar services received on the same domestic screen (and loudspeaker). Different regimes apply depending on the transmission path followed by a particular service: broadcast television is subject to Ofcom whereas a moving-image service accessed through a browser is not. Furthermore, the Act includes eight specific clauses (56–63) on telephone numbering but does not apply to[3] Internet naming and numbering.

How can we account for these contradictions? Perhaps, by exempting the Internet from the provisions of the Act, the UK Government sought, and achieved, a covert large-scale liberalization of a substantial and growing portion of the electronic communication sector. Perhaps the Secretaries of State's refusal to extend regulation to the Internet was a pragmatic decision to keep as tightly closed as possible a particularly messy can of worms. Perhaps the Government's pragmatism came from a recognition that in important respects the Internet is beyond UK control because control lies elsewhere – notably in the United States. Or perhaps the Government just went with the flow, with the pervasive utopian sentiment that not only is the Internet ungovernable but the Internet *should* be ungovernable, as one of the prophets of the Internet, John Perry Barlow, proclaimed:

> Governments of the Industrial World, you weary giants of flesh and steel, I come from Cyberspace, the new home of Mind. On behalf of the future, I ask you of the past to leave us alone. You are not welcome among us. You have no sovereignty where we gather. (Barlow 1996)

But the absence of consistent, effective and coherent regulatory bite on the Internet in the UK does not mean that governance is absent. As Lessig (1999: 220) said: 'When Governments step aside, it is not as if nothing takes its place. Paradise does not prevail.' What has filled the gap when government, at least in the UK, has stepped aside? To understand UK Internet governance we need to understand three things. First, that there are different forms of Internet governance and here I shall use Thompson's three part distinctions between hierarchical, market and network governance for discussion of Internet governance in the UK. Second, the Internet infrastructure is organized differently from the infrastructures of 'legacy media': Internet organization is disaggregated and horizontally layered rather than vertically integrated. And third, there is an inescapable international dimension to Internet governance that has not yet been, and perhaps will never be, subject to international agreement expressed in a formal international treaty.

Network organization

The arguments about network and self-regulatory organization of the Internet made by Barry, Castells and others chime with Foucault's (2002[1978]) influential propositions about governmentality: that is the idea that important practices of governance take place outside the formal institutions of the state and notably through internalized habits and rituals of self-regulation. What characterizes governmentality in network organizations? Putatively, co-operation, trust, solidarity and loyalty are the attributes of network organization, Thompson claims (2003: 112), following Riles (2001), that networks have a kind of 'elective affinity' with self-regulation; with 'bottom up type of organizational arrangements…[that] strongly connect to 'private interest governance' and the sphere of non-governmental organizations'

(Thompson 2003: 30). Internet organization and governance does indeed display such characteristics but these are manifest only in *some*, not all, parts of the Internet and in only some moments of Internet history.

Network organization, with its attendant shared values and commitment to consensus building, was characteristic of the 'early moment' of the Internet: a moment when commercial use of the Internet was proscribed; when governance took place through RFCs (Requests for Comment – the governance propositions drafted by Internet 'insiders' such as Jon Postel and Vint Cerf and which were circulated to the Internet community for revision, rejection and/or adoption); and when Internet infrastructure and services to users were 'free' at the point of use. 1994/5 is a convenient date to mark the end of this period: this was the date when NSFNET ceased to be generally available as a backbone infrastructure, when domain name registration in the US was first priced and when, in the UK, commercial ISPs (e.g. CompuServe, AOL, Demon, Pipex) began to operate as serious businesses with significant customer bases. However, in the UK at least, network organization (with rules, practices and institutions characteristic of the 'early moment') continues to characterize some important parts of the Internet. Cooperation, trust, solidarity and loyalty are notably evident in the not-for-profit Internet exchange LINX (the London Internet Exchange), in 'knock for knock' peering (versus the priced interconnection characteristic in voice telephony), the Internet Watch Foundation, the non-profit distributing status of the UK's registry Nominet and so on. These examples suggest that network self-governance remains a key, but not necessarily dominant or enduring, organizational characteristic of the contemporary UK Internet.

How do network attributes – cooperation, solidarity, trust and loyalty – play out when the network in question is made up of different, sometimes competing, firms working through markets and under different political jurisdictions (i.e. subject to different hierarchies)? Perhaps through a shared ideology or, put another way, at a different social site. Instead of being embodied in formal network institutions, such as self-regulatory agencies, these values are sustained in social networks and a shared ideology. A striking feature of findings from interviews the author conducted in 2003 was the extent to which interviewees referred to the 'interests of the Internet'. This culture of self-regulation and shared purpose chimes with the utopian, indeed anarchistic, culture of the Internet. But this culture and these practices may lead to governance being performed, *faute de mieux,* by unaccountable (i.e. required neither to report or give reasons for their decisions nor submit to election or other means of being held to account by their citizen and consumer constituencies) and incompetent (in the sense of being unable to resist capture of the Internet by powerful firms) institutions. Self-regulating organizations by definition tend to exclude those who do not share the dominant values of the self-regulating community (or network). See the persistent critique of self-regulatory network governance by Sandy Starr in *Spiked* (Starr 2003) and the (2003) arguments of the Scottish Advisory Committee on Telecommunications (SACOT) for the strong and effective presence of independent regulators and against regulation by interested parties.[4]

Starr's and SACOT's concerns are echoed elsewhere. Richard Hooper referred to the 'strong historical/cultural association of the internet with no censorship and no content regulation' (Hooper: 2005 np). And Geoff Huston (formerly a senior executive with the Australian incumbent telco, Telstra, and now Executive Director of the Internet Architecture Board),[5] proposed that:

- The Internet ethos of collaboration as the mechanism for policy formulation has failed to meet the demands of an environment of widespread deployment across many market sectors. Collaboration simply does not scale.
- Industry self-regulation is perhaps more an expression of faith in the outcomes of the competitive market as being an efficient distributor of a public resource of service than it is a well-understood mechanism to achieve the desired objectives in all situations. Industry self-regulation is a faith, not a science.
- The established communications industry players perceive a substantial threat to their existing mode of business within the guise of the Internet.
- The traditional methods of policy formulation in the public sector are attuned to gradual and well-researched changes to a relatively static policy framework, and a very strong tendency exists to preserve the status quo within the process. Public policy often comes as too little, too late (Huston 2002: 15).

The Internet's self-regulatory governance structures may not be well adapted to securing long-term public interest objectives. And it remains an open question whether important interests vital to the long-term health of the Internet in the UK are well served by the UK's emphasis on self-regulation. Perhaps the present relatively benign order is unstable and may metamorphose into the concentration of control seen in other related sectors such as broadcasting but, because of the UK Government's reliance on self-regulatory governance, without countervailing hierarchical regulatory institutions. This would be cause for concern even if it were only the Internet as presently configured that was at issue. But many aspects and elements of the Internet are paradigmatic of, and will form part of, what are called Next Generation Networks (NGN).[6]

Horizontal v Vertical

The Internet is not only an important phenomenon in itself but is also paradigmatic of a general shift[7] in the provision of electronic communication services from circuit to packet switched systems. Consider the evolution of mobile telephony from circuit switched second generation GSM (Global System for Mobile Communications) to the hybrid circuit/packet switched architecture of 2.5G, GPRS (General Packet Radio Service), which has a packet switched core and then to 3G (Third Generation) which has moved further towards a fully packet switched architecture. Together with the transition from circuit to packet switching goes a shift away from a vertically integrated to a disaggregated sector structure.

Table 1: Indicative comparison of vertically integrated network and NGN.

	Vertically integrated network (e.g. wireline telephony) examples	*New Generation Network*
Access	In firm: dial tone and call routing	Disaggregated: ISP.
Transport	In firm: wired local loop and trunk network.	Disaggregated: local loop unbundled and backbone network(s) routing dependent on traffic volumes. Wired and wireless.
Control	In firm: numbering and directory enquiry.	Disaggregated: DNS, search engines.
Content	In firm: e.g. speaking clock, cricket scores.	Disaggregated: Internet and www content providers.

Broadcasting too has characteristically followed the vertically integrated model: e.g. the BBC has provided content through its own orchestras, makes programmes using its own staff and facilities, transmitted programmes from its own transmitters. In broadcasting too we see moves towards disaggregation – e.g. independent production, sale of transmission networks though in the Pay TV sector in particular there have been moves towards vertical integration e.g. the vertical integration of production, scheduling and control (vie EPGs and CAS).

New loci of control and dominance are characteristic of Next Generation Networks (NGNs) and governance (hierarchical, market or network/self-regulatory) is an issue not only *within* each layer but also in the connections *between* layers. Interfaces between network layers, such as APIs (Application Programming Interface) – the interface between network and customer intelligence – have the potential to become bottlenecks and incumbents, whether telcos or proprietors of dominant standards, such as Microsoft, may resist moving to emerging generic standard APIs such as Parlay and JAIN (Java Advanced Intelligent Networks). In a study for the European Commission, Devoteam has argued persuasively that:

> So far, market power has been associated with a certain market share related to networks and transmission services. With NGN, market dominance may also be derived from controlling more limited sets of functions and capabilities that are necessary for the provision of services to end users. One example is the system of domain name servers, which perform translations from domain names to IP addresses. The ability to use domain names is fully dependent upon this function and in this sense, the number translation function constitutes a *control point*. In a hypothetical situation where the domain name translation would be controlled by a commercial profit seeking organisation, there would be obvious dangers of abuse of dominant position. (Devoteam 2003: 100)

Moreover, in contrast to vertically integrated circuit switched networks, where bottlenecks, such as the local loop, have been fairly easy to identify, loci of control may be anywhere in a NGN architecture. A shift towards a new network architecture not only creates new loci of power (opening up the question of whether generic competition law and regulation – the application of hierarchy to redress failure of market governance – will be sufficient to secure the public interest) but is also a shift which makes applications, services and firms associated with the emerging new order dependent on incumbent 'legacy' firms because 'legacy' infrastructures are still indispensable. Whereas in a vertically integrated network operators had an interest in managing network congestion and ensuring good quality of service now, with the emergence of NGNs using 'legacy' infrastructure provided by incumbent firms, there are powerful disincentives to incumbents providing high quality of service. For example, provision of a sufficiently high quality of service to make voice over internet protocol (VoIP) circuits practicable is unattractive to incumbent telcos because of the revenue loss they are likely to experience with a migration of traffic from circuit switched to IP networks.

Castells makes an analogous point (though his meaning remains somewhat fugitive). And he generalizes from a well-founded observation about the changing characteristics of network to a more speculative larger-scale observation about society and social power:

> '[N]etwork morphology is also a source of dramatic re-organization of power relationships …Since networks are multiple, the interoperating codes and switches between networks become the fundamental sources in shaping, guiding, and misguiding societies. The convergence of social evolution and information technologies has created a new material basis for the performance of activities throughout the social structure. This material base, built in networks, earmarks dominant social processes, thus shaping social structure itself. (Castells 1996: 471)

Hierarchy and markets

Hierarchical governance, the province of Barlow's weary giants of flesh and steel, embraces the activities of Government, law and statutory regulation. For the UK electronic communications sector, including the Internet, the key agency is Ofcom (the Office of Communications).[8] Ofcom has concurrent powers to regulate competition with the UK's principal competition regulator, the Office of Fair Trading, and is the lead regulator for the communications sector. And it is Ofcom's competition powers that are most relevant to Internet governance. These powers chiefly derive from transposition of the EU telecom liberalization and regulation Directives promulgated in 2002.[9] As the No. 10 Strategy Unit (ie the Prime Minister's office) has stated: 'In dealing with SMP,[10] Ofcom's powers will be largely determined by the EU regulatory framework. This framework restricts the majority of regulatory activity to those instances where there is SMP as identified by the process of market reviews' (Strategy

Unit 2002: 66). The Prime Minister's Office Strategy Unit gave examples of anti-competitive behaviour that Ofcom would be expected to regulate, including: leverage of SMP through horizontal or vertical integration; cross subsidies or price squeezing; differentiating product availability; differentiating level of service; differentiating availability of information; bundling different products; leverage of customer base; managing profits; and generally obstructive behaviour ['strategic incompetence'] (Strategy Unit 2002: 68).

Well-functioning market governance is equated with effective competition. In a well-functioning market the market's invisible hand (Smith 1776) governs firms' behaviour and establishes an equilibrium in which prices and long-run costs converge. In such circumstances, firms secure rents (i.e. profit beyond the levels required to maintain the system in equilibrium) only if they innovate and are thereby able to create and capture a new market where they can capture rents in the, theoretically, short period before other firms imitate them and re-establish a competitive equilibrium. This compressed sketch of competition theory is important because it shows, contrary to assumptions in some contemporary literature on the governance of electronic communications, that self-regulation is not an exclusive property of network governance but may also obtain in market governance regimes. In theory, both markets and networks may be self-regulating – it is, however, an empirical question as to whether in any particular instance a homeostatic, self-regulating, system, the *telos* of competition theory, actually exists.

The standard method of applying hierarchical governance to the market is through competition law. The relevant UK statutes are the Competition Act 1998 and the Enterprise Act 2002 which are now complemented by the sector specific Communications Act 2003. However, several commentators have remarked that competition law is too slow to provide effective remedies. The Director of Public Policy of AOL UK (interviewed 28 July 2003) asserted that the 'problem lies in the timing of the regulatory process. It may take up to 3 years for judgement'. This estimate is supported by the testimony of the Office of Fair Trading's then-Director of Competition Enforcement who stated: 'cases have taken longer than we expected when planning for the introduction of the Act. A realistic estimate for an infringement decision ranges from one year – in a very straightforward case – to 3 years or possibly even longer. Perhaps there are no "straightforward' infringement cases" (Bloom 2003: 5).

The Layered structure of the Internet

If one important aspect of convergence is the projection of Internet structures, practices and cultures onto legacy media, another is the reciprocal application of legacy regimes onto the Internet – interdependency is both retrospective and prospective. The Internet may therefore be considered paradigmatic of important general shifts[11] in the governance and organization of electronic communication services: from the vertically integrated organization characteristic of legacy electronic media to a disaggregated, horizontally layered, sector structure; from circuit to packet switched; and from hierarchical to network governance. However, both interdependency between the Internet and legacy media and the Internet's disaggregated structure suggest that Internet governance is better considered not as a single regime but rather as a series of regimes applying differently to the different layers. I have earlier referred to the Internet as a series of layers and contrasted this disintegrated form of organization to the vertical integration characteristic of voice telephony and broadcasting. This distinction is convenient but over-simplified. The layers of the Internet may be conceived in a technical and in a market sense.

There are two established descriptions of the Internet's technical layers – the four layers of the Internet protocol (IP) – applications, transport, Internet and network access and seven (physical, data link, network, transport, session, presentation, application) which derive from the Open Systems Interconnection Reference Model (OSI) designed for telecommunication systems in general, i.e., not solely for the Internet (see Wikipedia entry on Data Link Layer). The OSI model is seldom replicated in real world situations. As Wikipedia states, 'real-world protocol suites often do not strictly match the seven-layer model. There can be some argument as to where the distinctions between layers are drawn; there is no one correct answer. However, most protocol suites share the concept of three [i.e. neither seven nor four RC] general sections' (Wikipedia). Moreover, OSI and IP layers do not necessarily correspond to either market sectors (albeit also fuzzily demarcated) or to functional layers which make up our everyday experience of the Internet as a public communication system. How far does the market provide effective homeostatic governance of the UK Internet? How far does competition exist in new generation, layered, telecommunication networks?

The different layers of the Internet are distinguished by effective competition in varying degrees. How far can each be considered to be homeostatically self-regulating? There are challenging difficulties in answering this question. The OECD 2001 report suggests that answers will differ between different countries. Not least that, because markets are changing fast, conclusions drawn from a snapshot at a particular time may soon be outdated. Moreover, a definitive answer to this question would require a comprehensive market analysis based on rigorous definition of markets, followed by an analysis of each market thus defined. Such an analysis goes beyond what is possible here; however, an indicative analysis follows.

Whilst I have distinguished between hierarchical, market and network forms of governance, it is important to recognize that agents in any or all of the Internet layers may be influenced (whether consciously or not) by the possibility of another form of governance being visited upon them. If network and market governance regimes do not work to the satisfaction of government or citizens (or both), hierarchy may replace them. The 'shadow'[12] of hierarchy always lies over market and network governance systems and often shapes the behaviour of such agents in such systems of governance.

Let us conceive of the Internet as made up of distinct horizontal layers (Barua et al. 1999) as schematized in the table below and consider, in the context of UK arrangements, each layer in turn. My distinctions are organizational and sociological rather than technical and they derive from analysis of the UK Internet in 2003. The matrix below offers a schematic account of the discursive analysis which follows.

Table 2: UK Internet layers.

Layer	*Market governance (extent of competition)*	*Network governance*	*Hierarchy (covered by Communications Act 2003)*
Control – DNS	No. Monopoly.	Yes – Nominet '4th way'.	No – excluded from Communications Act 2003 (though provisions of general law apply).
Access – ISPs	Yes. Competition between many firms.	Yes – self regulatory ISPA code.	Yes – if markets don't work provisions in Communications Act 2003 apply.
Internet Exchanges and Network Access Points (IXPs and NAPs).	Yes. Competition – but LINX dominance.	Yes. LINX MoU.	Yes – if markets don't work provisions in Communications Act 2003 apply.
Transport	Wired backbone – competition but diminishing. Local access – wired some dominant suppliers but competition from resale assisted by regulation and competition from wireless – few providers but growing.	No.	Yes – if markets don't work provisions in Communications Act 2003 apply.
Content	Competition – but strong presence of perceived 'negative externalities' hence walled gardens of some firms to secure competitive advantage.	Yes. IWF/ICRA self-regulation.	No – excluded from Communications Act 2003 (though provisions of general law apply). Forays by Government (see, among others, Home Office and Scottish Executive 2005) and individuals (e.g. Godfrey v Demon* case) to exert hierarchical authority.

*Case No: 1998-G-No 30 in the High Court of Justice, Queens Bench Division, (Handed Down at Leicester Crown Court), before Mr. Justice Morland, 26 March, 1999; and Godfrey v. Demon Internet Ltd, Queens Bench Division, (1999) The Times, April 20, [Judgement March 26].

Control

Consider how far markets act as effective, homeostatic, self-regulatory governance mechanism in the central areas of the Internet. In the control area, notably the DNS, of Internet naming and numbering the market is recognized not to be an effective governance mechanism. The same is true in the analogous case of telephone numbering. Unique addresses, secure and reliable routing systems and an authoritative dispute resolution mechanism are all required and the market is not well suited to providing these attributes of a numbering system.

As is well known, Internet addressing is organized hierarchically whereby the 'A' root server, which is at the top of the DNS addressing hierarchy, directs traffic to top level domains.[13] The 'A' root server is located in the US (where a further 9 of the 13 root servers also reside). Moreover, the potential power of the US accruing from location of the 'A' server and the majority of other root servers, and reflecting the historical development of the Internet, is strengthened by the global coordination of Internet addressing which resides with the US-based Internet Corporation for Assigned Names and Numbers (ICANN).

ICANN was established under a Memorandum of Understanding (MoU) with the United States' Department of Commerce (DoC). However, though therefore embedded within a hierarchical structure of governance, ICANN has been shaped by its origins under a 1997 US Presidential Directive which required the US Department of Commerce to govern the DNS through market ('private and competitive') and network ('self-regulatory') arrangements. The Presidential Directive stated, among other things, that the DoC was to 'support efforts to make the governance of the domain name system private and competitive and to create a contractually-based self-regulatory regime that deals with potential conflicts between domain-name usage and trademark laws on a global basis' (USGAO 2002: 7).

The establishment of ICANN followed the abortive attempt of IAHC (the Internet Ad Hoc Committee), which included representatives of major Internet institutions such as ISOC, IETF and other international bodies such as WIPO, ITU and the International Trademark Association to establish an equitable and robust DNS and to respond to the dominance Network Solutions (NSI) had established in the registration of US domain names. The IAHC proposed seven new TLDs (.arts, .firm, .info, .nom, .rec, .store, .web) and creation of 28 registrars to compete with Network Solutions (which in 1992 had been contracted by the NSF to register domain names in the .com, .net, .org, .gov, .edu TLDs). NSI, the European Commission and other bodies objected to the IAHC proposals and aborted its initiative. Self-regulatory governance of the DNS (through IAHC) did not work in this case because powerful international interests and commercial monopoly interests were not in accord with IAHC. Hierarchical governance, through the President of the United States, established the status quo which (sometimes uneasily) combines market, hierarchical and network governance.

ICANN operates outside the remit of an international treaty or intergovernmental agreement[14] and determines whether, and if so which, new top level domains (TLDs) are established (see, for example, ICANN 2000). Via the Internet Assigned Numbers Authority

(IANA), ICANN continued to assign allocation of Generic top level domains (gTLDs)[15] to a US-based corporation Network Solutions Inc (NSI), a company which was subsequently acquired by a for-profit corporation VeriSign (which also administers the 'A' root server). ICANN assigned the allocation of country code top level domains (ccTLDs) to four regional registries. In turn, these have assigned blocks of addresses to national Internet registries (APNIC for Asia, ARIN for the Americas, LACNIC for Latin America and the Caribbean and RIPE for Europe and parts of Africa and Asia.), in the UK to the national registry, the non-profit distributing company, Nominet. It is generally accepted that, like telephone numbering, the DNS does not lend itself to governance through the operation of markets. But, perhaps not surprisingly, there are live concerns about the extent, balance and orchestration of different methods and institutions of DNS governance. Here it is instructive to compare the operation of the US and UK national registries.

The US registry, VeriSign, has shown itself ready to use its monopoly power to advance its commercial interest. In September 2003 VeriSign redirected erroneously-addressed messages via its own commercial Site Finder web site. ICANN responded by requesting VeriSign to suspend its redirection 'service'. Initially, VeriSign refused but after a further communication from ICANN demanding suspension of redirection (itself perhaps inspired by China briefly withdrawing from the global DNS system) VeriSign complied (see, for example, Leyden 2003) The VeriSign redirection imbroglio of September/October 2003 suggests that national registries potentially have very significant market power and that ICANN, whether conceived as an institution of hierarchical or network governance, may not command sufficient authority alone to secure the compliance of the most powerful national registry in the DNS. However, ICANN's authority, when augmented by the prospect of VeriSign's loss of the 'network externality' benefits of a single, integrated, global Internet (a loss which would have been incurred had China permanently seceded from the established DNS) and perhaps complemented by US Government pressure on VeriSign, was sufficient to secure VeriSign's eventual compliance.

Like VeriSign, the UK registry, Nominet, also has monopoly power in a key area of the control layer of the Internet. The locus of VeriSign's power is the gTLD and the locus of Nominet's the UK's ccTLD. Nominet's stated mission is to control, manage and operate the .uk country code Top Level Domain in the interest of the UK Internet community as a whole. In order to do this it consults regularly with representatives of consumer groups, industry and government bodies (Nominet nd). Nominet is a non-profit distributing company and claims to be 'cost and not profit oriented' with cost-based pricing of services. A Nominet interviewee, (interviewed 1 September 2003), claimed that Nominet does 'what needs to be done centrally' (i.e. focuses on its core task and does not expand beyond that) and does not expand into provision of for-profit services: it offers 'no added-value services' and seeks to 'cover costs and maintain a prudent reserve'.

Nominet is controlled by a Council of Management comprising two executive directors (both *ex officio* and one of whom shall be the Managing Director of the company) and four non-executive directors – the non-executives are elected by Nominet's members at the company's annual general meeting. Anyone interested in the Internet is eligible to become a Nominet member by paying a one-off joining fee of £400 (plus VAT) and an annual subscription charge of £100 (plus VAT). Most of the 2800 members are Nominet clients and voting is weighted so that members registering most names have more votes – that is, Nominet's big customers are more influential than are its small customers. In late 2003 relative voting power varied between 1 and 795 votes. Nominet also has a Policy Advisory Board (PAB) which comprises two of the non-executive directors, five representatives of appointed organizations (such as the CBI and Companies House) and eight representatives who are elected by Nominet members. Nominet also provides a dispute resolution service Nominet's Executive Chairman – Dr Willie Black (interviewed 1 September 2003) claimed Nominet as a leading instance of what he termed a '4th way'[16] – that is, a well-run, reasonably-priced and efficient private organization, 'managing a valuable resource' and operating in circumstances where supply is constrained, responsive to its users but not formally regulated by external body. The key characteristics that Dr Black identified as distinguishing a '4th way' organization are:

- Fair, reasonable and non-discriminatory trade practices
- Efficient
- Cost- not profit-based pricing
- Public service ethos.

Nominet's monopoly market power is not only mitigated by its non-profit status but also the possibility of acquiring a gTLD address (e.g. .com instead of .uk) from VeriSign.[17] And, because Nominet is not covered by the provisions on 'electronic communications network' and 'associated facilities' in the Communications Act 2003 (Chapter 1, clause 32), Nominet is also effectively outside hierarchical governance.[18] Its autonomy was underlined by the Office of Fair Trading (OFT) decision not to pursue a complaint made against Nominet by Scotnom. Scotnom sought to establish a .scotland registry, to administer a new .scotland domain and complained that Nominet acted anti-competitively in considering this matter.[19] However, the OFT found (on 15 April 2003) that there was 'not enough evidence to launch a formal investigation' (OFT 2003).[20]

In conclusion, in the control layer, network governance, with some influence of competition from the market sector, has produced a well functioning layer where Nominet's monopoly power is tempered by:

- Nominet's '4th way' vocation
- Competition among second level domain registries
- Competition from gTLD registry
- Competition from other national registries (i.e., a UK-based company or individual could acquire an address from a ccTLD registry other than Nominet).

Access

Table 3: Estimated market shares of narrowband unmetered (including partially unmetered) ISPs in the Hull area.

	Residential share	*Business (SME) share*
Karoo	65%	46%
AOL	27%	27%
Freeserve	3%	7%
Demon	1%	5%
Hull24	0%	5%
Other	3%	11%

Oftel consumer research (2003b).

The review by the Office for Telecommunication (Oftel) of the wholesale unmetered narrowband Internet termination market (Oftel 2003b and 2003c), a key element of the access market,[21] found that no single firm (other than in the geographical market around Hull/Beverley served by the incumbent Kingston Communications) had SMP. However, in Hull the incumbent telco's own ISP, Karoo, was dominant.

Accordingly, Oftel directed Kingston to provide network access to competitors, not to unduly discriminate against competitors, to publish a reference offer, notify charges, and publish technical information.

In the UK, the ISP trade association ISPA (Internet Service Providers Association) estimates (interview ISPA 4 September 2003) that there are more than 300 ISPs trading – however this number represents a fall from a number once in excess of 1000. Moreover, three ISPs (AOL, BT, Freeserve) each account for around 20 per cent of the market and the sector thus has a long tail of small companies of which a representative of a large ISP (interviewed 28 July 2003) commented 'losses are so bad small ISPs can't even merge'. However, low barriers to entry have enabled new firms to enter the ISP sector (e.g. Tiscali in 2001).[22]

In conclusion, in the access layer, a combination of hierarchical and market governance has produced a well-functioning layer.

Internet exchanges

Consideration of this level illuminates the difficulties that sometimes exist in differentiating layers. Where does the boundary lie between the putative Internet exchange and the transport layers? Internet exchanges are key junctions at which traffic is handed from one transport provider to another – in one sense they are part of the transport layer. But the distinct institutional and governance characteristics of the exchange and transport layers, different firms, different balances between hierarchical, market and network governance, suggest that these layers should be considered separately.

The London Internet Exchange, LINX, clearly dominates the UK Internet exchange market with around 60 percent of UK Internet traffic passing through the LINX. However, although LINX is not subject to specific hierarchical governance, and its market share suggests it is not subject to strong forces of market governance, SMP exercised by LINX is mitigated by:

- Competition in the UK (from other UK-based Internet Exchanges such as Manap) and international competitors
- LINX's '4th way' governance arrangements.

Like Nominet, LINX is a not-for-profit organization which prices to recover costs. Its customers are members of LINX and are 'expected to contribute towards the running of LINX by volunteering for work required to run and manage LINX' (LINX MoU 3.1) and to abide by the LINX Memorandum of Understanding (LINX 2003). In turn, they are eligible to participate in the governance of LINX. LINX's objectives (LINX MoU iii) are to:

- Provide efficient interconnectivity within the UK for the Internet (core activity)
- Promote the interests of its members (non-core activity).

Clearly, LINX's objectives and constitution are characteristic of a mutual organization with membership open to all interested parties who pay fees and fulfil technical operating requirements.

In conclusion, in the Internet exchange layer, a combination of network self-governance and market governance through competition has produced a well-functioning layer.

Transport

At the time of writing there is evidence to suggest the UK Internet transport works reasonably well. There are a number of competing transport providers (notably Energis, Cable and Wireless, BT, Thus, NTL/Telewest). And Oftel (2003e) has estimated that in November 2003 the UK had more than 100 DSL service providers with ADSL, accounting for about 53 per cent of the broadband market of around 3m UK subscribers at the time of the survey. Technological change, notably through wireless transmission (wifi, satellite), promises to augment competition. However, Devoteam has advanced a plausible alternative account of likely European trends – notably a decline in competition in the European transport sector to as few as 3–5 players in the next few years (Devoteam 4.3.3 p 86).

Some concern has been voiced both about the decline in peering,[23] relative to paid transit, and about possible abuse of market power by incumbents. However, of LINX's some 120 members, most will peer with anyone though a few will peer only with operators passing on more than a certain amount of traffic (interview LINX 15 July 2003). Moreover, a representative of a large ISP (interviewed 28 July 2003) contended that BT exercises SMP in transport and claimed that BT is a 'problem on the access side', is 'squeezing out rivals', that 'everyone relies on BT's infrastructure' and also claimed that 'BT sells on retail minus, everyone wants cost plus but Oftel determined to use retail minus' and that BT was thus able to squeeze competitors' margins. Another commentator made an analogous argument claiming that 'if there is a commercial bottleneck in the UK, it's a shortage of high capacity leased lines - not in London but outside London…it all comes back to the Oftel policy of encouraging infrastructure build'. In 2001 Oftel (2001) reviewed the UK Internet transport market and concluded that the market was effectively competitive. More recently, however, Oftel (2003d) concluded that BT has SMP both in provision of inter-tandem conveyance and in-transit on fixed public narrowband networks in the UK (excluding the Hull Area)[24] and Ofcom (bolstered by the new hierarchical authority with which the Communications Act 2003 had endowed it) acted, in mid 2005, to effect a 'virtual separation' between BT's retail and wholesale divisions.

There is some uncertainty, therefore, about how well the UK Internet transport market works.[25] Experience in the UK suggests that extensive regulatory intervention has been required to redress the market power of incumbent telcos. Oftel has intervened on a continuing basis to create conditions in which quasi homeostatic markets have developed. For example, Oftel's valedictory (published less than three weeks before it was subsumed into Ofcom) *Internet and Broadband Brief* of 10 December 2003 resumed its interventions designed to secure effective competition in UK Internet connectivity. Headlines include Oftel's direction of May 2000 to BT to introduce FRIACO (Flat Rate Internet Access Call Origination)[26] which, Oftel claimed, led to the UK enjoying among the cheapest prices for Internet access in the world; extensive and intensive liaison between Oftel, BT and other operators to implement local loop unbundling (LLU);[27] Oftel's Direction (23 December 2002) on Partial Private Circuit (PPC)[28] prices and service level agreements and Oftel's investigation into BT's IP Stream (a family of BT broadband products) price cuts which, following discussions between Oftel and BT, resulted in BT reducing the price of its wholesale Datastream product (Oftel 2003f: 21). Ofcom's brokering of virtual separation in BT (Ofcom 2005) provides another case in point.

In conclusion, in the transport layer, a combination of hierarchical and market governance has produced a well-functioning layer (though one which may revert to a state of dominance).

Content

Prima facie, the content layer is extremely competitive. There are no obvious barriers to entry and innumerable suppliers but, in the UK, there may be dominance by the BBC. An independent report, the Graf report, on the BBC's role in the Internet content sector was published in the summer of 2004. Its author, Philip Graf, commented that 'the process of independent review is not, in my opinion, a very efficient one…The Charter review should seek to find a better regime for regulating services such as BBC Online' (Graf 2004: 6) and observed that though financial information about BBC Online was 'opaque' (Graf 2004: 9) it was 'very generously funded by comparison to its commercial competitors' (Graf 2004: 11).

Graf's findings provided few solid foundations for a challenge to KPMG's earlier conclusion (in a report commissioned by the BBC) that 'despite BBCi's evident popularity, we consider that it has had relatively little commercial impact to date' (KPMG 2003: 9). Graf brought in a 'not proven' verdict arguing that 'the nature and complexity of BBC Online's services, and the evidence available to the review' meant that the hypothesis of no adverse market impact could neither be proven nor disproven. Nonetheless, Graf judged that BBC Online may have 'crowded out' new entry to the online market but that overall 'it seems unlikely that BBC Online has eliminated effective competition' (Graf 2004: 58). Moreover, Graf found that the BBC's own internal procedures and processes of governance had been deficient. He observed, for example, that 'The Board of Governors does not appear to have sufficiently scrutinised the service's value to the public and its impact on the market' (Graf 2004: 83).

However, concern about the governance of the Internet content layer has focused more on the negative externalities thought to arise from dissemination of harmful content than on competition issues. The availability and effects of unlawful pornographic material, particularly images of child sexual abuse (child pornography), unlawful solicitation of children for sex in Internet chat rooms, and the defamation of individuals through content published on the Internet, have been particularly salient concerns. That some of this material and activity is/are unlawful means, by definition, that hierarchical governance operates in the content layer – although it may not be completely effective. In a curious and notable recent intervention (Home Office and Scottish Executive 2005) the Government has signalled its concern about the availability of lawful content (but of a kind which the Government deems undesirable) on the Internet and has sought to encourage self-regulatory action by ISPs and other relevant parties in order to suppress such admittedly lawful, but putatively undesirable, content.

The content layer also has particularly prominent institutions of network, self-regulatory, governance, notably The Internet Watch Foundation (IWF) which exemplifies the 'historical/cultural association' between the Internet and self-regulation to which Richard Hooper referred (Hooper 2005).

The IWF was established in 1996 by two Internet bodies, the trade association – the Internet Service Providers Association (ISPA) and the London Internet Exchange (LINX) together with a charitable foundation, the Safety Net Foundation. Initially, the IWF focused on 'R3', that is *rating*, *reporting*, and *responsibility* issues and operated a hot-line to allow UK Internet users to report material which they believed to be illegal,[29] it promoted rating of Internet content[30] and the availability of filtering devices and supported initiatives to make Internet users, and others, better informed and more competent in dealing with Internet content issues – responsibility. Latterly, the IWF has adopted three priorities:

- To foster trust and confidence in the Internet among current and future Internet users
- To assist service providers to combat the abuse of their systems for the dissemination of criminal content
- To assist law enforcement in the fight against criminal content on the Internet.[31]

The IWF is governed by a board of ten members, of whom three are industry members, (selected by its Funding Council – made up of IWF funders) and six are non-industry members (formerly selected by invitation but latterly through an open selection process involving press advertisements and an interviewing panel which includes independent representation) and an independent chair. The IWF is largely funded by Internet service providers, mobile telephony operators and a small number of other organizations (in and outside the Internet sector).[32] It works by establishing and encouraging good practice throughout the UK Internet sector and by assisting in and promoting the operation of relevant UK law. It has succeeded in commanding the support and respect of much of the sector and policy community (though libertarians have expressed concern about the possible chilling effect on free expression of a number of IWF policies and recommended practices)[33] For example, a DTI interviewee stated (4 August 2003) that the IWF model 'set up here, has been widely replicated around the world' and that 'There's lots of pornography[34] on the Internet but almost none comes from the UK'. The IWF chair stated that 'we have and have had the full support of Government for what we do' and that both the DTI and Home Office were involved in setting up the IWF, funded a review of IWF governance after the IWF's first two years and were consulted on the IWF's own review of its governance practices and procedures. The IWF and Government had, the Chair claimed, 'a very close relationship but not one which is institutionalised'.

No concerns have been raised by the UK ISP sector in respect of the takedown of unlawful images (notably of child abuse), but the ISP sector (ISPA interview 4 September 2003) is concerned that the 'takedown' practices mandated in consequence of the judgement in Godfrey v Demon Internet Ltd[35] (see Akdeniz 1999) expose ISPs to legal action (and to adverse judgements) if they do not promptly respond to all 'take down' requests by prima facie interested parties or, if they do so respond, freedom of expression on the Internet will be lethally chilled. In ISPA's view there is insufficient authoritative guidance on key matters such as who is qualified to give a notice of offence leading to a take down and what constitutes a notice on which they should act.[36] The IWF Chair, on the other hand, observed (27 July 2004)[37] that '[t]he problem with the Godfrey case was the arrogance of the industry, they wouldn't even respond to Godfrey'.

In conclusion, in the content layer, a combination of hierarchical and network governance has produced a well functioning layer.

Between the layers

Analysis of governance, and the extent to which a self-regulating homeostasis exists, and/or is possible, *within* each layer of the Internet supply chain is an important element of my analysis. However, it's also important to consider the interfaces *between* layers. How are these controlled? Essentially, the general adoption of TCP/IP and HTTP protocols has simplified interfacing between layers and inhibited the accumulation of market power by owners of proprietary standards (see discussion of Open Systems Interconnect on Wikipedia). Wikipedia also conveniently lists some alternative standards and applications for linking and interfacing between layers (Wikipedia on OSI model) which support my contention that control of connections between layers is not concentrated and hierarchical governance is not so significant an issue between layers as it is within some layers.

Conclusion. From layers to vertical integration?

> If technology companies owned the newspapers (and, not impossibly, one day they will – although I wouldn't bet on this outcome), they would not be entirely happy until they owned the town, or at least the shopping areas. It is not at all a secret that the competition among technology companies on the Internet is to own the network itself. It is perhaps the natural insecurities of most nascent industries – railroads, movies, oil, long before software – that made them monopolistic. (Wolff 1998: 155)

The generally well-functioning governance of the contemporary UK Internet can be attributed, in part at least, to the successful development of self-regulatory, network, governance practices. But this success does not derive exclusively from network governance but rather from a flexible and shifting articulation of different modes of governance, market, hierarchy and network, across and between the different layers of the UK Internet. And in respect of all these modes of governance Ofcom the successor to Oftel,[38] plays an important role.

Ofcom is the main institution of hierarchical governance of the UK Internet. It is the lead regulator for the communications sector exercising concurrent powers to regulate competition (or, in governance speak, supplant market governance by hierarchy) with the UK's principal competition regulator, the Office of Fair Trading (OFT). Ofcom's competition powers chiefly derive from transposition of the 2002 EU telecom liberalization package (see CEC 2002 and European Parliament and Council 2002a, 2002b, 2002c, 2002d) into the Communications Act 2003, as the No 10 Strategy Unit stated: 'In dealing with SMP, Ofcom's powers will be largely determined by the EU regulatory framework. This framework restricts the majority of regulatory activity to those instances where there is SMP as identified by the process of market reviews' (Strategy Unit 2002: 66).

The Strategy Unit's analysis points to an interrelationship and interdependency between different modes of governance. And specifically to an assumed *inverse* relationship between hierarchical and market systems of governance: as effective competition develops so hierarchical governance should wither away. Hence Ofcom's 'bias against intervention' (Ofcom 2004: 3) and its doctrine of exercising hierarchical authority only when homeostasis, whether market or network, fails. In keeping with its 'bias against intervention' Ofcom has also sought to foster self-regulation. This is clearer in its relationship to the broadcasting sector (where regulation of television advertising has been devolved to the self-regulatory Advertising Standards Authority – ASA) than in respect of the Internet (where self-regulatory bodies were in place before Ofcom came into existence and before the Internet became as salient a social force as it now is). Indeed, the strength of Ofcom's commitment to self-regulation of content is evident in Hooper's comment that 'you could argue that external sectoral content regulation of broadcasting is a recent and passing phenomenon in the UK, and we could gradually be returning to greater reliance on self-regulation' (Hooper 2005: np). But there are obvious connections between Ofcom and Internet self-regulation: for example, Roger Darlington, the Chair of the IWF, serves on Ofcom's Consumer Panel and it may be no coincidence that BT, the principal object of Ofcom's regulatory activity, has instituted a 'Cleanfeed' service to its Internet customers whereby access to websites identified by the IWF is blocked.

Although my analysis above shows the importance of both hierarchical and market governance in the UK Internet (and thus a qualification of the growing preponderance of network governance and its elective affinity with the Internet proposed by Castells, Thompson and others), network governance is undoubtedly a strikingly important aspect of the generally well-functioning governance and coordination of the UK Internet. It is particularly noteworthy in the:

- Control-Access Interface
  Where ISPs are represented on the Nominet Council

- Access-Internet Exchange Interface
  Where ISPs are represented on the LINX Council

- Access-Content Interface
  Where the IWF is (partly) funded by ISPs who are also represented on the IWF Council.

My argument thus far has focused on the Internet in the UK, and deliberately so. As Wilson 2005) has observed, discussion of Internet governance has neglected the national dimension. Although Internet governance is undoubtedly complicated by the Internet's international character, contentions such as Castells' (1996) – influential though they have been – that the traffic carried by the Internet is largely outside national regulation are surely overstated. Here is another Internet myth. And one, which sustains the myth of Internet self-governance, for Castells implies that if national governments, and thus hierarchical governance, are absent Internet governance, can only be undertaken through market and network arrangements.

But as examination of the UK case suggests, neither national nor hierarchical governance is absent. Nor is the Internet best understood as a single 'thing'. It is not a vertically integrated medium of communication with a single governance regime but a layered entity with multiple governance regimes in and between the layers. But how far is the layered, disaggregated, structure a permanent, structural feature of the Internet and how far a contingent characteristic? Perhaps the commercial uncertainties which derive both from the layered organization of the Internet and its uncertain governance regime (markets, hierarchies and self-regulation in shifting patterns and further complicated by uncertainties in international governance arrangements) are giving rise to an industry structure whereby functions are becoming internalized in the firm (Coase 1937).

Some aspects of UK Internet industry structure lend support to this hypothesis, notably the vertical integration of carriage and content in two of the UK's three largest ISPs: in mid 2003 BT and Yahoo linked, earlier AOL and Time Warner merged. And key features of both the historical (evolution of the sector towards public or private/regulated monopoly structure) and recent experiences in telecoms also lend support to this thesis. For example, the difficulties of contracting on acceptable terms for international transit of Internet traffic (due to the pricing of circuits differently from the voice telephony model of the sender and receiver each paying for half a circuit), has recently led to bypassing of the international settlements regime through the building out, or creation through merger and acquisition, of global networks – to internalization of functions within the firm. An (hierarchical) organizational form which echoes that of circuit switched systems where either the state sponsored the establishment of public monopolies (displacing private sector firms in the interests of achieving universal service) or tolerated establishment of regulated private monopolies in preference to governance through market institutions.

> The launch of BT Yahoo! Broadband signals the arrival on European shores of the broadband access provider/portal partnership model already prevalent in the US. It also signals a move away from content and online services for one of Europe's leading incumbent-owned ISPs. Both could have dire consequences for alternative broadband ISPs, now competing against not only a dominant access provider but also the leading portal. Partnerships between incumbent access providers and portals are nothing new in the US – indeed, they are fast becoming the norm for broadband access. SBC Yahoo! was announced as early as November 2001. Verizon and Qwest both have partnerships with MSN while BellSouth works with ISP EarthLink on its broadband services. However, such close partnerships are as yet unknown in Europe. (Dawson nd)

But this is not a fully satisfactory explanation. Although 3 firms, (AOL, BT and Freeserve), account for around 60 per cent of the UK ISP market and at least two of these are internalizing functions by vertically integrating, there are also many (albeit a declining number) of small and medium-sized ISPs operating in the UK. So too in other areas – there are a number of transit providers (notably BT, Cable and Wireless, Energis and Thus). And, where key bottlenecks exist, such as the Internet exchange (notably LINX) and registry functions (Nominet), in the UK (in contrast to the USA) these are controlled by non-profit distributing and/or mutual companies with strong user representation and/or control. A Coasian explanation seems therefore incomplete.

An alternative, and I think more plausible, hypothesis is that, by benign accident for there has clearly been no conscious design, the UK enjoys an uneven but appropriate matching of different regimes and institutions of Internet governance to different parts of the Internet supply and value chains. Where, prima facie, there is significant market power, e.g. in the local loop, there is an appropriate level of effective regulation (Oftel on BT). Where there are regulatory issues arising from offensive content, e.g. pornography, the sector itself (in partnership with Government) has developed institutions (notably the Internet Content Rating Association – ICRA, and the Internet Watch Foundation – IWF). To be sure, these UK (ICRA is UK-based but European in scope and funding) institutions are not fully competent to deal with a very international medium, the objections made by Starr (2003), SACOT (2003) and others (to which I have referred above) about the legitimacy of such arrangements are cogent, and various forms of unwanted content, e.g. spam, viruses and worms, remain untamed (though in the case of each of the latter there are clear commercial incentives for firms in the sector to devise effective measures against these forms of offensive and/or damaging content). But, improvised though the UK system may be, it seems to work better than Mueller judges the USA's Internet governance to be which he contends is characterized by 'poorly thought out improvisations' (Mueller 1999: 498).

But, concern for the interests of the Internet, to which interviewees testified,[39] may not be sustainable when firms from outside Internet history and culture enter Internet markets – e.g. Time Warner (now merged with AOL); incumbent telcos (e.g. British Telecom) and retailers (e.g. Dixons, which established and later sold Freeserve, and Tesco). How are conflicts managed when the network in question is not a 'private' organization (e.g. a self-organizing NGO, the focus of Riles' work) but a public communication network? How does self-regulation work when consensus (e.g. on content regulation) may not be widely shared and when firms with significant market power exercise their power? What happens when the pioneering generation who are bound together by a shared commitment to the 'interests of the Internet' are displaced by another with different commitments – probably to self-interest? And what of other governance challenges not yet met? Spam is a notable case in point and one where network governance seems the least likely potential mode of governance to provide a satisfactory solution. Nonetheless, the reservations I make above aside, it is striking how far network governance has pervaded the UK Internet and how well the '4th Way' has served it.

Mythical though the inevitably international character of Internet governance may be and mythical though an exclusively (or even preponderantly) network governance regime may be, like most myths, these myths of Internet governance have more than a grain of truth in them. Compared to the legacy media of broadcasting and telecommunications, the salience of network governance and the limits of national governance in the Internet are striking. Striking but Over emphasised. And Over emphasised because of the over-riding importance of the biggest myth of Internet governance – that Internet governance is new, unprecedented and distinct from governance of legacy media.

Notes

1. Notably, the Access and Interconnection Directive 2002, the Network and Services Directive 2002, the Framework Directive 2002 and the Universal Service Directive 2002. European Parliament and the Council of the European Union 2002a, 2002b, 2002c, 2002d.
2. Defined in section 7 of Clause 32 as one or both of '(a) the provision of material with a view to its being comprised in signals conveyed by means of an electronic communications network; (b) the exercise of editorial control over the contents of signals conveyed by means of such a network'.
3. The Government proposes to lay a Statutory Instrument before Parliament to ensure it has reserve powers to govern Internet naming and numbering activities undertaken in the UK should the need arise.
4. SACOT stated, inter alia, that 'Trade associations and other existing industry bodies are not suitable structures to exercise co-regulatory functions' (SACOT 2003:2).
5. The Internet Architecture Board (IAB) is a committee of the Internet Engineering Task Force (IETF). Its responsibilities include architectural oversight of IETF activities, Internet Standards Process oversight and appeal, and it is responsible for the management of publication of the RFC Series and the management of the IETF protocol parameter registry, operated by the IANA.
6. That is IP-based networks where layers, e.g. access, transport, control, services, are independent and multi-purpose (voice, data, access to services). Devoteam 2003 provides an excellent account of the architecture of emerging NGNs.
7. The direction of this change is clear – its pace may lag because of the strength of legacy networks, incumbent inertia, the generally superior current quality of service over circuit switched networks, etc.
8. Ofcom was established under the Communications Act 2003 and replaces five earlier regulators – the Broadcasting Standards Commission (BSC), the Independent Television Commission (ITC), the Office of Telecommunications (Oftel), the Radio Authority and the Radiocommunications Agency.
9. See European Parliament and Council 2002a, 2002b, 2002c, 2002d, and CEC [Commission of the European Communities] 2002.
10. Significant Market Power – i.e. the ability of a firm or firms to act anti-competitively.
11. The direction of this change is clear – its pace may lag because of the strength of legacy networks, incumbent inertia, the generally superior current quality of service over circuit switched networks, etc.
12. I am indebted to Grahame Thompson for this idea and metaphor.
13. County codes, such as .de (Germany), .uk (United Kingdom), .za (South Africa) are known as ccTLDs (country code top level domains) and other top level domains, such as .com, .net, .info, .arpa are known as gTLDs.

14. However, ICANN has a (significantly named) Government Advisory Committee (GAC) which provides a forum for the representation of other states' interests.
15. VeriSign has handed management of the gTLD .org to the Internet Society (ISOC).
16. The notion of a '4th' way plays a variation on the 'Third way', associated with the politics of New Labour and Tony Blair (and reprised in Giddens' 1998 book of the same name) and which, notionally, mediated between the first and second ways of market and state co-ordination.
17. Or a different ccTLD, for many national registries (including Nominet) allocate addresses to persons not resident in the country in question – it is quite possible for a German company, or individual, resident in Germany to have a .uk address.
18. A DTI source (interviewed 4.8.2003) stated that though it might be arguable that some parts of Nominet might be covered by the associated facilities provisions of the Act, 'It's clear that Internet names are not telephone numbers'. Moreover, Nominet (interview 1.9.2003) contends that, even if the Communication Act 2003 provided Ofcom with powers to direct Nominet, because Nominet has intellectual property rights in the .uk address data base, no effective alternative to Nominet as a .uk registry could be established.
19. A .scotland domain could not, under ICANN's current operating practices, be established independently of Nominet for ICANN permits ccTLDs to be established only for states recognized by ISO. Customarily national domains are given the ISO country code as their country code (Australia changed from .oz to .au to conform to this doctrine). Curiously, the UK is an exception to this rule, for gb is the ISO code however ICANN uses .uk, the ccTLD that Nominet administers.
20. This is not an unusual finding by the OFT. Its then-Director of Competition Enforcement, Margaret Bloom, has estimated that only about 5% of complaints to the OFT 'convert' into cases where there are reasonable grounds for suspecting an infringement of the Competition Act 1998 (Bloom 2003).
21. In mid 2003 around 78% of Internet homes used narrow band connections for Internet access see http://www.statistics.gov.uk/pdfdir/int0903.pdf accessed on 29.1.2004.
22. Tiscali UK launched in July 2001 following acquisition of Liberty Surf, World Online, LineOne and subsequently Tiny Online and Gateway ISP to form the fourth largest ISP in the UK.
23. Peering and transit can be distinguished in the Internet transport layer. Peering is the exchange of IP traffic between networks; transit is a pay-for version of the same. In the utopian, early, moment of the Internet, peering was the norm. Operators handed on traffic to each other on a 'knock for knock' basis. Latterly, peering has been supplanted by priced transit and, where peering still obtains, often transport providers will peer only with their equivalent peers. See, inter alia, Cable and Wireless' peering policy at http://www.cw.com/our_network/peering/peering_europe.html accessed on 8.1.2004. Now available at http://web.archive.org/web/20040603191624/http://www.cw.com/our_network/peering/peering_europe.html accessed on 26.7.2009. Cable and Wireless appears to have removed this document from its website some time between 2004 and 2009.
24. This finding, among other things, demonstrates that the distinct layers I have identified above can, for some purposes, be usefully further disaggregated.
25. For persuasive testimony of the dynamic character of transport markets, on the difficulty of defining markets, and thus the difficulty of giving an account of the extent to which transport markets function well, see Giovanetti 2000 and Giovanetti and Ristuccia 2003.
26. FRIACO is an unmetered wholesale product that allows other network operators to offer their own unmetered Internet access products in competition with incumbents.
27. However, by Nov 2003 only 7,800 loops had been unbundled. Further regulatory proposals on LLU are anticipated in 2004.

28. PPCs are the key wholesale components of leased lines which telecoms operators buy from BT so they can offer their own services directly to end users. The prices set by Oftel for PPCs are typically 50% lower for connection and 20% lower for rental than BT's previous charges.
29. Notably material which contains images of child abuse, anywhere in the world; contains adult material that potentially breaches the UK Obscene Publications Act; contains criminally racist material in the UK.
30. Notably by the Internet Content Rating Association (ICRA) see www.icra.org.
31. See http://www.iwf.org.uk/about/policies/remit2003.htm accessed on 17.9.2004. The IWF appears to have removed this document from its website some time between 2004 and 2009. Its mission is now stated as: 'To work in partnership with internet service providers, telecommunication companies, mobile operators, software providers, the police, Government and the public to minimise the availability of online illegal content, particularly child sexual abuse images'. See http://www.iwf.org.uk/public/page.114.htm accessed on 16.6.2009.
32. The most recent IWF Annual Report available (that for 2002 at http://www.iwf.org.uk/about/annual_report/annual2002.htm accessed on 14.1.2004) shows an annual income of approximately £0.5m which derives from 22 identified funders – a small number of the firms active in the sector – and the IWF has experienced financial difficulties in consequence of its narrow funding base.
33. See, among others, http://www.cyber-rights.org (accessed on 14.1.2004). Starr's (Starr 2003) remark is representative: 'Internet users are quite capable of deciding for themselves what to read, watch, listen to and download, and whether they think it's any good to boot. The imposition of new responsibilities, in order to safeguard users, can only insult their intelligence and undermine their freedom'.
34. That is unlawful images of child abuse rather than lawful adult pornography.
35. Case No: 1998-G-No 30 in the High Court of Justice, Queens Bench Division, (Handed Down at Leicester Crown Court), before Mr. Justice Morland, 26 March, 1999; and Godfrey v Demon Internet Ltd, Queens Bench Division, (1999) *The Times*, April 20, [Judgement March 26].
36. ISPA (interview 4.9.2003) stated its preference for an indemnity regime similar to that provided in the USA Digital Millennium Copyright Act. The lack of legal certainty left ISPs vulnerable and was 'an ongoing worry'.
37. Making clear that issues such as those raised by the Godfrey v Demon case were not within the IWF's remit.
38. Ofcom was established under the Communications Act 2003 and replaces five earlier regulators – the Broadcasting Standards Commission (BSC), the Independent Television Commission (ITC), the Office of Telecommunications (Oftel), the Radio Authority and the Radiocommunications Agency.
39. In summer 2003 the author interviewed 11 senior officials and managers from UK and international governance agencies (ICANN, OECD, DTI and Oftel), Internet firms and trade associations in access (ISPs), transport (telecom carriers), addressing and Internet exchange sectors. Subsequently other interviews were conducted.

Chapter 4

The BBC, the Internet and Public Value

Introduction

Development of the Internet in the UK has been strongly, and largely positively, influenced by the BBC. From 1997, the BBC has provided an extensive range of high quality web-accessible content and played an important role in incentivizing people to use the Internet. Its early entry and continuing commitment to the web has kept the BBC high in the UK Internet usage ratings. Alexa (Alexa Internet nd) scores the BBC 7th (and highest among UK-based sites) among the sites most used by UK-based Internet users and periodically the BBC has claimed that it's 'Europe's most widely visited content site'.[1]

The BBC's website (now BBC Online) was launched in the mid 1990s. Latterly, the BBC's iPlayer (which – for users with a UK IP address – provides online access to the previous 7 days of BBC radio and television) and within a year has come to account for about 7 per cent of UK Internet peak traffic. 248m items of content have been accessed through the iPlayer in less than 11 months since its launch on Christmas Day 2007. PC users account for around 85 per cent of iPlayer viewers, Mac users for about 10 per cent and iPhone and iPod Touch users a further 3 per cent. 15- to 34-year-olds account for 37 per cent of iPlayer viewers, 35- to 54-year-olds, 43 per cent and over 55s, 21 per cent. The BBC's flagship soap opera *EastEnders,* watched by around 18.9m viewers monthly, attracts 457,000 viewers on the iPlayer. Other programmes, such as the children's spy adventure series *MI High,* have a higher proportion of viewers on the iPlayer: 145,000 watch on television whereas 30,000 watch on the iPlayer.

The BBC Director General, Mark Thompson, testified to the importance of the Internet to the BBC, and indicated how it might come to supplant conventional broadcasting, stating that: 'broadcasting has not been a very efficient way of getting the right programmes in front of the right people…the iPlayer will make it much easier for people to catch up with recent programming' (Hansard 2008: Q 24).

Impact of Internet on broadcasting – increased competitiveness and therefore increased pressure on BBC

The Internet has had an important reciprocal effect on the BBC, though its impact has been somewhat indirect. The Internet's main effect on broadcasting has been to threaten the financial viability of advertising-financed media, both newspapers and broadcasting. Advertising-funded media are experiencing an intense crisis as advertising migrates to the web (the economic crisis is amplifying this effect by reducing overall advertising expenditure). The Internet is taking bigger portions of a smaller cake leaving less for broadcasters. Moreover, Internet use is replacing television viewing and radio listening – 26 per cent of UK Internet users claimed to use TV less (though 11 per cent claimed they used television more) and 20 per cent claimed to use radio less (though 16 per cent claimed they used it more). The Internet provides a better advertising medium than conventional broadcasting – linking advertisements to searches (e.g. via Google or Yahoo) ensures they are targeted effectively to potentially receptive potential purchasers – and it also provides a host of alternatives to conventional broadcasting (whether legitimate, such as iTunes, or illegitimate, such as streamed films via PirateBay).

The impact of the Internet on conventional broadcasting is a global phenomenon – although more marked in the UK than elsewhere. In its 2008 *International Market Report* Ofcom (2008a) reported that all six countries (France, Germany, Italy, Spain, UK, US) covered saw a significant increase in time spent on the Internet between 2004–2008 but growth was highest in the UK at 21 per cent. Ofcom also found that migration of advertising online had also been faster in the UK and that the Internet's share of total advertising expenditure was, at 19 per cent, higher in the UK than elsewhere.

These rapid changes in UK broadcasting have led to an unravelling of the long-standing regulatory 'bargain' between advertising-funded terrestrial television broadcasters, i.e. ITV/ Channel 3, Channel 4 and *five*/Channel 5 whereby the broadcasters deliver public service programming (e.g. children's, religious and news programming) in exchange for spectrum at less than market prices and a licence to enter a lucrative advertising market (and, latterly, for regulatory advantages such as prominence on electronic programme guides (EPGs), 'must carry' rules and so on). These changes have led to a precipitous fall in ITV's share price (from 86.6p per share on 21 December 2007 to 39p per share on 24 December 2008) and to a financial crisis at Channel 4 where a 'funding gap' of between £100m and £150m is foreseen by 2012. Commercial radio is also experiencing a similar funding crisis (radio advertising fell by 15 per cent in 2008) which has resulted in a spate of mergers.

In strictly economic terms, this Internet-driven crisis has improved the BBC's position relative to its advertising-financed public service rivals (for its income from licence fees does not depend either on the general vitality of the economy or on its competitiveness relative to the Internet) but the BBC, too, has suffered from the fall in consumption of conventional broadcasting and, in television, from the growing competitive success of pay-tv (notably Sky). However, most significantly, this improvement in the BBC's relative position has intensified other broadcasters' concern at the privileged position they perceive the BBC to hold. ITN (the news supplier to the two main advertising-financed public service channels – ITV and Channel 4), for example, has charged that 'Generously funded by the licence fee and operating without commercial restraint, the BBC's expansionist strategy poses a threat to plurality' (ITN 2008:np). Such criticisms are particularly telling because the BBC has lost much of its former legitimacy in consequence of a succession of fines for unethical behaviour[2] and several reports (notably those commissioned by the BBC Governors and the BBC Trust – though the Hutton Report was also significant) which have found shortcomings in the BBC's reporting and editorial policies and practices.[3]

The Internet has thus been both the means for the BBC successfully to extend the range and accessibility of its services and the trigger for intensified, and highly critical, public scrutiny which has brought into question the size, range and character of the BBC's own activities and conduct. One of the main policy and rhetorical strategies the BBC has deployed to deal with the increasingly hostile environment in which it operates is its embrace of 'public value'.

Public value

In 2004 the BBC published its 'manifesto' for renewal of its Charter[4] *Building Public Value* where it proclaimed that:

> It [the BBC] must apply the test of public value to everything it does – its services, its commercial activities, its scope and scale. (BBC 2004a: 5)

From one perspective, this invocation of 'public value' seemed unexceptional – is this not what public bodies are for – to provide value to the public(s) that finance them? But from another point of view the BBC's embrace of public value is surprising. For public value is a specific notion (or fashion) of public management successfully mobilized by the US scholar and Harvard management theorist Mark Moore (Moore 2005). Moore proposed that public value is a practice whereby providers work with users to produce outcomes that genuinely meet users' needs and is based in two principles – co-production (i.e. co-decision by users and providers) and contestation (i.e. competition). The BBC's *Building Public Value* specifically cited Moore (as did a number of other UK state agencies' contemporary mission statements) and seemed therefore to embrace these radical principles as numerous commentators acknowledged (see Elstein 2004).

But how was the BBC to enact co-production and contestation? In important senses neither was compatible with the core of the BBC's ethos and mandate. Classic, one-to-many, broadcasting, of the kind offered by the BBC, makes co-production intrinsically difficult. Not only is there no face-to-face contact between users and supplier but the independence at the heart of the BBC's public service broadcasting vocation and mandate weighs strongly against the collaboration in governance intrinsic to co-production. As for contestation, the 'standard defence' (see Graham 1999: 17–46) of public service broadcasting and the BBC rests on the argument that competition, that is contestation, cannot thrive in the irremediably imperfect broadcasting market and that public service broadcasting exists because competition cannot secure the public interest.

The BBC was (and is) to be independent, so how could it engage in co-decision? And, if it was to remain a public service broadcaster (rather than a me-too echo of commercial broadcasting) how could it accept the imperatives of competition? Clearly something else was meant (and it is now hard to know what that was since *Building Public Value* is no longer available on the BBC's website). The faint and somewhat distorted echoes of the radicalism of *Building Public Value* resonate in the contemporary BBC principally as management and regulatory procedures, notably the Public Value Test (PVT), and, intermittently, as an unspecific and unquestioned customary piety acknowledging, formally at least, the importance of the citizen-user of BBC services.

The Public Value Test

One of the major changes implemented in the 'new' BBC Charter (which took effect in January 2007) was the creation of a new body, the BBC Trust, which replaced the BBC Governors (a body which had existed from the inception of the BBC as a public corporation in 1927) and was more clearly separated from the BBC management (now the BBC Executive) than the Governors had been. The Trust was charged with an explicit regulatory role with the administration of a 'Public Value Test' (PVT) as one of its main instruments of control.

The PVT replaced the 'approval' power previously held by the Department of Culture, Media and Sport (DCMS), the Government department responsible for the BBC and thus has contributed to a modest, but welcome, strengthening of the BBC's independence of Government. Thus far there have been four formal, full scale, PVTs conducted (Online services, HDTV, Gaelic Digital Service, local video services)[5] three of which resulted in approvals (the local video proposal was provisionally rejected by the Trust but the Trust's indicative decision is, at the time of writing, subject to public consultation). There are two elements to the PVT: a Market Impact Assessment (MIA), undertaken by Ofcom, and a Public Value Assessment, undertaken by the BBC Trust, which are considered together when the Trust undertakes a PVT. As well as the Public Value Test, the BBC's new performance management system includes service licences issued by the Trust which define objectives for all BBC services and will be undertaken at least once every five years. Chris Woolard, a member of the Trust secretariat, described (interview 4 May 2006) the service licences as 'mini PVTs' (though the BBC undertakes the market impact assessment, not Ofcom).

The PVT for on-demand services (notably the iPlayer)[6] authorized making broadcast programmes available via the BBC website for 7 days after transmission and live streaming of broadcast programmes. The Trust judged that because 'digital technology presents opportunities to increase greatly access to BBC content and thereby provide greater value to licence payers' the new services should, with safeguards for rights holders, be approved.[7]

The PVT is an important and worthwhile regulatory initiative but it is far from being an institutional enactment of the rallying cry for reinvigoration of the public sector through self-organizing, collaborative governance which Moore made of public value doctrines (and which might serve the BBC well at a time when there seems to be a lack of a sense in BBC staff that public service broadcasting should be different from and better than commercial services).

BBC regulation, or non-regulation, of its Internet activities could be said to have provoked the implementation of the PVT. In 2004 an independent committee, set up by the Government and headed by Philip Graf (now Deputy Chairman of Ofcom), reported on the BBC's role in the Internet content sector. Graf found notable weaknesses in the BBC's regulatory and approvals process and judged that 'the process of independent review is not, in my opinion, a very efficient one…The Charter review should seek to find a better regime for regulating services such as BBC Online' (Graf 2004: 6). Essentially, Graf's committee was asked to decide whether the BBC's Internet services were adversely affecting other, commercial, Internet provision. It found that BBC Online was 'very generously funded by comparison to its commercial competitors' (Graf 2004: 11) but that 'the nature and complexity of BBC Online's services, and the evidence available to the review' meant that adverse market impact could neither be proven nor disproven. Nonetheless, Graf observed that 'The Board of Governors does not appear to have sufficiently scrutinised the service's value to the public and its impact on the market' (Graf 2004: 83).

Further support for Graf's suspicions, and industry dissatisfaction with the BBC's perceived anti-competitive behaviour by the BBC (notably its 'crowding out' of commercial rivals), came through a European Commission judgement that the BBC was in receipt of state aid that had not been properly notified to and approved by the EC.[8] A UK company, Research Machines, and 17 other companies complained that the BBC's online delivery of educational services (the so-called Digital Curriculum) was unfair and anti-competitive. Research Machines, like Graf, also criticized the pre PVT approvals process, it said: 'The way the DCMS has openly worded its approval makes it awfully difficult to hold the BBC to account'. The controversial service in question, BBC Jam, was closed in 2007 (Keers 2003).

Policy challenges

The BBC has a widely-admired and much-used and valued portfolio of online services which complement and extend its conventional radio and television broadcasting. It has a new governance regime, centred on the BBC Trust, which administers a formal Public Value Test (which in principle and practice is somewhat detached from the more fervid and transformatory rhetoric of *Building Public Value* and Mark Moore) to adjudicate on management proposals for major new services. And the BBC exists as a securely (and, in the eyes of many, generously) funded body at a time when recession and structural change driven by the Internet is devastating the business models and threatening the corporate survival of its rivals. In this context, the key UK policy issue is not whether the BBC should continue as a provider of online services – there is close to universal agreement that it should – but whether, in both its online and offline modes, it is too big and too dominant and thus an enemy of the pluralism and diversity which constitutes one of the main objectives and reasons for being of public service media.

The question of how media pluralism[9] is to be secured is posed both positively and negatively by the Internet. Positively, the Internet offers (and has provided) striking opportunities for new, and different, information providers to enhance diversity and pluralism. Negatively, the Internet has triggered an acute crisis in 'legacy' media and threatens the viability of established information and news providers. This changed context, with both positive and negative implications, puts in question the status of established forms of public intervention in the UK media – of which the BBC is by far the most important.

Ofcom has a duty under the Communications Act 2003 regularly to review the state of public service broadcasting in the UK. In its most recent review it identified the threats to advertising-financed public service media and the consequential risk of the BBC becoming the only UK source of public service broadcasting within an overall landscape of diminished pluralism, diversity and quality of broadcasting (and Internet) services. Ofcom's melancholy prognosis has been vindicated by the intense crisis which now besets Channel 4 and also ITV and, perhaps, *five*. Ofcom put forward several possible scenarios to address these problems, including the creation of what it called a Public Service Publisher (PSP) which would fund provision of public service content for television (and potentially radio and the Internet).

Latterly, Ofcom has ceased to use the term 'Public Service Publisher' but instead refers to a possible 'refined competitive funding model', should 'audiences turn rapidly to new platforms and forms of content', in which 'the BBC would remain as the cornerstone of provision, but additional funding would be opened up to a wider pool of providers'.[10] There is room for debate about how fast audiences are turning to new platforms and new forms of content (but, as cited above, the BBC Director General's recognition that 'broadcasting has not been a very efficient way of getting the right programmes in front of the right people' suggests this transition might be quite fast) but the crucial question is, of course, where 'additional funding' might come from.

Higher levels of taxation seem inconceivable in the context of the 'credit crunch' as does an industry levy (an option identified, perhaps only for it to be rejected, by Ofcom) and few alternative options other than redistributing the television licence fee, which the BBC currently enjoys exclusively, seem to exist. The BBC fiercely resists 'top-slicing' the licence fee (even though it was top-sliced from 1927 to 1961 and, in respect of the BBC's role in ensuring successful execution of the Government's policy of digital switchover, could be said to be top-sliced today) and, in respect of the current urgent need to provide funding for Channel 4, has offered various forms of 'partnership' with Channel 4 and other organizations (including sharing the iPlayer, digital production technology and regional news facilities). Other options canvassed (but not by the BBC!) include Channel 4 taking over the BBC's commercial activities and enjoying the profits which currently accrue to the BBC – top-slicing by another name.

There is room for doubt about how far 'partnership' offers a viable way forward. It is not clear that either party to such partnerships would be willing, and thus potentially successful, partners. Moreover, the UK Competition Commission has recently (on 4 December 2008) provisionally ruled that a proposed joint venture between BBC Worldwide, ITV and Channel 4 (the so-called 'Project Kangaroo' video on demand service) is likely to lessen substantially competition in the UK video-on-demand market. Specifically, the Commission concluded that Kangaroo would result in a loss of competitiveness at a wholesale and retail level. But, although Project Kangaroo seems unlikely to get off the ground, the BBC continues actively to pursue innovatory online initiatives.

For example, early in December 2008, the BBC reported that it, together with ITV and BT (British Telecom), will work together to deliver on-demand TV over broadband and invited other public service broadcasters, device developers and ISPs to join them. The BBC Press Office claimed that this initiative 'would mean a new generation of subscription-free devices, carrying free to air channels and a huge selection of on-demand TV services like iPlayer and ITV Player, as well as the potential for films, shows and interactive content from a range of other providers in standard and high definition' (BBC 2008b).

Conclusion

There is an important symbiotic relationship between the BBC and Internet development in the UK. The BBC has successfully provided an enormous range of often high quality content online, both 'static' web-based of the kind organizationally delivered by BBC Online and the 'dynamic' content accessed through the iPlayer. It is a notable achievement to have established an Internet presence that includes both the UK-based website most often accessed by UK users and, in the iPlayer, an application that accounts for 7 per cent of peak UK Internet traffic less than a year after its launch. The Internet has invigorated the BBC and the BBC the UK Internet. But, the changes to broadcasting which the Internet has brought about are so fundamental as to threaten (or promise depending on point of view) the shape, size, mandate and identity of the BBC.

The Internet has indirectly brought the BBC's size, salience and funding into question by facilitating a migration of advertising revenue away from 'legacy' broadcast and newspaper media to the Internet – to Google and eBay – and has thus, indirectly, focused concern on a BBC whose secure funding and substantial size reveal it as out of proportion to declining rivals. The BBC's Internet initiatives have both focused attention on its dominance and potential (perhaps actual) anti-competitive behaviour and have called into existence a new regulatory order, badged as based on public value principles, administered by the BBC Trust. Most fundamentally, the Internet, in the long run, puts in question the BBC's funding. The licence fee is payable only if television programmes are watched or recorded 'as they are being shown on television'.[11] If television programmes are downloaded and watched at a time different from that of their live screening, then the licence fee is not payable. The iPlayer, and other video on demand services, makes possible just such non-synchronous consumption.

But in the UK, unlike in Germany, there is no controversy about whether the BBC should be online or not. In principle, if there is a need for public provision of content (e.g. on radio and television) then why not on the Internet too? And though scepticism may have grown in the UK about whether public provision is actually required, such sceptics are in a small minority and the threat to the economic viability of established commercially-funded media promises further to reduce their number. The BBC's success in developing a very extensive portfolio of widely-used online services gives rise to challenging second-order problems (e.g. who should pay for the online distribution capacity which the iPlayer is using, and how? How should the BBC balance the interests of small ISPs, buying capacity wholesale, with those of its own efficiency – an interest currently aligned with large ISPs' preferences for a 'fat pipe' rather than cache-based BBC iPlayer distribution strategy – see Rose 2008). But most important is the new salience of the fundamental first-order problems of UK public service media policy: how big should the BBC be? How far should public policy use the potential to increase diversity and pluralism in public service media offered by the

Internet? How, and to what extent, should such public media be funded? All these questions are fundamental to realizing public value in public service media, all have been raised by the impact of the Internet and all of them put in question the BBC's current dominance.

Notes

1. The BBC's current web-based offer can be sampled using the portal at http://www.bbc.co.uk/a-z/ accessed on 29.12.2008.
2. In December 2008, Ofcom fined the BBC £95,000 for conducting radio competitions unfairly (see http://www.ofcom.org.uk/tv/obb/prog_cb/obb124/issue124.pdf accessed on 12.12.2008). In July 2008, it had fined the BBC £400,000 in respect of eight separate breaches of the Ofcom programme codes. Ofcom commented 'In each of these cases the BBC deceived its audience by faking winners of competitions and deliberately conducting competitions unfairly' (see http://www.ofcom.org.uk/media/news/2008/07/nr_20080730 accessed on 12.12.2008). A year earlier, Ofcom had fined the BBC £50,000 for falsifying the results of a competition on the iconic children's programme *Blue Peter*. The BBC Trust stated that these 'were particularly serious as they resulted in children being misled to participate in a competition they had no chance of winning and in a child in the studio being involved in deceiving the audience' (see http://www.bbc.co.uk/bbctrust/news/press_releases/2007/ofcom_blue_peter.html accessed on 12.12.2008). The BBC was not alone: in December 2007, Ofcom fined Channel 4 £1.5m and had previously fined *five* £300,000 and had also fined GMTV, the advertising financed but formally public service broadcaster, £2m. And the largest advertising funded, for profit, but formally public service broadcaster, ITV, was fined £5.68m by Ofcom for misconduct in conducting 'phone in competitions (see http://www.ofcom.org.uk/media/news/2008/05/nr_20080508 accessed on 12.12.2008). Each and everyone (the tiny S4C excepted) of the UK's public service broadcasters were thus found deficient in trustworthiness by Ofcom in the period 2007-8.
3. The most recent of these reports is the King report on BBC coverage of the 4 UK nations. King's research found that, though the BBC was superior to other broadcasters, 'nearly one in five' of its reports on the UK and its nations 'were found to be vague and confusing and/or, less commonly, to contain implicit or explicit factual inaccuracies' (King 2008: 30) and that, in consequence, 'there clearly exists a substantial disconnect between the BBC and much of its existing audiences, let alone its potential audiences' (King 2008: 35).
4. The BBC's Royal Charter is its constitutional foundation and is subject to periodical review – usually once every ten years.
5. See http://www.bbc.co.uk/bbctrust/framework/public_value_test/decisions.html and http://www.bbc.co.uk/bbctrust/news/press_releases/2008/local_video_prov.html accessed on 20.1.2009.
6. BBC Trust BBC on-demand proposals: Public Value Test final conclusions. 2007. http://www.bbc.co.uk/bbctrust/assets/files/pdf/consult/decisions/on_demand/decision.pdf accessed on 31.12.2008.
7. See http://www.bbc.co.uk/bbctrust/assets/files/pdf/consult/decisions/on_demand/decision.pdf accessed on 29.12.2008.
8. See http://ec.europa.eu/community_law/state_aids/comp-2003/n037-03.pdf accessed on 30.12.2008.
9. See the study for the European Commission: *Independent Study on Indicators for media pluralism in the Member States – Towards a risk-based approach*. SMART 007A 2007-0002 at http://ec.europa.eu/information_society/media_taskforce/doc/pluralism/pfr_report.pdf accessed on 16.6.2009.
10. See http://www.ofcom.org.uk/consult/condocs/psb2_phase2/summary/ accessed on 31.12.2008.
11. See *Terms and Conditions of your TV Licence at* http://www.tvlicensing.co.uk/information/conditions.jsp accessed on 16.6.2009.

Chapter 5

Hierarchy to Homeostasis? Hierarchy, Markets and Networks in UK Media and Communications Governance

Hierarchies, markets and networks

Thompson (2003) has identified three modes of social coordination or governance – through hierarchy, markets or networks. Persuasive arguments have been advanced that hierarchical governance (and thus the role of states) is giving way to either or both market and network governance. Moran (2003), for example, proposes that in the UK hierarchical 'club' governance has been supplanted by market governance in the form of a 'hyper-innovation'[1] distinguished by privatization and liberalization. Whereas Taylor (2001) and others (see, for example, Barabasi 2002, Barry 2001, Castells 1996 and 2001, Keohane and Nye 1998) have argued that it is network governance that is growing in salience and that 'What is emerging at the moment is a new *network culture*' (Taylor 2001: 5. Emphasis in original) which responds to the complexity of modern societies which in turn, Taylor argues, mandates network governance. However, in contrast to hierarchical governance, both market and network governance share a normative self-regulating, or homeostatic, character: market governance through the influence exerted by the 'invisible hand' (Smith 1776) and network governance because of its intrinsic properties of reciprocity – if Thompson's account of network governance as distinguished by cooperation, trust, solidarity and loyalty is accepted (Thompson 2003: 112).

Why this putative shift to homeostatic coordination or governance? Because, it is argued, an epochal shift in social organization has taken place because contemporary social relationships are just too complex to be managed by hierarchical 'command and control' systems. 'The moment of complexity', for Taylor, constitutes a 'tipping point where more is different' and mandates a shift to network governance. Taylor (2001: 4) identifies the 'explosive development of cybernetic, information and telematic technologies since the Second World War' as triggering this 'tip' to networks. Castells, perhaps the best known proponent of this thesis, contends that network organization 'constitute[s] the new social morphology of our societies' (Castells 1996: 469) and similarly defines technological change as the driver of this transition: 'the 'new information technology paradigm provides the material basis for its pervasive expansion throughout the entire social structure' (Castells 1996: 469).

The references to Castells and Taylor cited above exemplify an often-made argument that media and communications have a crucial constitutive role in the growing salience of network governance and also that, in a kind of elective affinity, network governance increasingly characterizes governance of media and communications themselves. What empirical evidence is there to support these propositions? How far are they born out by the governance of media and communications in the UK?

Major changes in the governance of UK media and communications have certainly taken place in recent times. Although the print and film sectors remain privately owned and self-regulated (under the law) major changes have taken place in network media – that is, broadcasting, telecommunications and the post – which lend empirical support to propositions of epochal change. In 1955 UK broadcasting was undertaken by a publicly-owned monopoly, the BBC (lawful commercial broadcasting began in 1955), telecommunications was undertaken by two publicly-owned monopolies, Post Office Telecommunications and Hull Telephones (the latter confined to providing service in and around Hull, an area where Post Office Telecommunications was not permitted to provide service) and postal services were the sole prerogative of the Royal Mail.[2] Half a century later, there is no publicly-owned presence in telecommunications, where hundreds of private companies compete to provide a range of services; in broadcasting the BBC (together with other public bodies – Channel 4, S4C and the Gaelic Media Service) maintains a significant presence but competes against hundreds of private radio and television channels; and in postal services the Royal Mail also competes in a substantially liberalized market though against fewer private sector competitors than have entered broadcasting and telecommunications markets.

Although these dramatic changes in UK media and communications have been accompanied by the invention of new agencies of hierarchical governance (notably the regulators Ofcom and Postcomm – new regulator of the Post Office) it seems obvious that there has been a substantial shift away from hierarchical governance. But the shift seems to favour market, rather than network, governance. Does this suggest that the claims of Castells (1996: 469) for a 'new social morphology' and Taylor (2001: 5) for a 'new network culture' are poorly founded?

Network governance

However, some recent developments in the UK, as elsewhere, do lend prima facie support to Castells' and Taylor's propositions. There is a clear shift towards self-regulation, or co-regulation, in areas of media and communications where formerly hierarchical 'command and control' regulation obtained. For example, the statutory regulatory agency for electronic communications, the Office of Communications, Ofcom,[3] has 'outsourced' regulation of television advertising to the private sector self-regulatory body, the Broadcast Committee of Advertising Practice (BCAP).[4] BCAP, or, sometimes, CAP (Broadcast), states 'We regulate the content of all TV and radio commercials on channels and stations licensed by Ofcom. We also regulate advertising on interactive television services, TV shopping channels and Teletext services' (see CAP nd: Broadcast). BCAP's parent body (the Committee of Advertising Practice) refers to its sponsoring industry, UK advertising, as setting 'the standard in successful self-regulation' (CAP nd).[5] Previously, Ofcom stated that it was formulated through 'extensive consultation with broadcasters, viewers and listeners and other interested parties' (Ofcom 2005: 2) however, this statement does not form part of the currently posted version though Ofcom's commitment to consultation is palpable. Not only does the new code state that Ofcom 'expects to consult' on any subsequent changes to the code but Ofcom continues to consult extensively: in the first two months of 2006, for example, Ofcom had opened nine new consultations and in the preceding year, 2005, it undertook 79 separate consultations (Ofcom nd).

Such changes are particularly marked, as one might expect in emerging media such as the Internet rather than in established or 'legacy' media. Indeed, many elements in the institutional structure and practice of Internet governance in the UK suggest that hierarchy is not sovereign. A DTI (Department of Trade and Industry) source (interviewed by the author 4 August 2003) testified to the subtle efforts given to drafting the Act so that Internet services were neither caught by provisions for television-licensable content services nor for telephone numbering. As another DTI interviewee (interviewed by the author 14 July 2003) stated: 'there's an underlying feeling that we're not in a telecoms situation. Overcontrol puts someone out of business and someone else in i-space takes over'.

Not only was the Communications Act 2003 (an act to create a consolidated regulatory regime for broadcasting and telecommunications under an integrated 'converged' regulator, the Office of Communications – Ofcom) drafted to exclude the Internet but key bodies such as Nominet, (which administers the .uk domain), and LINX, the London Internet Exchange, (through which around 60 per cent of UK Internet traffic passes), operate under a network governance regime whereby their customers form their governing bodies.

Nominet and LINX seem to well exemplify the characteristics of network governance which Thompson identified, that is self-regulation based on relationships of cooperation, trust, solidarity and loyalty (Thompson 2003: 112), and to bear out Thompson's claim, following Riles (2001), that networks have a kind of 'elective affinity' with self-regulation and with 'bottom up type of organizational arrangements…[that] strongly connect to 'private interest governance' and the sphere of non-governmental organizations' (Thompson 2003: 30). Indeed, the importance of network governance in the Internet sector suggests that network governance will grow in general salience as the architecture and organization of electronic communication networks in general become more Internet-like. See, among others, Devoteam's (2003) well evidenced and persuasive account of the development of New Generation Networks. Another interesting and informative case in point is TM Denton's (1999) account of the supercession of 'Bellhead' by 'Nethead' mentalities and arrangements (see Chapter 10).

Moreover, several synoptic scholarly studies, such as those undertaken by the University of Oxford's Programme in Comparative Media Law and Policy (PCMLP) and the Hans Bredow Institut of the University of Hamburg, have identified a growing recourse to self-regulation (or co-regulation) for media and communications. PCMLP found, in a study of Internet regulation across the world, that 'Authorities in Europe and elsewhere in the developed world have responded…by resisting calls for statutory regulation and encouraging the industry [i.e. the Internet RC] to regulate itself' (PCMLP 2004: 3). In the UK self-regulation of Internet content is undertaken by the Internet Watch Foundation (IWF). The Hans Bredow Institut's study of *Co-Regulatory Measures in the Media Sector of the EU* (Hans Bredow Institut 2006) similarly identified the growing salience of 'regulated co-regulation' more generally in media and communications across Europe.

However, the undoubted growing contemporary empirical salience of civil society and network governance in media and communications is not the whole story. Neither market nor hierarchical governance is absent – even in the Internet. And, whilst distinctions between hierarchical, market and network governance have considerable analytical and heuristic power, actual regimes often display a complex, hybrid, character rather than the purity of theory.

Market governance

It is a truism to observe that one of the 'grand narratives' of UK governance over the last quarter of a century has been a rebalancing towards market and away from hierarchical governance (see, for example, Moran 2003). This has been manifested in a re-engineering of the internal relationships of public sector bodies to embody the precepts of 'new public management' (NPM) on private sector lines (Osborne and Gaebler 1992) as well as in reshaping the outward facing relationships of public bodies through liberalization and privatization. These trends have resonated through the media and communications sector where market entry has become easier under the combined impact of Government policy, which shifted rapidly from the control of entry via the licensing of firms to a regime of general authorization and promotion of entry, and technological change which mitigated capacity constraints[6] that had formerly inhibited market growth.

In the residual public sector, notably the BBC and the Royal Mail (now a public limited company), top managers – respectively John Birt (Director General of the BBC, 1992–2000) and Adam Crozier (Chief Executive of the Royal Mail, 2003–present) introduced NPM-type measures and the both the BBC and the Royal Mail have been charged with meeting commercial as well as public interest targets. Moreover, promotion of competition has been constituted as a central element in communications regulators' mandates (and thus applying to the public sector bodies in so far as they are under regulators' oversight). For example:

The Postal Services Act 2000 (5.1) provides, among other things, that:

> [T]he Commission shall exercise its functions in the manner which it considers is best calculated to further the interests of users of postal services, wherever appropriate by *promoting effective competition* between postal operators. (OPSI 2000: Ch.26. Emphasis added)

The Communications Act 2003 (3.1) provides, among other things, that:

> It shall be the principal duty of Ofcom, in carrying out their functions –
>
> (a) to further the interests of citizens in relation to communications matters; and
>
> (b) to further the interests of consumers in relevant markets, where appropriate by *promoting competition*. (OPSI 2003: Ch.21. Emphasis added)

Indeed, one could claim the media sector as the path breaker in opening up the now familiar UK mix of market and hierarchical governance embodied in both the Postal Services and Communications Acts. The Independent Television Authority (ITA),[7] which was established in 1954 to oversee the introduction of commercial, advertising-financed, television to the UK (the first European country to have commercial television) is often seen as the first of the UK's North American-style regulatory agency and thus as the first such agency in Europe.

Homeostasis

We might reformulate the propositions (Castells 1996, Moran 2003, Taylor 2001, etc.) of migration towards network and market governance regimes rather as a teleological migration towards homeostatic governance. For both network and market governance regimes offer, at least in theory, a *telos* of a self-regulatory, homeostatic, equilibrium independent of hierarchy. A good example of this presumption is to be found in the UK Cabinet Office's[8] Strategy Unit's (2002) analysis of Ofcom's powers; this shows an anticipation of an *inverse* relationship between hierarchical and market systems of governance: the better market governance works, the less hierarchical governance will be required. Hierarchical governance will, in this vision of its operation, 'wither away' as a competitive homeostasis develops:

Sector Specific	
Retail price controls (RPI[9]-x) or rate of return regulation	All diminish with increased likelihood of competition
Wholesale price controls (RPI-x) and service level agreements	
Wholesale price controls (cost plus) and service level agreements	
Requirements to allow interconnection	
Co-regulation with industry	
Alternative dispute resolution (ADR)	
Self-regulation by industry	
Competition Law	
Investigation under the Competition Act 1998	
Referrals to the Competition Commission	

(Strategy Unit 2002: 80).

The Strategy Unit maps a path leading towards homeostatic market governance: the market's invisible hand (Smith 1776) will govern firms' behaviour and establish an equilibrium in which prices and long-run costs converge. In such circumstances, firms secure rents (i.e. profit beyond the levels required to maintain the system in equilibrium) only if they innovate, e.g. in content or services, and are thereby able to create and capture a new market where they can again secure rents in the, theoretically, short period before other firms imitate them and re-establish a competitive equilibrium. This compressed sketch of competition theory suggests, contrary to assumptions in some contemporary literature on the governance of electronic communications, that self-regulation is not exclusive to network governance but may also be found in market governance regimes. In theory at least both markets and networks may be self-regulating – it is, however, an empirical question as to whether in any particular instance a homeostatic, self-regulating, system, the objective of competition theory and, putatively, a constitutive element of network organization, actually exists.

The return of the repressed – hierarchy

However, we are far from a homeostatic arcadia, whether of network or market governance, in the real UK media world. Even though market and network governance do have a striking empirical and doctrinal salience, no one could imagine hierarchical governance was absent from UK media and communications when confronted with the 590 pages, 411 clauses and 19 schedules of the Communications Act 2003!

Hierarchical governance continues to play a large part in governance of UK media and communications though the salience of the new regulators Postcomm and Ofcom reflects a number of potentially conflicting assumptions and values. Notably that:

- there are important public interests that may not be secured through the operation of well-functioning markets (e.g. universal postal, telecommunication and broadcasting services at affordable prices)
- the presence of dominant legacy firms (such as British Telecom (BT), the Royal Mail and the BBC – created as public monopolies) mandate effective regulation to allow effective well-functioning markets to emerge
- there are important positive and negative externalities associated with media content that require effective regulation by an expert sector-specific agency such as Ofcom (though it is important to note that such regulation applies unevenly across the whole media sector and more strongly to television than to print, radio or the Internet)
- markets will fail in a technical sense and may become dominated by one or few firms and thus threaten the diversity and pluralism important both to free and democratic societies and to economic efficiency.

Although the presumption that well-functioning markets are likely to more effectively secure the public interest than will command and control regimes (hence Ofcom's and Postcomm's duties to promote competition) underpins contemporary UK media and communications regulation (indeed, it does not seem too much to argue, the contemporary market regime was devised to remedy the failures of hierarchical governance) also recognizes that markets may fail. Accordingly, the Communications Act 2003 reserves hierarchical powers for the Secretary of State (notably in respect of universal service and radio frequency spectrum management); Ofcom is charged with significant duties of content and media ownership regulation; and government intervenes in broadcasting on a massive scale to redress perceived market failure (the BBC alone receives more than £3bn of public funding annually). These measures have largely been formulated to address any failure in market governance. But what of failure in network governance?

Network Failure

The concept of failure in network governance seems novel – whilst there is an abundant literature on hierarchical and market-governance failure, the possibility of systemic failure in network governance does not seem to have been identified in the scholarly literature. The intoxicating discovery of epochal change in the form of a putative general transition towards the adoption of network governance and coordination regimes has left lacunae both in empirical (to assess how far such epochal claims may be substantiated) and in theoretical (to consider how far features of other types of governance regime are likely to be found in network governance) enquiry.

The concept of governance failure is well established in respect of both hierarchical (ossification and lack of innovation, weak efficiency incentives, poor responsiveness to users, susceptibility to producer capture, etc.) and market (exclusion of the poor, abuse of significant market power, capture by owners and/or managers, etc.) systems of governance: the complexity of communication and media governance arrangements in the UK (not least the length and tortuous character of the Communications Act 2003) reflect attempts to guard against both types of governance failure (as well as historical accretion, contingency, the effects of interest group lobbying and a host of other factors). But there is no equivalent notion of 'network failure', though the growing salience of network governance suggests that a matching concept of 'network failure' could be elaborated with advantage.

'Dark networks', such as the Mafia or al Qaeda (see Glasius and Kaldor 2002: 24–25) may be instanced as examples, perhaps provide an instance of one type of 'network failure' whereby unwelcome social consequences attach to the system of governance in question: a type of governance failure analogous to the exclusion, or under-representation, of the interests of the poor under market-governance regimes. Another may be the tendency for the values of networks to converge with the interests of those networked; this seems to be an intrinsic quality of network governance – not surprising perhaps that those networked construct and operate the network so as to advance their own interests! But, as regulatory functions are increasingly shifted from hierarchical (discharged by statutory regulators) to network governance (discharged by self- or co-regulatory bodies such as BCAP and the IWF) this form of network governance failure may become both more important and more controversial.

The late Sir David Calcutt's (second) review of UK press regulation and privacy issues identified a notable instance of network governance failure. Calcutt found the newspaper industry's self-regulatory body, the Press Complaints Commission, deficient. He stated:

> The Press Complaints Commission is not, in my view, an effective regulator of the press. It has not been set up in a way, and is not operating a code of practice, which enables it to command not only press but also public confidence. It does not, in my view, hold the balance fairly between the press and the individual. It is not the truly independent body that it should be. As constituted, it is, in essence, a body set up by the industry, financed by the industry, dominated by the industry, and operating a code of practice devised by the industry and which is over-favourable to the industry. (Calcutt 1993: xi)

Calcutt's critique of an instance of network governance through co-regulation was echoed in a more general sense by the now defunct Scottish Advisory Committee on Telecommunications (SACOT). SACOT argued persuasively that 'Trade associations and other existing industry bodies are not suitable structures to exercise co-regulatory functions' (SACOT 2003:2). Moreover, as well as the objections raised by Calcutt and SACOT, network governance may insufficiently take into account the views and interests of those at the margin and of the marginalized; see, for example, the persistent critique of self-regulatory network governance by Sandy Starr in *Spiked* (e.g. Starr 2003). Starr's general critique applies neatly, as he argued in a later commentary (Starr 2005), to the Government's recent attempt to win informal support through co-regulation what formerly (and perhaps should formally) be done through hierarchy: that is the suppression of thus far lawful communications – what the Home Office and Scottish Executive labelled 'extreme pornographic material' (see the Home Office and the Scottish Executive 2005) in their Consultation on the Possession of Extreme Pornographic Material.

Network governance failure thus seems, at least as a provisional judgement, to inhere in a structural tendency to govern through self-selecting and self-confirming groups of agents acting informally. In instances such as these we see how closely network governance may approximate to the characteristics of the 'club' form of hierarchical governance which Marquand described (see also Moran 2003) as a system based on shared understandings, assumptions and trust as follows:

> The atmosphere of British government was that of a club, whose members trusted each other to observe the spirit of the club rules; the notion that the principles underlying the rules should be clearly defined and publicly proclaimed was profoundly alien. (Marquand: 1988: 178)

Hierarchy rather than homeostasis?

It may be only in the heady atmosphere generated by epochal claims of transition to new social morphologies or discovery of hyper-innovation that the claim that hierarchy is back would be news: many might rather think it had never gone away. But epochal claims demand attention and have the merit of signalling that changes have been made. Hierarchy may be back (or never have gone away) but it is back in a different way – and is different because circumstances have changed. Why has governance of UK media and communications changed and how has hierarchical governance been re-articulated?

Technological change has changed the terms on which contemporary governance of media and communications may be conducted and the Internet epitomizes the two most important changes. First, media are converging, the boundaries between hitherto distinct media are blurring, meaning that policy and regulation, hitherto based on distinct and different technologies (such as print, wired one-to-one electronic communication and wireless one-to-many electronic communication), must change. Convergence has two faces, new, hybridized, media are coming into existence and there is also an increasing substitutability between media that have hitherto been separate (Werbach 1997).

Second, 'national' communication sovereignty is eroding; satellite transmission has abolished the relationship between cost and distance of communication and has made national control of radio frequency communication more difficult. And this, together with the factors of increased connectivity, greater traffic volume, browser access and digitization of content have made national control of access to Internet-delivered content more difficult.

It is easy to exaggerate both the impact of changes such as these and their novelty. Governments and hierarchical governance still dispose of significant power – firms are located in specific jurisdictions and are thereby subject to governmental influence and authority, governments cooperate across borders and so on. And there are historical precedents both for the emergence of new media of communication and for the internationalization of their sphere of operations. However, such prudent scholarly cautions against large-scale generalization aside, there is much to suggest that matters have changed significantly and in terms of governance, national political authorities' ability to manage media and communications sectors and markets has diminished.

Effectively, governments now have three governance strategies open to them:

- Liberalize and go with the flow in the hope that hierarchical governance at the margin together with market and network governance will produce acceptable outcomes
- Subsidize to secure desired outcomes
- Share sovereignty in order to exercise some, albeit, shared power.

The UK has adopted all these strategies.

Liberalization

The first strategy – liberalize and manage at the margin – clearly informs the regime governing most of UK media and communications (though the length and complexity of the Communications Act 2003 reminds us that managing at the margin can be a complex business). Effectively, this is a recipe for market governance lightly leavened by hierarchy ('regulation with a light touch') and conveniently signals that the clear analytical distinction between the three distinct modes of governance, hierarchy, market and network, identified by Thompson is not always found in practice. Patricia Hodgson, (speaking in her role as the last chief executive of the Independent Television Commission (ITC) before the ITC was subsumed into Ofcom),[10] enjoined Ofcom to 'focus on its competition duties; minimise burdens, sustain competition and much will follow' (Hodgson 2003: 14). There are three main areas of difficulty associated with the liberalization strategy arising out of the failure of light touch hierarchical and/or network governance to reliably redress market failures.

The first kind of difficulty arises from the tendency towards excessive delay when generic post hoc competition law, notably the Competition Act 1998 and Enterprise Act 2002, rather than sector specific *ex ante* regulation is applied – 'justice delayed is justice denied'. Several commentators have remarked that competition law is too slow to provide effective remedies. The Director of Public Policy of AOL UK (interviewed by the author 28 July 2003) asserted that the 'problem lies in the timing of the regulatory process. It may take up to 3 years for judgement'. This estimate is supported by the testimony of Margaret Bloom, when the Office of Fair Trading's Director of Competition Enforcement, who stated: 'cases have taken longer than we expected when planning for the introduction of the Act. A realistic estimate for an infringement decision ranges from one year – in a very straightforward case – to 3 years or possibly even longer. Perhaps there are no "straightforward" infringement cases' (Bloom 2003: 5). The uncertainty to which such delays give rise may also be amplified by the delays occasioned by the, otherwise laudable, lengthy consultations which characterize Ofcom's practice. For example, the Broadcasting Code, to which I refer above, took effect on 25 July 2005 more than 18 months after Ofcom's establishment. Moreover, the importance of consultation has grown with as regulatory discretion has increased.

The second kind of difficulty was also identified by Patricia Hodgson when she referred to the increase in regulatory discretion arising from Ofcom's mandate. She observed that 'Ofcom has reminded us that Parliament asked it to deregulate whilst giving it some 260 duties, double those of its parent bodies' and concluded that the regulator cannot but exercise discretion in prioritizing when it is charged with dealing with so many objectives. 'How can a regulator be asked to reconcile competing political goals when, by definition, the regulator is unelected?' (Hodgson 2003: 9). In negotiating this uncomfortable contradiction Ofcom has, she claimed 'Wisely…committed itself to less but more effective regulation, aiming at strategic interventions to achieve bundles of results (Hodgson 2003: 10). Hodgson noted that power, and the ability to exercise it on a discretionary basis, had shifted from government and the civil service to the regulator 'this transfer of talent and responsibility to a "fourth arm" of government must have affected the civil service. Three successive governments have now shown mounting impatience with the civil service, by-passing it with regulators, quangos and political advisors' (Hodgson 2003: 12). The exercise of regulatory discretion, if it is not to be capricious and ill-informed, also tends to make regulation slow, for the regulator must gather evidence and may consult widely.

The third area of difficulty arises at the intersection between regulated market governance and network governance in liberalized regimes. Consultation, self- and co-regulation may be seen as different points on a continuum of joint activity by regulator and regulatees. In varying degrees, all of these practices may lead to governance being performed by unaccountable (i.e. required neither to report or give reasons for their decisions nor submit to election or other means of being held to account by their constituencies) and incompetent (in the sense of being unable to resist capture by powerful) institutions. And it is in this terrain, ranging from consultation through co-regulation to self-regulation, that the analytical distinctions between hierarchical, market and network governance may become impenetrably blurred.

How do the network attributes identified by Thompson (2003) – co-operation, solidarity, trust and loyalty – play out when the network in question may be made up either of different, sometimes competing, firms and/or between firms and regulator(s)? Perhaps through a shared ideology, or put another way, at a different social site. Instead of being embodied in formal network institutions, such as self-regulatory agencies, these values are sustained and reproduced in social networks bound together by a shared ideology. As remarked earlier in connection with the idea of network failure, self-regulating organizations tend to exclude those who do not share the interests and values of the self-regulating community (or network).

The apparent opening-up of governance implied by network governance through self-regulation and co-regulation is echoed in hierarchical institutions, whether Government or regulator, increasingly having recourse to consultation (and pseudo-consultation). Few could do other than applaud such an opening towards the voices and perceptions of those who will be affected by Ofcom's decisions. Consultations go some way towards mitigating the closure and return to some aspects of 'club' governance (see Marquand 1998 and Moran 2003) that inevitably attends the exercise of regulatory discretion. But there is room for some reasonable doubt about the ability of a representative range of those affected by Ofcom's decisions effectively to contribute to consultations on so wide a range of issues, almost all of which require respondents to possess considerable expertise if they are to identify their own and others' interests and represent them appositely. True, the practice of consultation has stimulated civil society networks such as Ofcomwatch but not only are the voices heard in consultations overwhelmingly those of businesses likely to be materially interested in the topic in question but there are opportunities for responses to be conditioned by the framing of questions on which respondents' views are sought. And the translation of representations elicited in consultations into rules and practices remains the prerogative of those running the consultation.

Subsidy and the limits of the liberalization

The second strategy option, the strategy of exercising hierarchical power by subsidizing desired activities in media and communications rather than legislating to inhibit those which are not desired, has a long history dating, at least, from the subsidies paid by seventeenth-century governments to their supporters. More recently, and with less partisanship, newspapers and printed works have been favoured with postal and VAT concessions and commercial broadcasters (notably Channels 3 and 5) have been awarded spectrum at favourable rates in exchange for public service content and coverage. Subsidies such as these of course condition the development of markets and technologies: the same content provided in both a printed and an electronic medium is subject to different financial regimes – print is exempted from VAT, electronic is not.

Subsidy is concentrated in the audio-visual sector and particularly on public service broadcasting (PSB). The BBC receives by far the largest support from taxation[11] exceeding £3bn a year (in 2004, licence fee funding amounted to £2,940,300,000 and funding for the World Service from the Foreign and Commonwealth Office amounted to £225.1m). In 2004, S4C (Sianel Pedwar Cymru – a Welsh language public television service financed by advertising and state subsidy) received £101,264,000 and the Gaelic Media Service £8.5m. Further support to the audio-visual sector was channelled, largely as lottery awards, through the UK Film Council which, in 2004–5, disbursed £31,788,000. Such initiatives represent a hybrid form of governance: use of hierarchy to rebalance market forces. Subsidy in UK media and communications thus flows, overwhelmingly, to the broadcasting sector (though the BBC disbursed £69.2m on its website, bbc.co.uk, in 2004, somewhere between the £71.3m devoted to the BBC radio service Radio 4 and the £53.8m spent on the BBC radio service Radio Five Live). For it is in broadcasting that media and communication markets are thought most to fail and in broadcasting that the liberal (or, in Moran's terms, hyper-innovatory) paradigm is most thought to be flawed.

British debate about public service broadcasting over the last two decades has been dominated by the notion of market failure. In 1986 the Peacock Report (Peacock 1986) looked forward to a future, before the end of the twentieth century, when technological change meant intervention would no more be required in broadcasting than in print. Market failure, and thus the need for publicly supported PSB, would come to an end. In governance terms this meant the prospect of a dramatic diminution of hierarchical, and a corresponding growth in the importance of market, governance.

In response to the Peacock analysis, Andrew Graham (1999) and others built a powerful 'standard defence' arguing that market failure in broadcasting and thus a need for PSB, would continue despite technological change. DeLong and Froomkin's (1999) account of the 'new economy' suggests why the 'standard defence' is powerful. They proposed that the new economy – notably the information sector (including broadcasting) – is intrinsically different from the 'old economy' because the new economy does not conform to what they identify as the 'three pillars' of the market system – excludability, rivalry and transparency.

The 'New Economy' is an economy of non-excludability, non-rivalry and non-transparency. Non-transparency, that is the property of new economy goods and services whereby their characteristics are not fully evident before consumption (i.e. that they are experience goods) has latterly not been a major influence on media policy and governance for this non-transparency/experience goods aspect of the new economy is long established (books, other written works and indeed speech are all non-transparent before consumption). However, the other two properties identified by DeLong and Froomkin (non-rivalry and non-excludability) have been important shaping factors.

Free-to-air broadcasting is an outstanding case in point. It is non-rival because one person's consumption of a broadcast does not deny another a consumption opportunity. If I eat an apple it is not available for someone else to eat but if I watch a television programme it is still possible for others to watch it without loss to me (or anyone else). It is non-excludable because a free-to-air broadcasting service makes available to all what it makes available to one. In contrast, pay television returns to the old economy by excluding potential users who could enjoy the goods and services offered at no additional cost were they not artificially excluded from doing so. Welfare is reduced and additional costs are built into the system as the intrinsic non-excludability of the broadcasting medium is circumvented. Pay television converts a public good – as economists call this class of non-excludable goods – into a private good.

However, this standard defence of PSB might be thought to prove too much. For it applies as much to free-to-air commercial broadcasting as to PSB and also applies to other elements of the 'new economy' such as printed works (the 'new economy' is of course not quite as new as many of its proponents assume) which are also non-rival and whose excludability depends on law, notably an effective copyright regime, rather than their intrinsic properties. The 'standard defence' therefore customarily invokes another gambit and refers to information goods which confer long term benefits but which no individual thinks worth paying for. Examples of such merit goods include high culture, scientific research, education, etc. Because free markets tend to undersupply merit goods it is generally accepted that the state should provide them – hence public funding for education, the arts, research, etc. And because broadcasting is a good way to distribute merit goods, state intervention in support of public service broadcasting is necessary and desirable. But although the 'standard defence' eloquently and persuasively makes the case for hierarchical intervention in the media, and particularly so in broadcasting, it provides few guidelines as to what a proportionate intervention might be.

Accordingly, in some quarters the principal recipient of subsidy in UK media and communications, the BBC has come to be seen as overfunded[12] – as an '800 pound gorilla' (as its former Director General, Greg Dyke (2003), characterized it in a rather unReithian way). In this view of things, the BBC is seen as using its size and market power aggressively, thus imperilling the emergence, or survival, of commercial competitors in radio, online or television services, with damaging effects on diversity and pluralism.

Subsidy to redress market failure may thus, at least in theory (and there is no consensus on whether this problem exists in practice), maintain rather than redress market failure particularly when external circumstances change – e.g. through technological developments. In this view of things, the BBC may be perceived as a disproportionately large intervention standing in the way of the putatively well-functioning electronic media markets which technological change has made possible. From the point of view of some proponents of market and/or network governance, the BBC thus appears as a dominant incumbent 'legacy' institution kept in place by hierarchical governance and which inhibits the emergence of homeostatic governance (whether through markets and/or through networks).[13]

Sharing sovereignty

The third possible governance strategy open to governments, the sharing of sovereignty has been reflected in the significant extent to which the UK's accession to the European Union has resulted in a reshaping of media and communications governance in the UK. The UK acceded to the European Communities (now the European Union) in 1972. In 1989 the European Communities' Television without Frontiers Directive (TVWF) was first promulgated. The Directive (European Parliament and the Council 1997)[14] made it clear that broadcasting was not exempt from the general rules governing economic life in the community and that Member States could not lawfully discriminate against broadcasting services emanating from another Member State. It is hard to imagine the presence of important UK-based services such as Sky Television, let alone offshore services like Atlantic 252, without TVWF. And without TVWF the UK would not have become a location of choice for 'footloose' European broadcasters, e.g. the commercial television services based in the UK which serve Scandinavian markets.

In early 2006, Ofcom listed between 600 and 700 Ofcom-licensed cable and satellite television services including, for example, 21 different MTV channels.[15] Chalaby (2002: 185) has estimated that around 80 per cent of transnational television channels in Europe are UK-based. If there is 'a race to the bottom', as Peter Humphreys has sometimes proposed (Humphreys 2005), it seems that the UK is winning.

Moreover, the EU's competition and telecom liberalization Directives have shaped significantly the UK regulatory environment. The impact of Europe extends beyond its influence on the structure and regulation of communications infrastructures. The European Convention on Human Rights and, to a lesser extent the European Convention on Transfrontier Television, have also contributed to the reshaping of communications governance in the UK. In principle, therefore, a sharing of sovereignty has the potential to extend the effectiveness of hierarchical governance which in the specific instance under consideration, the EU, has been exercised to secure better market governance.[16]

The actual practice of media and communications governance in the UK, though lending some empirical support to the propositions that hierarchical governance has been displaced by either or both market and/or network forms of homeostatic governance, suggests that the epochal changes in favour of Castells' (1996) and Taylor's (2001) notions of network governance and Moran's (2003) notion of market/hyper-innovatory governance are somewhat overstated. But the relative salience of hierarchy, markets and networks has certainly changed and the two latter forms of governance have undoubtedly risen in importance over the last fifty years. Moreover, the exercise of hierarchical governance has changed and has increasingly has been exercised through a sharing of sovereignty, through subsidy rather than inhibition.

Conclusion

In 50 years media and communications in the UK has changed from a series of public monopolies (the print sector of course excepted) to a substantially liberalized and pluralized environment. In 1955 the BBC's monopoly of UK broadcasting was broken with the establishment of ITV.[17] Post Office Telecommunications subsequently became British Telecom, which now competes against 300 or more suppliers of telecommunication services (including Cable and Wireless, formerly a public sector body which then provided telecommunication services only outside the UK's frontiers). The Royal Mail is now a plc and competes against a number of new entrants. And in broadcasting the BBC now competes against a host of radio and television channels including the publicly owned Channel 4, though the BBC still accounts for 55 per cent of radio listening (RAJAR 2006) and around 33 per cent of television viewing (BARB 2006).

Today, instead of the straightforward command and control systems of hierarchical governance which obtained 50 years ago for all UK media and communications except the print sector, governance is effected through a complex intersection of different systems, with both market and network governance assuming a much greater role than before. Complexity has further increased because of the effect of sovereignty-sharing which has been intimately linked with technological change in the sector. The direction of travel in media and communication governance is clear – in broadcasting, posts and telecommunications there has been a pronounced shift towards market governance (and in some sectors, notably the Internet, towards network governance and co-regulation). But the pace of change differs from sector to sector.

However, although the direction of change towards market and network governance is clear, hierarchy still plays a major role. The BBC retains a special status and the broadcasting sector is characterized by hierarchical governance to a greater extent than other sectors such as telecommunications or the Internet. But, unlike other publicly-owned providers of communication services such as the Royal Mail and Channel 4 and unlike all other providers of electronic communications services, whether broadcasters or telecommunication service providers, the BBC is not fully subject to the jurisdiction of an independent regulatory body and retains significant self-regulatory powers. The BBC, unlike all other media and communication enterprises, is not subject to market governance in respect of its funding – the licence fee is a tax (see ONS 2006). Moreover, the Communication Act 2003 provides a legal context which, though structured to foster and facilitate market governance in general, still includes important elements of hierarchical governance principally in respect of broadcasting.

But hierarchical governance is now practised somewhat differently from the way it was fifty years ago – the plethora of duties which the Communications Act 2003 lays on Ofcom means, necessarily, that regulation must be exercised with discretion. Hierarchical governance is also practised more transparently and with considerably more opportunities for intervention from below – whether manifested through the somewhat absurd online voting (promoted by the Department for Culture, Media and Sport [DCMS] and the UK Film Council soliciting support for the film sector) concerning allocation of lottery funds or through the by-now habitual public consultations on policy and regulatory initiatives.

However, in the UK, despite the rise of network governance (without, as yet, a clear recognition of its – like any other system of governance – disposition towards failure and the distinctive character of network governance failure), the move towards markets rather than administered systems and the attempts to diffuse hierarchical power through the establishment of a powerful independent regulator endowed with significant discretion, much power still resides with Government. For example, Government sets the level of the BBC licence fee, determines the terms of the BBC's Charter and appoints members of the BBC Trust (and members of the Channel 4 Board). Moreover, the Secretary of State has the power to direct Ofcom on a number of important issues including spectrum allocation and universal service and to otherwise influence the practice of regulation.

But governance of media and communications in the UK has opened up in several senses. The preponderance of hierarchical governance, which lasted unchallenged by networks or markets until the 1950s for broadcasting, until the 1980s for telecommunications and until the twenty-first century for postal services, has given way to a mixed governance regime of hierarchy, markets and networks. Hierarchical governance has become notably more open, e.g. through extensive consultations and significant increases in institutional transparency, though the exercise of hierarchy has at the same time become more discretionary and therefore less predictable and open.

Failures of hierarchy led to the embrace of markets (see Moran 2003) and technological change has seemed to vindicate (and necessitate) this change by opening up the possibility of markets working well, notably by reducing barriers to entry. Where there is a consensus that market failure is structural and endemic, notably in respect of broadcasting, a significant element of hierarchical governance –notably through the BBC, as the Secretary of State for Culture Media and Sport acknowledged when stating 'In pure competition terms, the BBC is an intervention in the market, and one of very large scale' (Jowell 2005: np) – obtains with the aim of mitigating market failure.

However, the possibility of failures in network governance appear to be less clearly identified and where such failures exist they are less clearly countervailed by other forms of governance. Homeostatic network governance has delivered real benefits but the danger of 'network governance failure', notably through capture of governance bodies by a narrow group of interested parties, has attracted far less attention than have the undoubted dangers of failure of markets and hierarchy.

The governance of UK media and communications does much to bear out contentions that market and network governance, homeostatic governance, is growing in salience relative to hierarchical governance. But hierarchy remains a very powerful force in governance, notably through the effect and implementation of the Communications Act 2003 (and the Postal Services Act 2000) and the force exerted by the BBC. But governance, whether network, market or hierarchical, does not manifest itself in a pure unalloyed form. Characteristically, the clear analytical distinctions made by scholars for heuristic purposes map poorly onto a complex and contradictory world of practice.

The multiplicity of different systems, and combinations of systems, of governance in UK media and communications (whether market, network or hierarchical command and control) together with the melding of national and supra-national hierarchical systems has, in important respects, made governance more opaque. In the UK the very multiplicity of agencies, the complexity of the relevant legislation, the uneven application of different regulatory and governance regimes to different media and institutional formations mean that governance has become harder to understand and increasingly challenging even for experts to master. In spite of doctrines of transparency (sometimes realized in little more than the posting of documents on websites) and inclusion (manifested in a plethora of consultations in which the power to frame questions and select arguments and evidence from responses in order to substantiate conclusions remains with those who manage the consultations) such complexity means governance remains to a significant extent closed to effective scrutiny and participation. It is therefore also closed to the pervasive adoption of governance arrangements characterized by the cooperation, trust, solidarity and loyalty which Thompson (2003: 112) nominated as distinguishing characteristics of network governance. As well as the specific governance failures in and of each of the analytically separate systems of hierarchical, market and network governance in UK media and communications, a general failure therefore arises from the complexity and multiplicity of the governance systems that have accreted around media and communications in the UK.

Notes

1. The rhetorical use of intensifiers such as 'hyper', and in related usages 'ultra' (as in 'ultra-liberal') may sometimes suggest that the argument is being tipped.
2. Both telephony and broadcasting *became* state monopolies rather than starting out as such. Both began as activities carried out by private firms licensed by the state. The Post Office assumed control of public telecommunications in the UK between 1911 and 1914 (Hull excepted) and the

BBC, first established as a private company – the British Broadcasting Company, became a public monopoly on January 1st 1927.

3. The UK's creation of a 'converged' communications regulator conforms to a growing practice in the European Union. Ofcom was preceded by FICORA in Finland and AGCOM in Italy. The UK model differs from the German integrated network industry regulation model (the Bundesnetzagentur electricity, gas, post, railways and telecommunications) in that it's an exclusively *communications* regulator.
4. The legal foundation for the establishment of CAP (Broadcast) and its role within the new broadcast co-regulatory system is the Deregulation and Contracting Out Act, 1994. This Act allows for a Minister or public authority to delegate or 'contract out' specific functions or duties to another person or organization. Ofcom has been given the power to contract out its functions under DCOA by Section 1(7) of the Act. The contracting-out process means that broadcast advertising Codes, previously known as the Radio Authority's Radio Advertising and Sponsorship Code and the Independent Television Commission (ITC) Television Advertising Standards Code, are now the responsibility of the Broadcast Committee of Advertising Practice (BCAP http://www.asa.org.uk/ASA_2004_rebuild/ASAAppBase/AnnualReport2004/cap_introreview.shtml accessed on 24.2.2006).
5. Ofcom's statutory Broadcasting Code can be found at http://www.ofcom.org.uk/tv/ifi/codes/bcode/bcode.pdf (accessed on 16.6.2009).
6. The most striking instance of technological change leading to greater market capacity has been in the use of communication satellites to mitigate shortage of terrestrial radio frequency spectrum, but other developments such as fibre optic cable and digital compression techniques provide further cases in point.
7. The ITA metamorphosed into the IBA (Independent Broadcasting Authority) and the ITC (Independent Television Commission) which was finally assimilated into Ofcom.
8. Essentially, the Prime Minister's department.
9. RPI is Retail Price Index.
10. Hodgson was previously Director of Policy and Planning at the BBC and later became Principal of Newnham College, University of Cambridge and a member of the BBC Trust.
11. On January 20th 2006 the Office of National Statistics formally classified the BBC licence fee as a tax (ONS 2006).
12. In 2004/5 the BBC received more than £3bn in public funding and earned a further c£624m (BBC 2005: 104–5).
13. The proposal to establish local television stations in the UK has stimulated a wealth of interesting commentary – several instances of which illustrate the difficulty in some circumstances of distinguishing between network and market governance and institutional arrangements. Both Ofcom's discussion paper 'Digital Local' (Ofcom 2006) and a grass roots statement (Hewson 2005) make clear that entry of civil society and network governance in the local television arena is likely to depend on ability to enter the relevant markets – a classic market-governance issue.
14. Latterly, the TVWF Directive has been replaced by the Audiovisual Media Services Directive (AVMSD) (see http://ec.europa.eu/avpolicy/reg/avms/index_en.htm accessed on 28.5.2009).
15. MTV, MTV (Ireland), MTV Base, MTV Base Africa, MTV Dance, MTV Denmark, MTV Espana, MTV Europe (North), MTV Finland, MTV France, MTV Hits, MTV Idol, MTV in the UK, MTV Music, MTV Nordic, MTV Nordic (Sweden), MTV Norway, MTV Polska, MTV Portugal, MTV

Pulse, MTV2 (compiled from Ofcom website at http://www.ofcom.org.uk/static/tvlicensing/cs/main.htm accessed on 28.2.2006).

16. The connection between the extension of market governance in the UK and the European Union is not invariable. It may well be that measures to address media concentration emanating from the European Union (see, among others, the *Study on Indicators for Media Pluralism in the Member States* commissioned by DG Information Society's Task Force on the Co-ordination of Media Affairs at http://ec.europa.eu/information_society/media_taskforce/pluralism/study/index_en.htm accessed on 29.5.2009 which points to a continuing EU concern with the limitations of market governance in European media and communications) will also shape outcomes in the UK. However, such measures, if implemented or implementable, may reassert hierarchy rather than re-articulate it in the context of market governance. More generally, see Collins 1994 and 2002.
17. ITV is the acronym for Independent Television usually used to refer collectively to the television channel formally known as Channel 3 and to the Channel 3 licensees. However, the limited company ITV currently holds only the majority of Channel 3 licences – strictly speaking neither STV (Scottish Television) nor Ulster Television is part of ITV.

Chapter 6

Trust and Trustworthiness in the Fourth and Fifth Estates[1]

> We live in an age of communication technologies. It should be easier than it used to be to check out strangers and institutions, to test credentials, to authenticate sources, and to place trust with discrimination. But unfortunately many of the new ways of communicating don't offer adequate, let alone easy, ways of doing so. The new information technologies are ideal for spreading reliable information, but they dislocate our ordinary ways of judging one another's claims and deciding where to place our trust. (O'Neill 2002a: Lecture 5)

Introduction

Trust, or its absence, is a current high fashion topic in the social sciences.[2] As attention has focused on consent, rather than duress, as the prime factor in social cohesion, so the putatively trust-eroding threats to social cohesion posed by globalization, movement of populations and the disruption of culturally, linguistically and historicallyembedded communicative communities (with the attendant, putative, erosion of the trust that is necessary for us to live socially) have risen in social scientific salience. It is with a certain amount of unease that any scholar will now cite Francis Fukuyama to sustain an argument but his claim that 'Now that the question of ideology and institutions has been settled, the preservation and accumulation of social capital will occupy center stage' (Fukuyama 1995: 362) makes the point eloquently. Onora O'Neill (2005)[3] makes a similar point in reverse, claiming that there is:

> a 'crisis of trust' in developed societies. Many who note this crisis claim that trust is obsolete: we have eroded the social capital that traditional societies had accumulated, so now have to do without it. In complex and sophisticated societies, trust can no longer provide the cohesion and compliance that it provided in traditional societies.

But, despite its contemporary scholarly salience, trust is, curiously, a relatively new focus for social science – as Luhmann (1988) observed, trust was not a topic addressed in mainstream sociology.

Trust, social science and the media

Perhaps the most striking contemporary instance of the boom in trust related work is Robert Putnam's celebrated *Bowling Alone* (see Putnam 2000 and bowlingalone.com). Indeed, Reeskens and Hooghe (2008) claim that:

> The booming of research on social capital started with Robert Putnam's seminal work on civic traditions in modern Italy (1993). As is well known, Putnam argued that the presence of social capital (measured as the prevalence of generalized trust, norms of reciprocity and networks of civic engagement) determined the performance of local and regional government...The concept gained further prominence in the international literature when Putnam (2000) turned his attention to social capital in the United States...Notoriously, Putnam argued that generalized trust is diminishing rapidly and systematically in the US, at least since the 1970s. Since then, the empirical validity of this pessimistic claim has been highly contested [Stolle and Hooghe 2005]. (Reeskens and Hooghe 2008: 517)

Seymour Martin Lipset and William Schneider's (1983) *The Confidence Gap* (which focused on Americans' dissatisfaction with American leaders and institutions) has a claim to have anticipated the pervasive concern about erosion of trust attributed to Putnam's insights and Eric Uslaner's (2002a) *The Moral Foundations of Trust* and Richard Sennett's *The Corrosion of Character* (1998) provide further evidence of widespread scholarly concern. The putative erosion of trust and social capital in modern societies[4] has powerful implications for economics as well as social and political studies generally, as Uslaner recognized in claims such as these:

> High trusting societies have greater transfer payments, spend more on education, and have larger public sectors more generally. They also have more open markets–and 'better' government more generally. (Uslaner 2002b: 26)

> Trust helps us solve collective action problems by reducing transaction costs. (Uslaner 2002b: 2)

Clearly it is not just transaction costs that trust and high quotients of social capital reduce but also security, audit, search and other costs (see Guerra et al. 2003). Trust fills in for the incompleteness of contracts and thus both provides a rationale for internalizing functions within a stable organization, (because contact and mutual dependence is trust-engendering), and/or for only externalizing such functions to suppliers with whom long term and mutually dependent relationships exist or may be developed (see an extensive literature including Coase 1937, Luhmann 1979 and Williamson and Winter 1991). Onora O'Neill has rightly pointed both to the necessity of trust – somewhere in a system of accountability there has to be a locus of trust – and to the perils of alternatives to systems of trust, those she describes as the 'abstract systems of control and audit' (O'Neill 2002c: vii. See also Power 1997) which, latterly, have come in many instances to supplant the 'traditional approaches to compliance [which] relied heavily on cultures of trust' (O'Neill 2005: 1).

The large scale resonances of the putative decline in trust and trustworthiness are further manifested in the explosion of social scientific interest in risk and the 'risk society' (see, among others, Beck 1992,[5] Giddens 1990, 1999). The perceived decline in trust is often attributed, at least in part, to the influence of the mass media. Putnam's *Bowling Alone* is an outstanding instance: Putnam argued that the privatization of leisure, notably influenced by television, has hollowed out modern societies and eroded social capital.

Putnam's thesis has stimulated reassessment. Pippa Norris (2002[6] see also Norris 1996) argues that Putnam-like 'claims that it is the pervasive spread of television and privatized leisure in postindustrial societies that is driving any long-term erosion in social capital in general, and social trust in particular, does not seem to be supported by…cross-national evidence'.[7] Evidence is admittedly fragmentary and often commissioned and circulated by interested parties but Norris' point is well made.

Despite O'Neill's claim, in her *Autonomy and Trust in Bioethics*, that 'reported levels of trust in newspaper journalists are generally far lower than levels of trust in all holders of public office…Even lower than levels of trust in politicians' (O'Neill 2002b: 175), there is no consensus that either, on the one hand, trust and social capital have significantly and generally diminished or, on the other, that the media are either particularly mistrusted and/or are key agents in a general and serious decline in social trust.

In 2006, a poll of media users in ten countries (commissioned by the BBC, Reuters and the Media Center[8] and conducted by GlobeScan) found that 'Media is trusted by an average of 61 per cent compared to 52 per cent for governments across the countries polled'. Although respondents in the US and Britain trusted their governments somewhat more than their media (but see the findings of YouGov's 2007 poll considered below). Indeed, this survey found that 'Trust in media has increased overall over the last four years – in Britain up from 29 per cent to 47 per cent and in the US from 52 per cent to 59 per cent' (BBC 2006a: 2) and also found that two thirds of respondents thought the media reported the news accurately (BBC 2006a: 1). Martin Brookes, in his *Watching Alone. Social Capital and Public Service Broadcasting* (Brookes 2004), lends support to this view – he proposed that, contrary to Putnam's claims, television provides material for 'water cooler' conversation and thus builds, not diminishes, social capital. Further, Zhang and Chia's (2006) empirical testing of the thesis that the media are responsible for hollowing out society suggests that newspaper and television public affairs consumption was positively, not negatively, correlated with political participation (though they found the reverse in respect of Internet and entertainment).

Although there may be scant evidence of a consistent and convincing match between a pervasive social scientific (and public policy) concern about the media as a destroyer of trust and social capital (see the *compte rendu* provided by Bakir and Barlow 2007 around p 5) there is evidence that UK respondents perceive there to be a hierarchy of media trustworthiness, as a tabulation of 2007 YouGov poll evidence below suggests.

	% of respondents trusting a fair amount or a great deal.
Family doctors	87
Judges	64
Journalists on 'upmarket' newspapers	44
Television	35
Estate agents	11
Politicians	10
Second hand car salesmen	4

	% of respondents trusting a fair amount or a great deal.
BBC news journalists	56
ITV news journalists	47
Sky news journalists	38

Source: YouGov (nd)

But whether or not the media are trusted more than governments and/or are notably responsible for a contemporary decline in trust, all of this presumes that trust is a good thing – as indeed it is when the object of trust is *worthy* of trust. But when trust is misplaced, reposed in an untrustworthy person, process or institution, then there is too much trust, too much of a good thing. The trust-infused system of 'club governance' (Marquand 1988, Moran 2003), governance based on shared understandings, assumptions and trust between parties which Marquand described, talking of British government, as 'that of a club, whose members trusted each other to observe the spirit of the club rules' (Marquand: 1988: 178) (and which was epitomized, for Moran, by UK broadcasting) exemplifies the demerits of trust-based systems.

This high-level scholarly literature on trust, risk and the role of the media has focused on one-way, offline, conventional mass media rather than online media. Nonetheless, work by the 'big guns' of contemporary social science (Beck, Giddens, Putnam, Sennett et al.) on offline media complements a rather separate stream of work on trust and mistrust in cyberspace. The latter responds to and reflects what Mansell and Collins identify as 'considerable uncertainty about how trust in the offline world transfers into cyberspace and about the trustworthiness of elements of the cyberspace system' (Mansell and Collins 2005: 4). But here too there is some evidence of disconnection between alarm and evidence.

Despite pervasive concern about the Internet as a Putnam-like eroder of trust and a happy hunting ground for those who thrive on the abuse of trust, Mansell and Collins (2005: 37) observe (drawing on findings from the first annual Oxford Internet Survey of 2003) that '[e] xperience on the Internet tends to engender a higher level of cyber trust'. Findings from the most recent Oxford Internet Survey (OxIS 2007: 28) were consistent with those from 2003.[9] Though this finding needs to be considered in relation to Globescan's finding (BBC 2006a: 5) that only Internet blogs were trusted less than news websites as news sources – though, intriguingly, the most *mistrusted* news source was family, friends and colleagues.[10] Latterly, Dutton (2007) has argued that Internet-based information media have established themselves as a 'fifth estate' complementing and extending the fourth estate's (i.e. the 'legacy' mass media of the newspaper press and broadcasting) role of holding the powerful to account.

The sources of trust

What makes for trustworthiness in the media? Hewison and Holden (2004: 33–34) propose that:

> Trust is produced by a relationship between individuals or groups on the one hand, and public institutions where there is effective interaction and where the representatives of the institution are perceived to be straightforward and honest. Trust in an institution is enhanced where the institution is perceived to be independent, and trust increases the more 'local' the institution is perceived to be.

These criteria are roughly, if not completely, compatible with the empirical findings of the YouGov poll cited above. Although there is something tautological about identifying trustworthiness as a property of those 'perceived to be straightforward and honest', the criteria of effective interaction and localness seem likely to underpin the high perceived trustworthiness of family doctors; that of independence the high ranking of judges and the relatively high ranking of BBC journalists when compared to ITV and Sky journalists.

O'Neill presents a different account of the sources of trust. She argues in her Reith Lectures (O'Neill 2002a, 2002c) that trust is grounded in dialogue and face-to-face contact, that this direct personal contact was the basis of trust in pre-modern societies and that modernity (the 'information age' as she names it) no longer enjoys these trust-building rhythms and routines. She states:

> When Kings of old tested their daughters' suitors, most communication was face-to-face and two-way: in the information age it is often between strangers and one-way. Socrates worried about the written word, because it travelled beyond the possibility of question and revision, and so beyond trust. We may reasonably worry not only about the written word, but also about broadcast speech, film and television. These technologies are designed for one-way communication with minimal interaction. Those who control and use them may or may not be trustworthy. How are we to check what they tell us? (O'Neill 2002a: Lecture 5)

She thus images modern communication, that of the 'information age', as one-way and attributes two-wayness and interactivity (foundations of trust) as the exclusive prerogative of pre-modern, non-information age, media. This is, as I shall argue below, misleading, but O'Neill's contention that dialogue provides, through mutual checking and verification, possibilities of trust enhancement is potentially very productive. Although this dialogic capacity is largely absent (despite a few exceptions such as the readers' letters pages in newspapers, 'phone in' radio programmes and the occasional viewer response television programmes such as the UK's *Right to Reply*)[11] in traditional 'one-to-many' mass media it is potentially strongly present in the 'Web 2.0' generation of online media. Web 2.0 is not considered in the literature cited above – nor could it have been for Web 2.0 post dates (almost) all of it.[12]

Web 2.0,[13] user generated content, was well characterized by Tim O'Reilly, sometimes credited with first using the term 'Web 2.0', as 'applications that harness network effects to get better the more people use them' (O'Reilly 2006). Such applications often employ and foster collaboration and dialogue and the intrinsic character of Web 2.0 Internet practices may, if O'Neill is right about the trust-fostering attributes of dialogue, thus enhance trustworthiness and establish cyberspace, or at least an element of it, as no less, and perhaps more, trustworthy than its offline equivalent. O'Neill's focus on one-to-many, offline, mass media echoes Putnam et al. and precludes her from considering the positive potential of Web 2.0, dialogic, media. Indeed she argues that 'The new information technologies may be anti-authoritarian, but curiously they are often used in ways that are also anti-democratic. They undermine our capacities to judge others' claims and to place our trust' (O'Neill 2002a: Lecture 5). Rather, she argues for changed media source behaviour in order to improve the authoritativeness, and thus trustworthiness, of media content. Her most persuasive and fully worked out arguments are to be found in her *Autonomy and Trust in Bioethics* (O'Neill 2002b). O'Neill's arguments lead her to propose a supply-side solution, a strengthening of authoritativeness (notably through the implementation of stronger and more binding codes of journalistic practice). But O'Neill's empirical focus on offline media and embrace of supply-side measures to improve the authoritativeness, and thereby the trustworthiness, of media does not negate the potential importance of her arguments in respect of some of the new media (in her words 'new information technologies') although, I believe, she underestimates and misperceives these. New online media offer a dialogic capacity, and thus a potential for engendering trust, superior to the 'one-to-many' mass media which form the main object of her attention. Interactive, Web 2.0, media thus potentially satisfy the normative criteria implicit in O'Neill's claim that:

> Well-placed trust grows out of active inquiry rather than blind acceptance. In traditional relations of trust, active inquiry was usually extended over time by talking and asking questions, by listening and seeing how well claims to know and undertakings to act held up. That was the world in which Socrates placed his trust – and his reservations about publishing. Where we can check the information we receive, and when we can go back to

> those who put it into circulation, we may gain confidence about placing or refusing trust. (O'Neill 2002a: Lecture 4)

O'Neill makes some sensible and constructive supply side arguments, considered below, for enhancing the trustworthiness of conventional mass media. Similarly, contributors to Mansell and Collins' (2005) collection also propose ways to make cyberspace more trustworthy (e.g. authentication and 'transitivity' – see O' Hara and Shadbolt 2005: 132–134 – that is the authentification of an unknown by a trusted known) and less vulnerable to criminal abuse. Adoption of such recommendations is both desirable and applicable to both on- and offline media but does not acknowledge Web 2.0 media's greater intrinsic potential trustworthiness (though, of course, whether this potential trustworthiness is realized is an empirical matter). No more in the online than in the offline world are trust-building practices of the kind canvassed by O'Neill and by Mansell and Collins' collaborators irrelevant.

A plurality of sources of trust is thus proposed. Hewison and Holden, non-tautologically, identify:

- Source independence
- Localism
- Effective interaction.

Their criterion of 'effective interaction' is synonymous with O'Neill's prescription of a dialogic relationship and their criterion of 'localism' also maps onto O'Neill's notion of dialogue, though Hewison and Holden's notion of source independence is not implicit in O'Neill's notion of dialogue but is a principle which she affirms elsewhere, see, for example, O'Neill 2004b:

> Reuters have taken various measures to back their 'Independence and Trust' principles,[14] which include freedom from bias…Their approach to self-regulation both prescribes standards and establishes certain structures and disciplines to support adherence to those standards…They impose some routine disciplines on their financial journalists, by requiring them to declare shareholdings in companies on which they report to their managers, and to refrain from dealing in those shares during the time in which they report. Reuters' journalists therefore face disciplines that those who work for the BBC… do not face. Journalists and editors working for…the BBC do not routinely have to declare their interests, or their conflicts of interest to their managers (let alone their audiences) or to withdraw from broadcasting on topics in which they have a financial interest. (O'Neill 2004a: np)

'Independence' thus inheres both in institutional status (e.g. the prohibition of Reuters passing 'into the hands of any one interest, group or faction') and in the practices of content sources (notably journalists and editors). These are procedural measures (designed to foster what I shall call 'authoritativeness') and are applicable to both on and offline media.

Trust, accountability and on and offline media

Trust hitherto has rested with established media brands. Because information is an 'experience good'[15] the reputation of providers is likely to be decisive in determining consumption and use. There are thus formidable advantages for incumbents for, almost by definition, it's 'legacy' providers that currently enjoy the highest levels of public trust. The UK public, for example, tends to trust the BBC more than other media. The BBC's own claim that 'The public trusts BBC news more than that of any other news provider' (BBC 2004b: 45) was supported by a YouGov poll which found, (in a poll conducted in January 2005), that the BBC is 'still the most trusted for news' (see Aitken 2007) and by the greater trust invested in BBC journalists (when compared to ITV and Sky journalists) in YouGov's 2007 poll.

The BBC has proposed that the trust it enjoys is fungible and provides a basis for assuming a role as gatekeeper in filtering other providers' content: as the wider UK news environment is becoming more crowded and confusing the BBC has claimed that its role as a 'trusted guide' will become increasingly important' (BBC 2004b: 8). The Alexa rankings for UK Internet 'top sites' (Alexa Internet nd) on 19 June 2008 identified the BBC as the top media site (ranked seventh, following search and virtual community sites such as Google and Facebook) followed by well-established and generally well-reputed sites established by UK national daily newspapers: the *Guardian Unlimited* (ranked twenty-fourth) and *The Times* and *Daily Telegraph* (ranked forty-second and forty-third). The 'page strength' ranking site SEOmoz[16] rated the BBC and online *Daily Telegraph* sites 10/10 and the online *Guardian* 9/10, *The Times* 8.5/10 (i.e. all were '[a]mong the most popular and important sites/pages on the web; you've achieved near legendary status'). These ratings suggest both the importance of incumbency and its fungibility across platforms.

Although O'Neill constructs trust as a product of dialogue, as an attribute engendered through contact and the resulting ability to check and verify propositions and to hold trust claimants to account, she also distinguishes between traditional notions and practices of trust. Dialogue is characteristic of trust-construction in traditional societies whereas trust-building in modern societies is based on formal structures of accountability and powers of sanction because large scale societies cannot generate a generalized trust through the face-to-face contact assumed to underpin its generation in families and in traditional societies. The mass media are thus seen as one of the main contemporary agencies through which power holders are held to account. They do the checking out of strangers and institutions, test credentials, authenticate sources, and enable us, at best, 'to place trust with discrimination' (O'Neill 2002a: Lecture 5). At its most sober (and therefore little known) this holding to account may be seen in the UK television Channel 4's excellent fact-checking web site where the evidence stated, or implied, in politicians' claims is subjected to verification – see Channel 4 News (2009). And it can be seen manifested more vivaciously in headlines such as those sported in the UK 'tabloid' *The Sun*, for example, (2 September 1995) 'I was bedded by head. Vice girl Sally tells all.' and (8 February 2008) 'What a Burkha. Archbishop wants Muslim law in UK.' These examples suggest, too, that trust can be differential and conditional: I may trust *The Sun* when it reports cricket scores but be more cautious about its assertion that 'Archbishop wants Muslim law in UK'.

But the extent to which the media may be effective institutions, because trusted, through which social actors are held to account, depends on how far the media themselves are trusted. Trusted media are those to whose account of the world users give credence over the long term. And though this credence and credibility resides principally in the extent to which media's representations of the world consistently are found to be reliable, the extent to which and manner by which the media are themselves held to account also sustains, or undermines, their credibility and thus their trustworthiness. Here I draw on Warnock's (1974) distinction between giving an account and being held to account as separate and complementary aspects of accountability. Such holding of the media to account may be through any or all of the institutions of law, competition, regulation external to the media and through endogenous professional norms and self-regulatory practices and institutions, such as readers' editors and media ombudsmen, through which stakeholders can hold the media to account and through which the media may give an account of themselves. Such mechanisms correspond to O'Neill's 'modern' paradigm where trustworthiness is constructed through formal, institutional and specialized structures of holding to account and exercising sanctions. They do not acknowledge the possibilities of a return to what O'Neill called the methods of the 'Kings of old' permitted by the dialogic character of Web 2.0 applications.

Barriers to entry have fallen, new providers have entered the digital world and a new form of provision (whereby users can post and amend content), variously called interactive,[17] 'Web 2.0', user generated content, or 'pull' content, which exhibits O'Reilly's network effect 'to get better the more people use them' (O'Reilly 2006) is now becoming both pervasive and indispensible. The dialogic potentiality of Web 2.0 media may mitigate, if not solve, some of the problems of trust which beset one-to-many mass media. To make such a claim may seem unusual in the context of the general emphasis of Internet studies which predominantly addresses the perceived problems and damaging potentiality of the media and the Internet in particular. There can be no doubt that there are significant negative issues to be addressed: fraud, spam, phishing and the dissemination of potentially harmful and/or offensive material (see, among others, Byron 2008, Mansell and Collins 2005) but attention to these has tended to mask recognition of the positive potential of the Internet and the trust-enhancing capabilities of networked online collaboration.

Slashdot provides an outstanding example of how these network effects, or 'participating user relationships' (Jones 2007: 177), can build trust and authority.

Slashdot.org was one of the first sites to build trustworthiness on contributors' input by appointing contributors as moderators who are empowered to award 'karma' points to other contributors. The level of 'karma' determines the salience of contributors' postings and karma scores may (if users of the site so wish) trigger filters enabling readers to exclude postings with low karma from those presented to them (see Slashdot nd). Slashdot has thus a self-regulating and ranking system which is based on peer review and ranking. As Tony Curzon-Price, Chief Editor of openDemocracy stated (interview 27 June 2008) 'something like this carries over to all successful online communities'. The buyer-ranking of sellers on eBay also exemplifies such network effects or 'participating user relationships' (Jones 2007: 177).

Although procedurally different, this sort of peer review and ranking system is analogous to that long established in the scholarly community. Badging identifies those most strongly legitimized in the scholarly community: professors outrank readers, readers outrank lecturers, doctors outrank masters and Harvard, Princeton, Cambridge and so on outrank the Open University. Such badging systems are fallible but perhaps no less fallible than other, generally well-merited ranking systems: just as the generally high esteem ceded to the journalism of *The New York Times* (NYT) does not invariably mean that NYT journalists adhere to the highest professional standards, so a Harvard professorial pedigree does not mean infallibility. But such peer-reviewed badging systems are often rightly successful in building and maintaining trust.

Web 2.0

Dutton (2007: 2) has referred to the Internet as a 'fifth estate' providing a 'new form of social accountability' and the rhetorical power of his metaphor directs attention to its substantive, dialogic, root in what he names as the fifth estate's 'online interaction between ever-changing networks of individuals' (Dutton 2007: 16) and which is characteristic of Web 2.0. The most striking example of a Web 2.0 application/service is Wikipedia. Alexa testifies to the extent to which UK Internet users have adopted Wikipedia, ranking it (21 June 2008) as the tenth most-visited Internet site, SEOmoz rates it at 9/10. At its best Wikipedia accelerates and makes more extensive and inclusive the collaborative processes of peer review, critique, factual correction and consensus-building that underpin offline scholarship. It has, at least potentially, an intrinsic self-correcting capacity. But at its worst (though this worst seems scarcely different from similarly abusive behaviour offline) Wikipedia is prey to systematic falsification and bias. Not surprisingly, controversy over how far Wikipedia (and user-generated content in general) can be trusted is rife and it has been the object of much odium expressed by professional journalists.

The UK House of Lords' Communications Committee Inquiry on the Ownership of the News of 2007/8 elicited the comment from Pierre Le Sourd, the London Bureau Editor for Agence France Presse: 'We have a written rule inside our company which forbids any journalist from using Wikipedia. We have the same thing, which has been updated last week, for Facebook because there was an incident last week with Bilawal Bhutto in Oxford where some newspaper picked up some pictures on the Facebook site about Mr Bhutto which turned out to be fake' (House of Lords 2008a: 30). M. Le Sourd's judgement was foreshadowed by Richard Dixon, the revise (*sic*) editor of *The Times*, who stated his 'default position' to be 'every article on Wikipedia is rubbish'. 'Why' he asked 'trust the vagaries of Wikipedia when there are web stalwarts such as the BBC, Know UK, the Internet Movie Data Base and the Ordnance Survey'?[18]

Dixon perhaps spoils his case by citing the Internet Movie Data Base (imdb.com) which, though now owned by Amazon, began as a 'Web 2.0' 'wiki'-type collaboration and uses a database which was, to a significant extent, user-generated. Moreover, few of the sources Dixon cites are as readily accessible as Wikipedia: in theory, KnowUK is available to any registered user of a public library in the UK but its log-on and security procedures have defeated more than one potential user. The Ordnance Survey makes its maps available free online (but non-printable) only up to scale 1:25000 – in many respects Google's free-at-the-point-of-use maps and satellite imagery[19] serve users better. And the BBC's massive (estimated at 6m pages) website is fully accessible only to users with a UK IP address – even though BBC licence fee payers sometimes travel beyond the borders of the UK! However, Dixon is surely right to point to institutions such as these, each with well-established supply-side norms of professional practice in information-collection, processing and presentation, providing a potentially authoritative alternative to Web 2.0 sources of content – though the Ordnance Survey's exclusion of 'sensitive' locations (such as military establishments) from its maps and a succession of challenges to the BBC's authority[20] suggest that 'gold standard' sources are not always unimpeachable.

Le Sourd's and Dixon's statements represent a familiar negative professional journalistic reflex as 'networked' (Beckett 2008a, 2008b) or 'distributed' (Bradshaw 2007) journalism changes news consumption, as well as news gathering and editorial practices, and exemplify both an understandable defensive interest, well captured in Greenslade's speculation that 'We are surely moving towards a situation in which relatively small 'core' staffs will process material from freelances and/or citizen journalists, bloggers, whatever' (Greenslade 2007) and a proper professional concern for the quality of news. Their responses represent one perspective in an often thoughtful and usually vigorous debate among journalists[21] but only one perspective. Others have embraced the networked Web 2.0 model anathematized by Le Sourd and Dixon. An issue of general importance arises from this discussion: we may identify two sources of authority, and potential trustworthiness, in information, both of which are, in different ways, reliant on peer consensus. The first employs user review to establish authority (with a corresponding expectation that authors will revise and amend in the light of convincing peer commentary), and the supply-side-biased second type of authority derives from authors' status as experts, a status which is in turn based on adherence to proven procedures and practices found to ensure a high level of correspondence between the real world and its representation. In fact, there are seldom pure instances of either form of authentication – most public information is authenticated through a combination, in varying degrees, of both methods.

Authority and trustworthiness

There is no necessary incompatibility between Web 2.0, 'wiki', information-generation and authentication and use of the procedures that have underpinned successful operations such as the BBC's and the Ordnance Survey's. Information may *both* be user-generated and be compiled and produced using procedures deemed likely to engender trustworthiness. Indeed, many sites including the IMDb, Wikipedia and a noteworthy UK-based content site openDemocracy combine user-generated content with expert editorial origination and amendment of content. However, despite the precarious economic position of some online content providers, the translation of dominant 'legacy media' from the analogue world to the digital world co-exists with the emergence of some striking new entrants. New voices range from individual blogs, contributions to social networking (see, among others, bebo and Technorati), user-generated content sites (see, among others, YouTube) to online media modelled on offline equivalents (for example *The First Post* at thefirstpost.co.uk). However despite the rapid proliferation of user-generated sites, only a small proportion of UK Internet users actually post content[22] and only 15 per cent use 'newspapers or news services' different from those they use offline (OxIS 2007: 69).

Interesting intermediate content sites, with neither the idiosyncratic character of blogs nor the traditional one-to-many, 'push' character of sites such as *The First Post*, include sites which collectively construct authoritative content through deliberation and/or 'natural selection'. A well-established group blog of this kind, which creatively expands a public sphere of expert (often nerdy) comment and debate on media regulation and policy, is www.ofcomwatch.co.uk . Another comparable instance is the blog on European media and communications policy, www.contentandcarrier.eu The UK Citizens Online Democracy (UKCOD), a charity, provides another type of hybrid website, mysociety, which, in turn, enables people to build 'websites which give people simple, tangible benefits in the civic and community aspects of their lives', notably by enhancing citizens' ability to secure information so that they can act more effectively as citizens and hold their representatives (including Members of Parliament) to account. 'Wiki' sites, and the multilingual Wikipedia[23] are further deservedly well-known examples of this intermediate type of content site.

Dialogue in online content provision – some UK examples

Wikipedia strikingly exemplifies the possibilities of the so-called Web 2.0, whereby the interaction of users generates content, exchange, collective deliberation and debate. 'Wiki', essentially, speeds up and opens up the processes of peer review and construction of an expert consensus that has underpinned the production and sanctification of knowledge. It remains to be seen how far the 'wiki' model of open access will supplant the more orderly and structured construction of expert consensus which has characterized established expert repositories of knowledge such as the *Encyclopaedia Britannica*[24] but though there have been egregious cases of abuse[25] of the openness of the wiki process there seems no reason to doubt the robustness of the general model as a variety of new entrants, which have seized the opportunities of digital online provision, have demonstrated. These have settled on varying mixes between dialogic, Web 2.0, and formal, supply-side systems of authority and trustworthiness-generation.

Consider these examples of current UK online providers[26] variously using text, audio and video:[27]

- The Independent Media Centre UK (Indymedia)
- Interworld Radio (IWR)
- openDemocracy
- 18 Doughty Street.

The Independent Media Centre UK (Indymedia) runs a moderated 'Web 2.0' site with a commitment to 'a world based on freedom, cooperation, justice and solidarity, and against environmental degradation, neoliberal exploitation, racism and patriarchy'.[28] Indymedia is a moderated site but which invites everybody to add their own comments at the end of each article. Comments can be used to:

- State an opinion about any given posting
- Add information
- Correct inaccurate or malicious information
- Rectify misinformation. (Indymedia Uk nd)

This invests Indymedia content with the transparency claimed by Malter (2001): 'Readers can see editorial decisions being made by others. They can see how to get involved and help make editorial decisions'. Indymedia is a global movement and, as the UK site claims:

> Independent DIY media projects are spreading around the planet at unprecedented speed. Triggered by discontent with the mainstream media and supported by the widespread availability of media technologies, groups all over the world are creating their own channels of information and distribution in order to bypass the (mainstream) corporate media. The idea behind most of these projects is to create open platforms to which everyone can contribute – not only a small media elite with their particular interests.[29] By eliminating the classic division between professional producers and passive audience, many issues and discussions that were previously suppressed become visible and available. (Indymedia UK ndb)

In classic 'Web 2.0' fashion Indymedia claims that its open, interactive, site 'erodes the dividing line between reporters and reported, between active producers and passive audience: people are enabled to speak for themselves'.[30] Nonetheless, Indymedia is clearly a media source with a preconceived view – transparency may be necessary for trustworthiness but is not necessarily sufficient for it.

A further case in point is the UK news and comment, e-zine site, openDemocracy, which began in 2001 as a non-profit interactive news, comment and deliberation site. openDemocracy is distinguished by its use of writers from the localities under consideration: 'we use African writers when an African issue is under consideration', by its commitment to 'non metropolitan voices' – 'we don't publish on the basis of a metropolitan outlook' and by its dialogic and debate format: 'we typically commission more than one piece' and 'we still regard ourselves as a debate site' (Hilton interview 7 February 2007).[31] SEOmoz ranked openDemocracy 9/10 and Alexa ranked the site 3,071 among UK users.

openDemocracy is, of course, not the only new voice to find expression through digital interactive media. But there are few other new digital content sites of the range and authoritativeness of openDemocracy which so successfully utilize the potential of the Internet for dialogue and collective deliberation. Hilton identified only one further European exemplar: Safe Democracy in Spain but Safe Democracy appears, at least in the English language version, to be less interactive and dialogic than openDemocracy.

Wikinews provides much better grounds for critiques such as those of Le Sourd and Dixon than does Wikipedia. Wikinews has not attained the salience of its parent (the SEOmoz ranking for wikinews.org is 5.5/10 with the comment: 'Your site is having an impact and may even be a leader in your field (depending on how big or small that field is). Keep on this path; it's clear that the effort you've put in is producing results') nor Wikipedia's reputation (albeit disputed by those such as Le Sourd and Dixon). As Tony Curzon-Price stated (interview 27 June 2008) Wikipedia has 'the luxury of moving slowly'. Wikipedia has around 5, 000 fact checkers (though fewer than 30 paid staff), who flag items in reports as requiring corroboration or their source identifying, who lock pages when abuse is suspected. It is, for Curzon-Price, 'a self-regulatory, self-selecting and self-validating community' operating a 'quasi industrialised *clearly* defined process'. Whereas Wikinews has many fewer such quality controllers and lacks the 'luxury of moving slowly' and is of 'extremely variable quality' and 'falls apart quite quickly'. Moreover, as McIntosh (2008: 206–7) relates, Wikinews has been subject to egregious 'troll'-ish behaviour by partisan interveners such as 'Neutralizer' and 'MrMiscellanious' *(sic)*.

Both Wikipedia and Wikinews are more transparent in important respects than are most offline media: readers of all stories can 'go behind' the stories to see the history of their editing, their source and the sources on which contributors have drawn.[32] Transparency does not necessarily establish authority, for example it does little to enhance Wikinews' authority and often reveals no more than Wikinews' reliance on established offline news sources. For example, on 27 June 2008 (timelined at 1500 UTC time) Wikinews Main (front) page stories and sources were as follows:

US Supreme Court rules DC gun ban unconstitutional (sourced from CNN and ABC news and the transcripts of 'District of Columbia et al. v. Heller', Supreme Court of the United States, June 26, 2008; 'Shelly Parker, et al., v. District of Columbia and Adrian M. Fenty, Mayor of the District of Columbia'. United States Court of Appeals for the District of

Columbia Circuit, March 9, 2007; 'Government Reform to Review D.C. s Handgun Ban'. Congressman Tom Davis, June 28, 2005).

US will remove 'terror' tag on North Korea (sourced from Fox and al Jazeera English news).

Mugabe says he's open to talks with Zimbabwe opposition (sourced from Associated Press, Bloomberg, Agence France-Presse, The Times and the Ghana Broadcasting Corporation).

EU regulation prevents sale of 'small' kiwi fruit in Bristol shop (sourced from BBC News Online and The Daily Telegraph).

Nonetheless, the growth of 'citizen' or 'networked' journalism (see, for example, Beckett 2008a) where both the contributions of non-professional journalists to news-gathering and formulation and, crucially, the 'wiki'-like fact-checking and dialogic verification of the output of professional journalists can, Beckett claims, 'help the news media address the crisis of trust in journalism as a way of re-building its relevance and authority' (Beckett 2008a: 62).

Supply-side measures to foster trust

Parallel to successful Web 2.0 content services based on dialogic models of trust building, other supply-side initiatives, to enhance trustworthiness of on and offline media, have also grown. In the online domain these have largely responded to public disquiet about the perceived potential of the Internet to expose children and young people to harmful content and contacts. The UK Byron Review's proposal for 'better self regulation' (Byron 2008: 3) and the successful establishment of the self-regulatory Internet Watch Foundation (IWF) are cases in point (see iwf.org.uk). But there have been few equivalents in online media to the (slow) growth in offline media of supply-side measures, such as editorial and journalistic codes and independent spokespersons, readers' editors/media ombudsman, to enhance the authority and trustworthiness of news and other information services.

The intrinsic properties of one-to-many, one-way, offline mass media mean that there are few opportunities for trust-building through the dialogic Web 2.0-like methods that are available online. It is therefore unsurprising that development of supply-side measures of trust enhancement are most evident in offline media, though it has to be acknowledged that their growth is both uneven and poorly generalized in the UK.[33] Indeed Onora O'Neill has argued that 'newspaper journalists face few disciplines that support public trust' (O'Neill 2002b: 175): 'there are no enforceable requirements for accuracy or coverage and balance; there are no enforceable requirements to refrain from writing on subjects of which they are ignorant; there are no enforceable requirements to distinguish reporting from commentary… There is a well-guarded 'right' to hide sources, that can be used to obstruct the reader's ability to tell whether there is any sources whatsoever, or (if there is) whether it can be trusted' (O'Neill 2002b: 176). And where more exacting norms are mandated (e.g. in the BBC), O'Neill argues that these are 'less demanding than those that apply in the professions or the public sector' (2002b: 176). Fundamental is the obligation to 'reject deception' (2002b: 185) and 'the habitual failure' of the media to provide readers (*sic*) with the 'means of checking and interpreting what they are reading' (2002b: 186).

O'Neill's fingering of the potential deficiencies of the BBC's norms was prescient. In July 2008, Ofcom fined the BBC £400,000 in respect of eight separate breaches of the Ofcom programme codes.[34] Ofcom commented 'In each of these cases the BBC deceived its audience by faking winners of competitions and deliberately conducting competitions unfairly' (see Ofcom 2008d). A year earlier, Ofcom had fined the BBC £50,000 for falsifying the results of a competition on the children's programme *Blue Peter.*[35]

O'Neill points up the general failure of offline media to engender trust both by listing the deficiencies of their performance and their norms and by comparing then adversely to her talismanic norm of face-to-face exchange. Dialogue, she claims, enables interlocutors to 'assess what we are told by backtracking and asking questions, by cross-checking and testing our understanding and our interlocutors' (O'Neill 2002b: 186). And 'Because written and broadcast communication is almost exclusively one way' writers and broadcasters should adhere to supply side 'conventions and standards' (O'Neill 2002b: 186–7) in order to establish their trustworthiness. Here it is important to signal the importance of the one way character of offline media for O'Neill's argument. They lack the dialogic character which enabled the Kings of old to assess their daughters' suitors and which underpin the notable strengths and achievements of Web 2.0 applications. Accordingly, to redress the deficiencies intrinsic to one way media, she (2002b: 190) proposes these norms:

- Declaration of 'relevant interests and conflicts of interest'
- Declaration of 'relations with lobbyists, political parties, companies and campaigning organisations'
- Publication of 'credentials of reporters writing on technical topics' and warning if reporters 'lacking the relevant competence' are assigned to a particular topic
- Declaration of 'full financial information about payments made to obtain material relevant to stories'
- Publication of corrections 'of equal length and prominence, perhaps written by third parties'
- Penalties for 'recirculating 'stories' shown to be libellous or invented.

All of these ethical and procedural norms seem sensible, constructive and proportionate – and relevant to public service broadcasting (as well as more generally) as the sad litany of Ofcom fines suggests.

The convergence of BBC values with those of the UK media more generally are interestingly evidenced by the BBC's own online instructional site designed to address the problems which have compromised the BBC's trustworthiness and occasioned Ofcom's fines (BBC 2009). One exercise on the BBC instructional site asks the student whether it is permissible to publish a statement under a 'star' name if the star in question has not actually written it. The question is posed in a self-instruction/self-test on issues of trust in an online context. We are asked to imagine a celebrity chef whose online statement (feature article) was written by a researcher after a telephone talk with the chef and the draft vetted by the chef before publication. And we are asked to decide whether this is acceptable. The 'right answer' is provided: the BBC states explicitly: 'There isn't a problem with anything that happened here'. Would we so conclude if the context was academic publication (a PhD thesis written by a retired professor after a talk with the PhD candidate)? Or a medical (a paramedic drafts and a doctor signs?) or legal (an intern drafts and a judge signs?) report? I think not. Doubtless all of these practices occur but few members of the professional communities in question would endorse them. The BBC exercise continues with further examples (e.g. the legitimacy of 'spoof' websites) where, I think, reasonable people might also reasonably form different judgements as to what is acceptable practice by those who seek to be regarded as trustworthy to those which are defined, by the BBC in its instructional exercises, as the 'right' answers.

All this is not to suggest that academic (or legal and medical) norms are 'right' and the BBC's 'wrong', only to state that the evidence is that professional criteria of trustworthiness are different in different professions and that broadcasters', and the BBC's, criteria are not always the most stringent. Indeed the BBC's 'right' answer in the example considered above is on all fours with the widespread 'ghosting' of articles in UK newspapers: few articles purporting to be authored by Gordon Brown are likely to have been written by the Prime Minister and so, too, may one reasonably doubt whether cricketer Matthew Hoggard (to name a personal favourite) or many other sports stars write the articles which regularly appear under their names.

O'Neill's proposals are congruent with the scrutiny, transparency, transfer of ownership from experts to stakeholders, evidence of identity etc.,[36] counselled by O' Hara and Shadbolt in the online domain (2005: 113, 130–37). However, they are proposed in the content of one-way conventional broadcasting and newspapers – circumstances where the opportunities that exist in dialogic, face-to-face, exchanges do not prevail. Whereas Web 2.0 content offers many (but not all) of the opportunities for authentification, interrogation, revision and consensus-building absent in one-way mass communication and present in face-to-face communication. Intrinsically, therefore, there are opportunities to establish the trustworthiness of information and comment mediated through 'Web 2.0' dialogic, cooperative, collaborations on content-production that are absent in the contemporary and conventional mass media.

To be sure, just as in face-to-face communication, contributors to Web 2.0 content can lie, act in bad faith, mislead and so on. This means that the norms and procedures which

O'Neill and others propose for the conventional mass media are no less applicable to online digital content production and dissemination. But Web 2.0 offers possibilities of establishing trustworthiness that are absent in offline and Web 1.0 media and thus the potentially beneficial combination of both dialogic and procedural (academic and journalistic) routes to trustworthiness. This dialogic potentiality is realized, albeit in different degrees, in a number of contemporary instances: Wikinews gives an account of its sources; Slashdot's content is explicitly peer ranked through the 'karma' point system; openDemocracy's content is characterized by debate, dialogue and collective deliberation and so on. True, the trustworthiness of few of these Web 2.0 media is supported by the stringent (albeit fallible) procedural practices of the best legacy media professional journalism (such as those which O'Neill identifies in Reuters' codes). But there are no reasons in principle why the dialogic legitimation of Web 2.0 content may not be further enhanced through appropriate procedural means – the 'moderation' of sites such as Wikipedia and Indymedia, imperfect and halting though it may be, suggests how this might be developed.

Conclusion

There can never be too much well-founded trust. Contemporary social science has characterized modernity as trust-deficient and has fingered the mass media, particularly television, as a prime cause of modernity's bankruptcy in social capital. O' Neill follows this current in situating the erosion of trust in the decline of face-to-faceness and dialogue (not many opportunities for chat if *Bowling Alone*!) but she is unusual in identifying persuasive measures to redress the deficiencies of offline, one-to-many (as she names them 'one-way') media. These procedural measures are applicable to online media but the potential of online media to provide for a return to the dialogic methods of the 'Kings of old', collaborative construction of knowledge and understanding, collective fact-checking and correction and the Socratic apparatus of 'question and revision' to which O'Neill referred (see 2002a: Lecture 5) have not been acknowledged. True, this potential may take a long time to realize in a context where few UK Internet users actually post content (OxIS 2007: 54 and 61). But, both procedural and dialogic means to foster and augment authority and trustworthiness are applicable to online media, though only the procedural are effectively accessible to offline media. Web 2.0 applications thus offer an unrecognized, and only fragmentarily realized, potential to rebuild social capital and augment trust and trustworthiness.

Notes

1. This article draws on the author's paper presented at the conference (Leipzig May 2007) on European Union Media Policy organized by the Bundesregierung fuer Kultur und Medien as part of Germany's EU Presidency, and published as *Wer bietet in der digitalen Welt zuverlaessige und*

vielfaeltige Informationen, und wie koennen Nutzer darauf zugreifen? Unterscheidliche Arten von Anbietern und ihre Funktion fuer die oeffentliche Kommunikation. In Schulz, W and T Held (eds) *Mehr Vertrauen in Inhalte.* (2008) Berlin, Vistas, and Duesseldorf. Landesanstalt fuer Medien. pp. 59–90. A shorter version is in *Communication et Strategies* 71/3; 57-78. 2008.

2. I found 212,760 hits in a keyword search using the search term 'trust' in the 'Social Sciences' section of Academic Search Complete; 254 hits in a keyword search using search term keywords of both 'trust' and 'economics' in both the 'Social Sciences' and 'Arts and Humanities' sections of Academic Search Complete on 15.6.2008.
3. I quote from the original English language version supplied to me as a textfile by the author rather than from the German language published version.
4. I do not distinguish rigorously between the terms 'social capital' and 'trust', although, for some purposes, a distinction between the categories may be important. I rely on precedent for not so doing, not least O' Neill's who stated 'Trust, it is constantly observed, is hard earned and easily dissipated. It is valuable social capital and not to be squandered' (O'Neill 2002a: Lecture 1).
5. Beck states 'Risks experienced presume a *normative horizon* of lost security and broken trust' (1992: 28).
6. Citation from unpaginated web source.
7. Norris' scepticism about cross-national validity of Putnam's, and Putnam-like claims is echoed by Reeskens and Hooghe (2008) who stated: 'Various authors have also investigated the concept of generalized trust in a comparative manner, showing strong and significant differences between countries. When limiting ourselves to Europe, research routinely shows very high social trust levels in the Scandinavian countries, with lower levels in the Catholic countries of Western and Central Europe, and the lowest levels being recorded in Southern Europe (Stolle 1998; Newton 1999). There is more disagreement, however, on how we could explain this pattern of differences' (Reeskens and Hooghe 2008: 517). See also Newton 1995.
8. At the American Press Institute – see http://www.mediacenter.org/pages/mc/trust_in_media/ for a range of pages of findings on trust and the media.
9. 2007 Internet users in the UK trusted the Internet more than did non-users (on a 10 point scale users rated the Internet at 6.8 whereas non-users rated it at 5.7). Perhaps too much importance should not be placed on this finding – it is intuitively likely that users will trust more than non-users and the greater credence that Internet users placed in both television (6.7 compared to non-Internet users 6.6) and newspapers (5.8 compared to non-Internet users 5.7) suggests that Internet users may also be slightly generally more disposed to grant credence to media claims than are non-users.
10. Internet blogs were trusted by 25% and mistrusted by 23% of respondents; news websites were trusted by 38% and mistrusted by 17%, friends family and colleagues were trusted by 62% and mistrusted by 30% (Globescan 2006: 5).
11. *Right to Reply* ran on Channel 4 from 1982 to 2001. Following racially-offensive behaviour by one celebrity performing on Channel 4's *Big Brother* show, Channel 4 promised a return of *Right to Reply* (see Channel 4 Press Release of 24.5.2007 at http://www.channel4.com/about4/pdf/c4response_cbb_review.pdf accessed on 16.5.2008).
12. Wikipedia, an outstanding instance of Web 2.0 media, dates from 2001.
13. See http://en.wikipedia.org/wiki/Web_2 accessed on 6.3.2007.
14. See the Reuters 'Independence and Trust' Principles. 'Reuters shall at no time pass into the hands of any one interest, group or faction'; 'the integrity, independence and freedom from bias of Reuters shall at all times be fully preserved' and 'Reuters shall supply unbiased and reliable news' See http://about.reuters.com/aboutus/editorial/independence.asp accessed on 16.2.2006.

15. A term attributed to Nelson (1970) but which signifies a much-used concept, referring to information gaps or deficits, particularly in information economics and policy (see, for example, Davies et al. 1999, Graham and Davies 1997 in respect of public service broadcasting). DeLong and Froomkin (1999) develop a similar notion contending that a key element in the difference between 'new' (information) and 'old' (tangible goods) economics is the inherent lack of transparency in new economics.
16. See www.seomoz.org. Page Strength scores are determined by collecting data from external sources such as Yahoo, Alexa, and Google. SEOmoz collects this data tens of thousands of times a day. http://www.seomoz.org/dp/page-strength-faq.
17. Although it focuses on established 'legacy' media, music, films, television, games, radio, magazine newspaper and book publishing (reflecting the authors' remit to consider the 'exploitation of digital content' (p 11), i.e. of established media, see the study for the European Commission '*Interactive content and convergence: Implications for the information society*'. At http://ec.europa.eu/information_society/eeurope/i2010/docs/studies/interactive_content_ec2006_final_report.pdf accessed on 10.3.2007.
18. Cited in '*You couldn't make it up*' by Jenny Kleeman, first published in hard copy in '*times2*' on March 2nd 2007. At http://women.timesonline.co.uk/tol/life_and_style/women/the_way_we_live/article1457697.ece accessed on 7.3.2007. See also the BBC's report of Jaron Lanier's charge that contributors to 'Web 2.0' sites adopt a 'mob mentality' at http://news.bbc.co.uk/1/hi/technology/6379621.stm accessed on 15.3.2007.
19. e.g. at http://maps.google.co.uk/maps?ie=UTF-8&oe=UTF-8&hl=en&tab=wl&q= accessed on 14.5.2007.
20. See, for example, the Hutton Report (Hutton 2004) and studies commissioned by the BBC Governors such as the Review of European Union coverage, Israeli-Palestinian impartiality review etc. See http://www.bbcgovernorsarchive.co.uk/docs/reviews.html accessed on 12.3.2007.
21. See, for example, Roy Greenslade's blogsat http://blogs.guardian.co.uk/greenslade.
22. The Oxford Internet Survey for 2007 found that 28% of UK users have posted images on the web, 16% have tried to establish a website, 15% have a website and 12% write a blog (OxIS 2007: 54 and 61).
23. Wikipedia claims entries in 250 languages (including the constructed language Klingon http://en.wikipedia.org/wiki/Klingon_language accessed on 27.2.2007, Bavarian, Cornish, Lombard, Occitan, Sorbian and Veneta http://www.wikipedia.org/ accessed on 27.2.2007).
24. See the report of '*Nature*'s comparative evaluation of the accuracy of Wikipedia and the '*Encyclopaedia Britannica*' Nature 438, 900-901 (15 December 2005) and the article is accessible online (for a payment) at http://www.nature.com/nature/journal/v438/n7070/full/438900a.html accessed on 16.6.2009. '*Nature*' found 'the difference in accuracy was not particularly great'.
25. See, among others, http://www.concurringopinions.com/archives/2006/01/wikipeding_cong.html and/or http://blogs.zdnet.com/Ou/?p=152 accessed on 27.2.2007.
26. The absence of systematic international comparative data on the issues addressed in this paper makes many of my arguments reliant on anecdotal and possibly unrepresentative data.
27. These examples are not necessarily representative – they are cited because known to the author and have not been selected as a representative sample of the total population of similar sites.
28. From http://www.indymedia.org.uk/en/static/mission.html accessed on 8.3.2007.
29. Interworld Radio (IWR) provides a similar service to Indymedia using the web to distribute sound-based information aimed at making 'a difference to people's lives by giving them access to information, stimulating debate, and improving communication'. From http://www.interworldradio.net/about/mission.asp accessed on 8.3.2007.

30. From http://www.indymedia.org.uk/en/static/mission.html accessed on 8.3.2007.
31. Isabel Hilton was editor-in-chief of openDemocracy at the time of the interview.
32. An intriguing, but uncommon, equivalent is the webcast of the editorial conference of the *Liverpool Daily Post* editorial news conference. At http://www.journalism.co.uk/2/articles/531560.php
33. For example, the first UK readers' editor/media ombudsman elsewhere was appointed in 1997 to *the Guardian* and its sister paper *The Observer* are the only UK newspapers to adhere to the Organization of News Ombudsmen and ombudsmen are established in various European newspapers and broadcasters e.g. in France, the Netherlands, Spain and elsewhere (see http://www.newsombudsmen.org/what.htm on 14.3.2007). Moreover, the self-regulatory code of the UK Press Complaints Commission (PCC) has been held to be both less stringent than other comparable codes and less adhered to (see, *inter alia*, the compilation of European codes of journalistic ethics at http://www.uta.fi/ethicnet/ accessed on 10.3.2007).
34. The BBC was not alone: in December 2007, Ofcom fined Channel 4 £1.5m and had previously fined *five* £300,000 and had also fined GMTV, the advertising financed but formally public service broadcaster, £2m. And the largest advertising funded, for profit, but formally public service broadcaster, ITV, was fined £5.68m by Ofcom for misconduct in conducting 'phone in competitions' (see http://www.ofcom.org.uk/media/news/2008/05/nr_20080508 accessed on 11.4.2009).
35. The BBC Trust stated that these 'were particularly serious as they resulted in children being misled to participate in a competition they had no chance of winning and in a child in the studio being involved in deceiving the audience'. See http://www.bbc.co.uk/bbctrust/news/press_releases/2007/ofcom_blue_peter.html accessed on 11.4.2009.
36. O' Hara and Shadbolt also refer to 'transitivity' of trust (see O' Hara and Shadbolt 2005: 132–34).

Chapter 7

Associative or Communal Society? The Globalization of Media and Communications and Claims for Communality

> A social relationship will be called 'communal' if and so far as the orientation of social action – whether in the individual case, on the average, or in the pure type – is based on a subjective feeling of the parties, whether affectual or traditional, that they belong together. A social relationship will, on the other hand, be called 'associative' if and in so far as the orientation of social action within it rests on a rationally motivated adjustment of interests or a similarly motivated agreement, whether the basis of rational judgement be absolute values or reasons of expediency. (Weber 1964[1922]: 136)

The argument stated

The globalization of media and communications has two main sequences for social identities and communities and therefore for possibilities of social inclusion. To the very large extent that modern societies have taken the form of the nation state, there has been a requirement that citizens share a culture and thereby an identity. When such national culture is eroded by globalization, social cohesion is thought to be threatened. The critical issue then becomes: can national societies – as inclusive, communal societies thus far have mostly been – successfully metamorphose into something different – associative societies? But there is a second, ethical consequence: if there is a right to a national identity, the globalization of media and communications is ethically objectionable because it denies the opportunity for full self-realization.

Introduction

The growing interdependence of hitherto separate economies, allied to complementary trends such as the implementation of military doctrines of collective security, the pooling of sovereignty in associations such as the European Union, international agreements such as the Law of the Sea and international travel (whether voluntary tourism or involuntary migration), together constitute the phenomenon of globalization.

Globalization is particularly pronounced in information and communication. The international division of labour, on which the growth in world trade depends, requires what Weber identified as 'extremely important conditions in the fields of communication and transportation' and specifically 'the services of the railway, the telegraph and the telephone'

(Weber 1964: 339). Also, the inherent economic characteristics of information tend to make the extension of information markets, through both time and space, more pronounced than markets in other traded goods and services. A succession of technological changes culminating in electronic transmission of sound and image has made possible successful exploitation of the highly distinctive economic characteristics of information, notably its imperishability and inexhaustibility: information does not decay and nor is it destroyed by consumption. Information can be stored, transmitted and reproduced at very low cost across time and space. It can be used many times and by many people without being exhausted. Moreover, if Bell's (1973), Porat's (1977) and others' contention, that the world is experiencing a transition to 'post industrial' or information economies where information itself becomes the key locus of power and an increasingly important traded commodity, is well founded then information and communication both grow in salience as a consequence of this transition and, as policy makers seek to accelerate such transitions, become ends in themselves. Not surprisingly, media and communications are one of the most globalized sectors of the world economy.

The Internet

The Internet, the most recent and striking new medium of information and communication, defies conventional statistical description and categorization but confirms the implacable globalization of media and communications. More than any other medium, the Internet has decoupled distance (and often time) from price. For those with Internet connections, communication with the other side of the world is as easy as communication next door. Moreover, its infrastructural architecture means the Internet is an inherently international – indeed global – system which confounds established models. As Paltridge observes:

> The Internet is turning traditional point to point communication models on their head. For example, in the world of public switched telecommunication networks (PSTN) there was generally a correlation between the amount of traffic exchanged between two countries and the amount of capacity allocated by infrastructure providers for this route. For the Internet the points of origin and termination of packets of data have very little relationship to the traffic that may be carried over any given route or to traditional PSTN traffic patterns. Consider that PSTN traffic between Singapore and Canada makes up less than one per cent of each country's outgoing international traffic. In December 1997, by way of contrast, nearly half of Singapore Telecom's international Internet capacity was deployed between Singapore and Vancouver. Similarly, in the PSTN world, telephone numbers were administered on a national basis. For the Internet more than two thirds of second level domain names registered by Canadian, French and Spanish users are administered in the US. (Paltridge 1998: 4)

The Internet has intensified the process of integration of media and communications markets through space (and time) which began with Gutenberg's 'invention' of printing with moveable types. The inherently imperishable and inexhaustible (non-rival) characteristics of information, allied to developing technological systems of reproduction (e.g. printing) which have low marginal costs of production (i.e. high 'first copy' and relatively low 'second and subsequent copy' costs) provide strong economic incentives to extend the markets for 'content' media such as printed works, films and recorded music. In 'carriage' media, such as telephony and mail, similar considerations apply. Once an infrastructure has been established, the marginal cost of an extra unit (whether another letter posted or another minute of voice telecommunications traffic) carried is close to zero (so long as the infrastructure is not loaded to capacity).

The globalization of media and communications, pre-eminently exemplified by the Internet, threatens (or promises) to erode the distinctions – particularly the repertoires of symbolic distinctions – out of which societies have been constituted. Society is not only what it includes but what it excludes. There can be no inclusion without exclusion and globalization threatens, or promises, to dissolve differences – particularly in the symbolic domain. Difference from others keeps social groups together. Not members' difference from others in the same group but their shared difference from outsiders makes individuals members of a group. Where symbolic differences erode, the integrity of established societies is weakened. Smith puts it pithily: 'where Esperanto failed, information technology might succeed' (Smith 1995: 17). If the symbolic bonds which engender the 'subjective feeling' that characterizes communal societies wear away, the question arises: can the inclusive society hold together without the glue of 'subjective feeling' of affiliation and as an 'associative' rather than a 'communal' institution? Further, are members of an associative society, one distinguished by 'rationally motivated adjustments' rather than by 'subjective feeling' (Weber 1964: 136), denied one of their rights (that is, their right to a collective identity in which the sentiment of affiliation with those like them can be enjoyed even if that same sentiment necessarily involves alienation from dissimilar others) in such a society?

Nationalism

Pre-globalization, the normative model of the inclusive society, was characterized by a matching, mutually-reinforcing, relationship between economic structures – the character of the markets within which labour was divided; political structures – the states within which rules of law were exercised; and cultural/linguistic structures within which collective identities were sustained. These 'inclusive societies' were national societies.

The creation of national states, sovereign entities distinguished by the principle that 'the political and the national unit should be congruent', was, Gellner proposed, the midwife to industrialization and the modern era: national sentiment was necessary for the transition to modernity (Gellner 1983: 1). Where sentiments of collective, national, identity existed, men and women could be reconciled to the traumatic exchange of the routines of the sun and seasons for those of industrial waged labour and the clock; to loss of a concrete, lived community for membership of an 'imagined' national community.

For Gellner, nationalism re-enchanted the world, compensating for the loss in social cohesiveness which accompanied increased logical cohesiveness (Macfarlane cited in Hall and Jarvie 1992: 125). By providing an ideological glue during the intense anonymization and social stress which accompanied modernization, a sentiment of collective national identity reconciled the modernized to their lot. Nationalism, in Gellner's scheme of things, made possible modernity. It was, and is, a 'common intellectual denominator' (Hall and Jarvie 1992: 3). Nationalism constituted the coupling of polity and culture in 'communal' societies as normative and necessary.

In spite of the importance leading contemporary theorists of nationalism have ceded to the mass media (see, for example, Smith 1991 and 1995), discussion for the most part consists of a genuflection to its importance rather than a situated discussion. Central to such a discussion is the question: do contemporary international trends in media and communications, and notably the growth of the Internet, threaten to make the inclusive society include too much? Addressing this question requires that we distinguish between two possible bases of social cohesion.

Associative and communal societies

Weber distinguished between 'associative' relationships characterized by 'rational free market exchange', and 'communal' relationships characterized by 'a national community' (Weber 1964: 136-7). He states:

> A social relationship will be called 'communal' if and so far as the orientation of social action...is based on a subjective feeling of the parties...that they belong together. A social relationship will, on the other hand, be called 'associative' if and in so far as the orientation of social action...rests on a rationally motivated adjustment of interests or a similarly motivated agreement...(Weber 1964: 136)

Weber's distinction echoes Meinecke's distinction between 'cultural nations and political nations' (Meinecke 1970: 10), a distinction reformulated by Smith (1991) as two types of nationalism – 'civic' and 'ethnic' nationalism. It is civic, or political, nationalism which is thought to bind together states (such as Canada, Finland, India, Switzerland, etc.) where citizens share neither a single linguistic/cultural identity nor a common ethnicity. Whereas, cultural/ethnic nationalism posits the clear necessity of congruence between culture and polity if societies are to be legitimate and durable. Social cohesion requires that societies must maintain an endogenous culture and resist exogenous cultural influence. Such an inclusive society must be made up of people *like us*. In contrast, civic nationalism emphasizes adherence to a shared body of law, social rules and conventions which are both exercised and accepted as being impartial between different ethnicities/cultures (or other social groups or collective identities). It can, potentially, deliver an inclusive society of people *unlike us* tolerant of difference and which guarantees rights independent of class, creed, culture or colour.

The ethics of associative and communal societies

Seen from this civic perspective, the globalization of media and communications could be regarded positively as a stage in the teleological progress towards completion of the project of modernity in which all would enjoy 'undifferentiated citizenship' as members of a global inclusive society built on associative lines (Kymlicka 1995: 174). Viewed thus, the blocking of globalization in the name of the national – for example, impeding the development of an international division of labour; restricting the circulation of exogenous information products; reserving full political and human rights to fellow nationals; and the anathematization of difference – appears as a rejection of the project of modernity and thus of the full realization of what Gellner (modernly) insisted is empirically, as well as epistemologically, 'one world' (Hall and Jarvie 1992: 216).

But some have argued that associative arrangements are both pragmatically and ethically inferior to communal arrangements. For David Miller, a communal society is ethically superior both because it provides for the realization of identity entitlements (the ability to fully realize ourselves through living with people like ourselves), and also because it is better adapted to the delivery of the reciprocal obligations necessary to societies carrying on carrying on. He doubts that commitment to reciprocal obligations is robust enough in an 'associative' or 'civic' society. The principle of cohesion is too anaemic and fragile to survive extreme conditions. Only in a 'communal' society, made up of like peoples, can exacting obligations reliably be discharged. Only then will people die for each other and for society itself. This points, of course, to a different regime for media and communications to that mandated by globalization.

The ethical case for communalism

Two chief issues thus arise from the choice between associative and communal models for the inclusive society. First a pragmatic issue – can culturally discontinuous polities survive? And if so, on what basis? I have put forward the pragmatic case for associative arrangements elsewhere (Collins 1999). Second, an issue of principle. Are communal societies morally superior to civic societies? Miller (and others) elaborates an ethical case for communalism and contends that there 'are strong ethical reasons for making the bounds of nationality and the bounds of the state coincide' (Miller 1995: 73), and that, in consequence, 'positive obligations to protect basic rights…fall in the first place on co-nationals' (Miller 1995: 79 – see also Miller 1989).

Miller further states that 'in a national community…unconditional obligations to other members…arise simply by virtue of the fact that one has been born and raised in that particular community' (Miller 1995: 42). Here Miller elaborates an argument – which Smith names socio-biological (Smith 1995: 32) – that the 'special obligations [owed] to fellow members of my nation' are not similarly owed 'to other human beings' (Miller 1995: 49) because of the intrinsically greater obligations owed to those to whom we are close – classically our family. This argument seems true but only by tautology, however a more important objection is that Miller's analogy does not acknowledge the importance of cases where a family is not made up of members of the same ethnic or national community, nor where a family member is rightly handed over to the law. Moreover, just as the social generalization of individual volitions may be hostile to social order and the general good, so too may the generalization of what a family wishes for itself be hostile to the interests of society at large. Family commitments can (vide the Mafia, for which the customary synonym 'The Family' is particularly appropriate here) be hostile both to social cohesion and to others' rights. And further, as feminism has taught us, the family is not universally recommended as a sound basis either for society or for social theory.

The family analogy further frays with the acknowledgement that nations can be multi-ethnic and that what counts is not shared descent but a 'common public culture' (Miller 1995: 25). Though the invocation of 'common public culture' in modern societies, of course, foregrounds media and communications. Shared experience may build firm bonds and social cohesion may be engendered by the common experience of being 'born and raised in [a] particular community' (Miller 1995: 42). Multi-ethnic states may indeed share a 'common public culture'. But the difficult case, pragmatically and ethically, is not the multi-ethnic state but the multinational state (Kymlicka 1995).

Nonetheless, Miller's focus on the relatively neglected ethical issues within a sophisticated context of recognition of the complex relationships of political, historical and sentimental factors make his arguments important. He poses the stark choice between extreme viewpoints:

> At one extreme stands the view that the nation should be the supreme object of our loyalty, that every other claim should be set aside in its favour. At the other extreme stands the view that we are citizens of the world, members of a common humanity, and that we should pay no more regard to the claims of our co-nationals than to those of any other human beings regardless of where they happen to reside. (Miller 1995: 3)[1]

Miller argues that nationalism is ethically superior to an abstract universalism because it rests 'on well established facts about human identity and human motivation' and that, accordingly, 'The onus is on the universalist to show that, in widening the scope of ethical ties to encompass equally the whole of the human species, he does not also drain them of their binding force' (Miller 1995: 80). Miller's conclusion is rooted in his analogy: family and its bonds of sentiment and obligation model the national community. But not only is this argument less powerful than Miller supposes, but the choice Miller poses between national communities and abstract universalism is forced and false.

Doubtless there are limits beyond which the bonds of obligation which hold societies together do begin to crack – societies cannot function without some shared values and shared communication systems – but ethics is a domain of 'oughts' rather than 'ises', a sphere of principle rather than pragmatics. Miller fails to make an ethical case for nationalism – to show that organizing political communities on national lines is how they ought to be. His argument that, 'Nations are communities of obligation, in the sense that their members recognise duties to meet the basic needs and protect the basic interests of other members', clearly implies that these obligations do not extend to non-members of the national community (Miller 1995: 83). This criterion, at a time of pervasive mobility of populations, hybridization of symbolic culture and transnationalization of almost every relationship – economic, political, social and affective – that one could name, simply excludes too much – not least the empirical cases of multinational states in which 'common loyalty' derives from 'shared patriotism, not a common national identity' (Kymlicka 1995: 13) and the claims in principle of those unlike us for the rights of 'undifferentiated citizenship' (Kymlicka 1995: 174).[2]

For more compelling ethical – though I believe still unsatisfactory – arguments for nationalism, and communal organization of societies, we must go to Taylor (1994) and for a humane, practical and ethical theory of citizenship and identity politics to Kymlicka (1995). Kymlicka argues for a weaker, less normative, public culture than Miller[3] for multinationalism and the accommodation of national identities within a single society and polity on the basis, not of a shared normative public culture, but of 'equality between groups and freedom and equality within groups' (Kymlicka 1995: 194). Accordingly, I turn now to the issues of principle implicit in rival, associative and communal, models of the inclusive society.

Considerations of principle

Whether society is to be communal or associative is not just a sociological/historical issue: it is also one of rights as, from different perspectives, Rousseau and Miller acknowledge (see also Gellner 1983: 1–2 and Trudeau 1968):

> If, therefore, at the time of the social compact there are opponents to it, their opposition does not invalidate the contract, but simply prevents them from being included in it; they are foreigners dwelling among citizens. When the state is instituted, residence is consent; to dwell in a territory is to submit to its sovereign. (Rousseau 1953 [1762] Book IV Chapter II: 117)

> A critically reflective person must adhere to some form of cosmopolitanism. (Miller 1995: 12)

These citations conveniently mark the limits of a spectrum of views on the extent to which difference should be acknowledged in an inclusive society. In terms of media and communications, this issue might be posed as: 'How far should society be organized so as to realize a collective identity for and of its members?' The ethical case rests on the proposition that, without a collective cultural roof under which a distinct identity may thrive, individuals are denied their entitlement to feel themselves. This is possible only if one feels part of a group of like members. Central to this group sentiment (and thus to boundary definition) is a shared language and culture, precisely what the globalization of media, communication and information is transforming. Without the ability to share membership of a group of like people, individuals are, as Taylor argues, denied a crucial element of self-realization. He states that a:

> crucial feature of human life is its fundamental dialogical character. We become full human agents, capable of understanding ourselves, and hence of defining our identity, through our acquisition of rich human languages of expression. (Taylor 1994: 32)

And difference itself, Taylor argued, is intrinsically valuable:

> Just as all must have equal civil rights, and equal voting rights, regardless of race or culture, so all should enjoy the presumption that their traditional culture has value. (Taylor 1994: 68)

Cultural rights

Similar arguments to Taylor's have been advanced in the policy domain. For example, Jacques Delors, when President of the Commission of the European Communities, stated (at the Assises de l'audiovisuel in Paris 1989) that:

> Culture is not a piece of merchandise like any other and must not be treated as such… culture cannot flower today unless control of the relevant technologies is assured. On the first point…we cannot treat culture the way we treat refrigerators or even cars. Laissez-faire, leaving market forces to operate freely is not enough. I would like to ask just one question of our American friends…do we have the right to exist? (Assises de l'audiovisuel 1989: 47-8)

Delors' arguments chime with Taylor's. Like Taylor he constitutes collective cultural identity as a right. Other public figures, such as Jack Lang[4] and Roberto Barzanti[5] (Barzanti 1990) have argued in the same vein. In 1988, for example, Lang objected to the preponderance of US programmes on European screens and argued:

> At a time when Europe, the cradle of Western civilisation, loses control over one of the main areas in which contemporary culture is being made, the audiovisual, one can no longer react aesthetically to such liberal or ultra liberal ideologies. Reality demands that concrete steps be taken. (Lang 1988: 20)

Elsewhere Taylor has provided an exposition of the propositions implicit in Delors' and Lang's statements:

> The core of the modern conception of rights is that respect is owed the integrity of the human subject. This obviously entails that the human subject has a right to life, to liberty; on Lockeian assumptions, also to property. But if we add the Romantic understanding of identity, as essential to human subjecthood, then plainly there is something else here to which we have a right, namely, that the conditions of our identity be respected. If we take the nationalist thesis that these are primarily our belonging to a linguistically defined nation, we have the beginnings of another justification of the rights of nations to political expression. (Taylor 1993: 45)

Taylor affirms, as intrinsic to a bundle of modern, largely individual, rights, the right to a collective identity and to the realization of that entitlement through public expression of identity. He argues that without, 'certain values, certain allegiances, a certain community…I could not function as a fully human subject' (Taylor 1993: 45).

Communal nationalism and identity entitlements

Taylor's formula chimes with Kedourie's famous statement that 'language is the means through which a man becomes conscious of his personality. Language is not only a vehicle for rational propositions, it is the outer expression of an inner experience, the outcome of a particular history, the legacy of a distinctive tradition' (Kedourie 1966: 68). If Taylor and Kedourie are right, then multilingual states are unlikely to be friendly to the full realization of a humanity in which the experience and expression of collective cultural identity entitlements are central. Clearly, a common European culture, necessarily expressed in and through a common language, would be at the expense of the majority of the European Union's languages and cultures and would devalue the 'fund of positive identification' to which Taylor (1993: 66) referred. But, paradoxically, the nearest to which Europe has come to a shared contemporary symbolic culture is in the English language media – notably television and film – where US programmes often predominate. Moeglin observed that of 12 transnational European television channels in 1990, five transmitted in English, another used English as one of its three languages, a seventh used no language and an eighth used several languages (including English). Moreover, of 96 national and regional television channels in the European Community (at the time Moeglin wrote) 24 used English, more than used any other single language (Moeglin 1991: 17).

The communalist doctrine of identity entitlement is hostile to the classic liberal principle of individual 'undifferentiated citizenship' (Kymlicka 1995: 174) specifying universal equality of human rights, and does not satisfy the conditions specified by Rawls – notably difference and pluralism – which characterize 'a well-ordered society' (Rawls cited in Kymlicka 1995: 187). Kymlicka argues that, 'Basic human rights such as freedom of speech, association, and conscience, while attributed to individuals, are typically exercised in community with others, and so provide protection for group life' (Kymlicka 1995: 3). This is not a wholly convincing claim: at best it is a truism and, at worst, it misleadingly constructs community activity as necessarily benign – the denial of rights is typically 'exercised in community' and justified in the name of community.

It is only within a society organized on national lines of congruence between polity and culture that such collective identity rights can be realized. Not within socio-political structures, such as the contemporary European Union, where polity and culture are incongruent: still less within societies in which a 'they' (and globalization, migration – whether voluntary or involuntary – and a host of other factors are increasingly constituting societies as made up of different 'thems' as well as by 'us') enjoy the same rights of 'undifferentiated citizenship' (Kymlicka 1995: 174) which are extended to 'us'.

Thus, an important aspect of contemporary media policy turns on the issue of whether collective identity entitlements can be reconciled with individual rights of 'undifferentiated citizenship' (notably to freedom of access to information emanating from outside the society in question). Proponents of restrictions on expression (for example, in official language laws such as France's lois Toubon and Bas-Lauriol) and on access to information and of expression (for example, the Canadian Content requirements in Canada's 1990 Broadcasting Act [Canada, 1991] and the European Union's 'Television without Frontiers' Directive [89/552/EEC amended by Directive 97/ B6/EC] European Parliament and the Council [1997]), have argued for such measures on the ground that the principle of free flow of information across (and within) political boundaries is an empty principle given the unequal character of these flows and the absence of any real dialogic character to these exchanges.

Such unequal relationships do not satisfy Rawls' criteria of common citizenship: 'reasonableness and a sense of fairness, a spirit of compromise and a readiness to meet others half way' (Rawls cited in Kymlicka 1995: 183). Moreover, they dissolve the sentimental bonds of communal societies and compromise both the durability and legitimacy of established national societies: they substitute a desiccated calculation of rational self-interest for the spontaneous sentiment of social solidarity.

Kymlicka argues that the central individual 'communication' right – notably freedom of access to information and to expression – is friendly to social cohesion, but his pragmatic argument is over-neat (Kymlicka 1995: 175). An assertion of group rights – and a right to a distinctive collective social and cultural identity in particular – is offensive to a central liberal precept: an individual's entitlement to be different without thereby incurring the fate of becoming a 'foreigner dwelling among citizens' (Rousseau 1953: 117). Thus, neither national information exclusivity nor untrammelled openness to globalization seems to satisfy Rawls' criteria.

Recognizing some of these problems, Miller implicitly softens his case for a congruence between polity and culture, and thus for a recognition of the superior claims of those to whom we are close over those from whom we are distant, by broadening his definition of the close. He does so by arguing that a multiethnic community may be a nation. But the issue of language severely tests Miller's argument, as it does general liberal arguments for an extension of the entitlements of 'undifferentiated citizenship' to speakers of any and all languages. The realization of collective identity rights in a well-functioning society necessitates a limitation on the number of official languages recognized within a single political community.[6] Both the principle of nationality and the principle of undifferentiated citizenship can be applied only to a limited extent.

Limits of the associative and communal models

The moral superiority of the principle of nationality is murkier than Miller claims. Kymlicka looks this problem in the face and argues that linguistic and cultural homogenization is morally and practically bankrupt. 'Globalisation has made the myth of a culturally homogeneous state even more unrealistic, and has forced the majority within each state to be more open to pluralism and diversity' (Kymlicka 1995: 9). Kymlicka does argue, however, that some forms of collective rights are not hostile to individual rights. He proposes that 'collective rights could refer to the right of a group to limit the liberty of its own individual members in the name of group solidarity or cultural purity' – limits which Kymlicka (and I agree) believes to be offensive because incompatible with individual freedom – and 'it could refer to the right of a group to limit the economic or political power exercised by the larger society over the group, to ensure that the resources and institutions on which the minority depends are not vulnerable to majority decisions' which Kymlicka (and I do not agree) also believes incompatible with individual rights (Kymlicka 1995: 7).

There are, then, cogent objections to the principle of nationality; so, too, are there to the principle of undifferentiated citizenship. Whilst there are multiethnic states (and nations), there are surely few nations or states in which a plurality of languages enjoy common currency. This question of practical limits has become more and more important, as populations have become more mobile and the size of political communities has grown. The practical implementation of the principle of undifferentiated citizenship is more challenging than its proponents customarily acknowledge.

Conclusion

If there is no justification for preferring identity entitlements over entitlements to undifferentiated citizenship, how can social cohesion be secured in pluralistic inclusive societies? Is there an alternative to a common culture? The way forward seems to lie in an acceptance of the priority of different principles at different levels of social and political organization. This, in a more or less explicit and systematic way, informs the practice of some actual existing heterogeneous societies.

The official *National Agenda for a Multicultural Australia* (Commonwealth of Australia 1989) and in particular the section 'What is Multiculturalism?' makes the argument well. Australia's 'national agenda' proposes decoupling polity and culture and distinguishing political obligations from cultural entitlements. All Australian citizens are obligated to 'accept the basic structures and principles of Australian society – the Constitution and the rule of law, tolerance and equality, Parliamentary democracy, freedom of speech and religion, English as the national language and equality of the sexes' (Commonwealth of Australia 1989: vii). All Australians are guaranteed 'the right…within carefully defined limits, to express and share their individual cultural heritage, including their language and religion' (ibid.).[7]

It is easy to identify the neuralgic points here, notably around language where establishing a national language clearly compromises putative rights to self-expression and public use of other languages. But the Australian model points to a practicable model for the inclusive society, one which is both communal and associative – communal at some points, associative at others. The full realization of rights is traded off against the pragmatic imperative of a society which does hang together. Australia's 'National Agenda' is a powerful testimony to a vision of a society based on universal political obligations and diverse cultural rights. It defines a basis for an inclusive society which respects rights to the maximum possible extent because it is communal and associative to different degrees at different levels.

This pragmatic striking of a balance seems inescapable. Considered in terms of communications, individual rights (for example, to freedom of information and communication) tend to conflict with collective rights (for example, to collective identities borne by language and culture). The claims of religion, and the choice between a confessional and a secular society, potentially offer an illuminating analogy. Kymlicka and Miller both observe that a seemingly irreconcilable contradiction between social cohesion (collective rights) and individual (confessional) rights was resolved by secularizing society and by making religion a private matter. (Kymlicka recognizes that secularization does not wholly solve the problem.)[8]

Globalization threatens the established basis on which inclusive societies have been constituted. It disrupts customary congruencies between polity and culture that have both notionally and normatively distinguished the inclusive society of the national state. Yet, so too does the most salient principled (rather than interested) response to globalization from identity politics. For the assertion, à la Delors and Taylor, of an entitlement to collective identity is, of necessity, assertion of an exclusionary principle. To be sure, this assertion of exclusivity may be asserted to different degrees at different times and in different places (contemporary France is, for example, a very different case from contemporary Pakistan or even contemporary Malaysia). It may be argued that a modest degree of exclusion (for example, at the levels set in the national audio-visual content quotas of Canada and the European Union) is required in the interests of cultural pluralism and diversity. But it is hard to resist the conclusion that, if the inclusive society is not to exclude too much, its public culture must both be looser and more pluralistic than heretofore. Symbolic culture embodied in the mass media can no longer be given the role of holding society together. The principle of social coherence in the inclusive society, if it is to be an ethical coherence, must be found elsewhere. Notably in associative rather than communal social relationships, but in associative relationships which acknowledge cultural diversity and difference and thus the legitimacy of claims for a realization of communalist sentiments at appropriate levels.

Notes

1. Residence, Miller's term, is of course not the issue. For the sentimental bonds we share with our co-nationals tend to endure even if we do not share a residence. Hungarians' sense of solidarity with Hungarian speakers in Romania and Slovakia; Irish Australians and Irish Americans affirm their sense of shared identity with the Irish living on the island of Ireland; Jews' solidarity with Israelis and Israel; Arabs' solidarity with Palestine and Palestinians are case in point. Moreover, the sentimental bonds of shared identity may obtain even when there is neither common citizenship nor common residence in question: the South Atlantic war of 1982 focused a sense of sentimental affiliation between many Spanish (and Italian) citizens and Argentines just as it did between many British citizens and Falklanders.
2. Miller qualifies the force of his argument later where he states: 'My claim is that in multicultural societies group and national identities should co-exist' (Miller 1995: 153). However, it is hard to see how his principle that 'everyone should take part...on an equal footing' (Miller 1995: 153) can be reconciled with his prior, and more central argument, that the principle of nationality is an organizing principle of political communities which necessitates a shared (normative) public culture.
3. Kymlicka (1995: 73) challenges an earlier version of Miller's arguments as assimilationist.
4. Lang became Minister of Culture of France in 1981, a post he held for most of the next decade: he was Minister of Culture from 1981–86 and from 1988–93 Minister of Culture and Communication. He was succeeded (as Minister of Culture) by Jacques Toubon.
5. An Italian MEP who served as Chairman of the European Parliament's Committee on Youth, Culture, Media and Sport.
6. A notable exception seems to prove the rule: South Africa, after the end of apartheid, changed its language policy from recognition of Afrikaans and English to recognition of 11 official languages. But formal recognition of 11 languages has been accompanied by the effective elimination of Afrikaans as a language of public life and a quasi-universal use of English.
7. Gellner makes a similar argument (1998: 79).

8. As he shows in his discussion of the Amish who secured the right to withdraw their children from public, secular schooling in the US on the grounds that 'religious affiliation is so profoundly constitutive of who they are that their overriding interest is in protecting and advancing their identity and that they have no comparable interest in being able to stand back and assess that identity. Hence there is little or no value (and perhaps even positive harm) in teaching Amish children about the outside world' (Kymlicka, 1995: 163).

Chapter 8

Rawls, Fraser, Redistribution, Recognition and The World Summit on the Information Society

> The 'struggle for recognition' is fast becoming the paradigmatic form of political conflict in the late twentieth century...Cultural domination supplants exploitation as the fundamental injustice. (Fraser 1997: 11)

> Imagine, then, a hypothetical initial arrangement in which all the social primary goods are equally distributed: everyone has similar rights and duties, and income and wealth are equally shared. This state of affairs provides a benchmark for judging improvements. If certain inequalities of wealth and differences in authority would make everyone better off than in this hypothetical starting situation, then they accord with the general conception. (Rawls 1999: 54–5)

Introduction

The 2003–2005 World Summit on the Information Society (WSIS) was the first formal UN summit on communications and addressed three chief issues:

- Internet governance
- The 'political chapeau'/Tunis Commitment[1]
- Use of Information and Communication Technology for Development (ICT4D).

Internet governance, (notably the role of the US-based Internet Corporation for Assigned Names and Numbers, ICANN, in governing the global Internet addressing system – the domain name system, DNS), was an intensely contested issue at the WSIS and its discussion dominated much of the proceedings of the Summit and its pendant Working Group on Internet Governance (WGIG). These disagreements, and their intensity, may seem surprising because the Internet is a global infrastructure which generally works well and also because this rather abstract issue took at least rhetorical precedence over the concrete question of access to and distribution of resources: Internet governance rather than ICT4D took centre stage at WSIS.

Why should this be so? Can contemporary political philosophy resolve this puzzle? And, in particular, how far can John Rawls' *A Theory of Justice* (a work whose widely acknowledged influence on contemporary political philosophy has run alongside some scepticism as to how far Rawls' system, and his 'difference principle' in particular, can help with real world political problems) illuminate the events of the WSIS and WGIG? Further, how far can Nancy Fraser's arguments for the importance of 'recognition', a concern neglected by Rawls, clarify the WSIS/WGIG conflicts?

Rawls, Fraser, redistribution and recognition

The late John Rawls' *A Theory of Justice* (first published in 1971 and revised and republished in 1999) is widely regarded as the most important work in political philosophy to appear in recent years and to offer powerful and innovatory arguments for the importance of redistribution in securing justice and fairness. Rawls' academic home, Harvard University, plausibly stated in its obituary notice after Rawls' death in 2002 that 'Rawls is considered by many to be the most important political philosopher of the second half of the 20th century' (Harvard University nd). Wikipedia, with similar plausibility, claims that:

> Many academic philosophers believe that Rawls made an important and lasting contribution to political philosophy. There is general agreement that the publication of *A Theory of Justice* in 1971 led to a revival in the academic study of political philosophy. Rawls's work has crossed disciplinary lines, receiving serious attention from economists, legal scholars, political scientists, sociologists, and theologians. Rawls has the unique distinction among contemporary political philosophers of being frequently cited by the courts of law in the United States and referred to by practicing politicians in the United Kingdom. (http://en.wikipedia.org/wiki/John_Rawls accessed on 18.10.2006)

And Sandel (1982: 13) comments '"revisionist" deontology captures the spirit of much contemporary liberalism and finds its fullest expression in the work of John Rawls' and acknowledges 'the voluminous critical literature' (Sandel 1982: 15) which Rawls' work has attracted. Martin (1985: vii) remarks that '*A Theory of Justice* (1971) is already something of a classic'.

Rawls' influential theory of justice rests on an imagined agreement between people whereby they, we, would spontaneously choose to distribute social primary goods as if we were doing so from behind a 'veil of ignorance' (Rawls 1999: 119). The distribution that emerges from behind the veil of ignorance is, for Rawls, the 'original position' an 'initial status quo which insures that the fundamental agreements reached in it are fair' (Rawls 1999: 15). And from the original position Rawls derives two principles of justice: a principle of liberty where 'each person is to have an equal right to the most extensive basic liberty compatible with a similar liberty for others' and a principle of difference whereby 'social and economic inequalities are to be arranged so that they are both (a) reasonably expected to be to everyone's advantage and (b) attached to positions and offices open to all' (Rawls 1999: 53).

The re-distributive implications of Rawls' difference principle and the practical consequences of Rawls' proposition that 'the social order is not to establish and secure the more attractive prospects of the better off unless doing so is to the advantage of the less fortunate' (Rawls 1999: 65)[2] have attracted much attention. A measure of the celebrity of Rawls' *A Theory of Justice* (1999) is the extent to which his arguments have been the subject of extension and qualification. Robert Nozick's *Anarchy, State and Utopia* (1974) is perhaps the most celebrated instance of an engagement with Rawls' arguments (see also Honderich 1975, Sandel 1997) but latterly Nancy Fraser's arguments for the importance of 'the struggle for recognition' (Fraser 1997: 11) have proven influential.

Fraser's themes are partly foreshadowed in Rawls' own development of his arguments. Rawls (1999: 386) stated that 'perhaps the most important primary good is that of self-respect' and observed that one of the revisions he would make, were he further to revise *A Theory of Justice* (after his reworking of the 1971 text in the 1999 text), would be to rework his discussion of property-owning democracy and a welfare state in the light of the idea of citizens being able to 'take part in social cooperation on a footing of mutual respect' (Rawls 1999: xv). Respect and recognition are closely intertwined and Rawls' revisionary intentions perhaps suggest an acknowledgement of the substance of such criticisms.

But Rawls' possibly insufficient consideration of the matters of respect and recognition is not the only qualification which has been entered about his work. Others have argued that he constructs the problem of justice at an individual rather than social or political level and that, in spite of the celebrity of *A Theory of Justice,* Rawls' system cannot readily be applied to real world political problems. Honderich, for example, in one of several robust engagements with Rawls beginning with his review of *A Theory of Justice* in *Mind* (Honderich 1975), contended that the imagined contract 'behind the veil of ignorance' which Rawls placed at the centre of his system was asocial (and thus apolitical) because the contracting parties imagined by Rawls were '*identical* with each other' (emphasis in original) and that consequently their imagined distribution of endowments using the difference principle was only an instance of the 'binding sort of agreement that occurs when you agree with yourself' (Honderich 2001: 212). Sandel, less truculently, makes an analogous point when proposing that 'Political philosophy seems often to reside at a distance from the world' (Sandel 2005: 156) and goes on to substantiate his general contention through a discussion of Rawlsian liberalism and its antecedents.

However, Fraser treats the politics of Rawls' arguments more generously (and, as I shall try and show below, the difference principle can illuminate at least one very concrete socio-political issue) in arguing that something important is left out by Rawls – notably the claims of recognition. Her arguments are framed to extend and complement Rawls (rather than, as did Rawls' most celebrated interlocutor Robert Nozick, to open up a radically different frame of reference) and she argues that although the struggle for recognition deserves more salience, its importance does not extinguish the question of distributive justice, and the struggles for redistribution, which were Rawls' primary focus. Rather she states 'Cultural domination supplants exploitation as the fundamental injustice' (Fraser 1997: 11).

How far can Rawls' and Fraser's notions of redistribution and recognition inform our understanding of telecommunication and Internet policy and of the WSIS and WGIG in particular? What was taken to be the 'fundamental injustice' and what, in these domains, would count as the 'social primary goods'? And how, if at all, would Rawls' difference principle, the proposition that inequality is justified only when all benefit (albeit unequally) from such inequalities, and Fraser's notion of 'recognition' apply to telecommunications and Internet policy?

The digital divide and redistribution

There is now an abundant scholarly literature on the 'digital divide' – a term which is now pervasive[3] (notable instances include Compaine 2001, Golding and Murdock 2001, Hargittai 1999, Hargittai nd, Norris 2001, 6 and Jupp 2001) – and in the light of this literature we might plausibly claim that connectivity, the ability to communicate, is the relevant 'primary good'.[4] If so, a Rawlsian might ask whether the manifest inequalities in global capacities and competencies in connectivity and communication can be justified on the grounds that these inequalities co-exist with improvements to the communicative capacity of the worst off.

It seems there is a potential (albeit as yet not fully realized) to do so. Average and marginal costs tend to fall rapidly as electronic communication infrastructures are built out and network utility for all users rises as networks become extended. This suggests that, although the digital divide[5] seems to be best explained as a manifestation of a general divide between rich and poor (see Hargittai 1999, Norris 2001),[6] there may be more promising opportunities to reduce the divide in communications than in other domains of significant wealth disparities such as health, housing and education. There is both theoretical and empirical evidence which suggests that this is so.

In a hypothetical electronic communication network (costing, let us say, 2 cost units) of two users, the costs of the network must be borne by these two who are connected and, if the costs are shared equally, then each user pays one cost unit. If a third user joins the network there may, depending on network architecture, be no additional costs (e.g. if wireless propagation of signals is used) and in most scenarios the cost of supplying the third user is less than the one cost unit born by the first pair of users, the 'early adopters'. Moreover, the potential utility of the network for all users rises as new users join the network (see Collins 2005 for a fuller account of this 'network externality' relationship).

Clearly, 'early adopters' in the scenario sketched are advantaged relative to those who lack connectivity and are left behind, 'digitally divided' from the connected. But in Rawlsian terms there need be nothing necessarily offensive about the advantages enjoyed by the early adopters. For, by bearing the costs of initially establishing the network, early adopters make possible the later connection of others at lower costs and prices. Of course, for this potential to be realized, much depends on variables such as the speed of network rollout, the pricing and cost-allocation policies of network operators, access to electricity, attainment of literacy and numeracy and so on. It is not difficult to imagine, or identify real world examples, scenarios where the relatively disadvantaged do not enjoy in timely fashion and at reasonable and affordable prices the potential benefits which under different policies they might enjoy.

But surely a potential to satisfy Rawls' difference principle exists. Much depends on the judgement taken on what is an acceptable time scale for the disadvantaged to have access to the benefits enjoyed earlier by others. And, once an acceptable time period is identified, there are many intervening empirical variables to affect and constrain the realization of such potentiality. As indicated above, factors which are strictly exogenous to the domain of telecommunications and Internet policy (such as attainment of literacy and access to reliable supplies of electrical power) can be decisive. But there are also important endogenous factors, Paltridge (OECD 2006: 14) has testified to the power of incumbent telcos 'to exercise monopoly power over domestic or international facilities' and thus make 'broadband pricing…[a] source of criticism from users and regulators'. He observed that 'The greatest cost barriers to any country connecting to global networks is not traffic exchange relationships in competitive environments, but monopolists charging high prices in the absence of such competition' (OECD 2006: 31).[7]

Nonetheless, there are not a few real world examples where initially unequal access to social primary goods in electronic communications has made possible widespread sharing of benefits: the strikingly rapid dissemination of mobile telephony in South Africa is one example personally known to the author.[8] Mobile telephony rapidly developed from being a rich (white) man's toy to a socially pervasive and by now indispensable medium.[9] And the spectacular global growth of Internet traffic and connectivity provides another case in point. The growth of access to the Internet has been, and continues to be, remarkable. As Paltridge (OECD 2006: 4) observes 'the Internet has become a critical and integral part of economic and social life. This has been made possible by the phenomenally successful growth of the Internet, as a network of networks. In 2005 more than 20,000 networks with independent routing policies provided connectivity…supporting close to a billion users around the world'.

In September 2006, World Internet Statistics[10] estimated that 16.7 per cent of the world's population had Internet access. Access grew across the world; although regional disparities were striking (access in 2006 ranged from 69.1 per cent in North America to 3.6 per cent in Africa) there was a pervasive overall growth in global Internet access: access in Africa grew from 4,514,400 in 2000 to 32,765,700 in 2006 (a growth of 625.8 per cent) whereas in the same period in North America, growth (of course, from a higher initial base) amounted to 112 per cent. Quality of service (QoS) is less easy to compare regionally – a leading source, Internet Traffic Report (nd) does not report on response time or packet loss ratios (two significant QoS indices) for Africa (North America has the best QoS rating at 88 and Asia the worst at 58 (against a global average rating of 81).[11] In respect of other significant indices, Paltridge (OECD 2006: 4) notes the fall in costs of connectivity, from an average of $1,000US per month in 1995 for a permanent 56/64kbs connection to a monthly cost in 2005 of less than $30US for a connection of vastly greater bandwidth.[12] Paltridge (OECD 2006: 41, Figure 8) also identifies a growth in Internet Exchange Points (IXPs) between 1994 to 2004 rising, for OECD members, from fewer than 10 to more than 140 whereas for the rest of the world the number rises from 0 to more than 40.

Data of this kind may be less than completely comprehensive in respect of the benefits which accrue to the least advantaged in consequence of the financing of infrastructures by, and building of facilities for, the better-off. OECD members are very different from sub-Saharan Africa. But reliable data is both less readily available and less complete for Africa than it is for other parts of the world. Nonetheless, there seem few reasons to doubt that the fall in prices of connectivity, thus opening up Internet access, which has arisen primarily in consequence of demand from relatively wealthy users offers benefits to the relatively poor – even the illiterate and those without access to mains electricity can (and do) benefit from VoIP (Voice over Internet Protocol) cellular telephony services. A Rawlsian, who was prepared to accept a reasonable (and there is much room for discussion about what constitutes 'reasonable' in this context) delay in the realization of the potential for the worst-off to benefit from access to electronic communication networks, might see the established rate of closure of the 'digital divide' as consistent with the 'difference principle' and compatible with a Rawlsian notion of justice. Certainly, the faster the divide closes the better, and there is much to impede or prevent its closure, but the existence of a digital divide and differences in the rate of diffusion of new communication technologies and practices (such as mobile telephony and Internet connectivity) are not in themselves necessarily unjust.

Justice, recognition, redistribution and the WSIS/WGIG

The novel salience of the Internet (albeit after nearly 40 years of Internet history!), the high, but uneven, levels of growth in Internet access and the influence of the Internet on established structures and relationships in telephony (e.g. the substitution of VoIP for conventional voice telephony and the rebalancing of financial transfers between states through changes to international telecommunication settlements regimes – see OECD 2006) all informed discussion in the United Nations' first summit on communications, the World Summit on the Information Society (WSIS) which took place in Geneva and Tunis between 2002 and 2005. The WSIS was notable both as the first formal UN summit on a communications issue and as the first UN summit in which civil society[13] enjoyed a formal status as participant.

The WSIS focused on two major themes:[14]

- Internet governance
- ICT (Information and Communication Technology) for Development (ICT4D).

Of the two potentially controversial issues, ICT4D (see Maitland 1984 and Weigel and Waldburger 2004) corresponded most closely to the Rawlsian issue of redistribution. In the context of the Summit, it was taken forward by a Task Force on Financial Mechanisms (TFFM), set up by the UN Secretary-General, which reported to the WSIS (WSIS 2005a) which in turn, in the Tunis Agenda for the Information Society at Clause 28 (WSIS 2005b) established a Digital Solidarity Fund to reduce inequality and diminish the digital divide. Though concerned with access to resources and thus closely linked to global inequalities, ICT4D was, in comparison to Internet governance, uncontroversial. On ICT4D matters, the Tunis Agenda, the principal formal outcome of the WSIS, specifically recommended promotion of wider access to, and use of, the Internet. Clause 27 of the Agreement identified several 'improvements and innovations in existing financing mechanisms' including 'Enhancing regional cooperation and creating multi-stakeholder partnerships, especially by creating incentives for building regional backbone infrastructure' and 'Providing affordable access to ICTs, by the following measures *including* (my emphasis) reducing international Internet costs charged by backbone providers, supporting, inter alia, the creation and development of regional ICT backbones and Internet Exchange Points to reduce interconnection cost and broaden network access'[15] (WSIS 2005b).

It remains to be seen how effectively these, and other, related provisions are implemented. Markus Kummer (Head of the Secretariat of the Working Group on Internet Governance and latterly the Executive Coordinator of the Internet Governance Forum Secretariat) described (on 31 August 2006 at a public session of a short conference, 'Internet Governance for Development: Focusing on the Issues' held at the Oxford Internet Institute – OII) (OII nd) the Tunis Agenda/Agreement as 'full of creative ambiguity' and a 'diplomatic compromise text'. These are often the characteristics of similar documents arising from formal international diplomatic negotiations. For some members of the WSIS, the Digital Solidarity Fund was the most important consideration[16] but it, and redistribution issues in general, were neither the most salient in discussions, nor most prominent in the text of the Tunis Agreement, nor the issues discussed with most passion and intensity at WSIS and WGIG sessions. Although the section on 'Financial mechanisms for meeting the challenges of ICT for development' received rhetorical salience in the Tunis Agenda (as the first section, clauses 3–28, following the preamble) Internet governance accounted for a higher proportion of the text of the Agreement and dominated, both in time and intensity, the WSIS/WGIG proceedings. Internet governance in the context of the WSIS is further notable because it is a matter which touches chiefly on issues of recognition (see Fraser 2000) rather than of redistribution.

Internet governance, recognition and the WSIS/WGIG

It was Internet governance that proved to be the least tractable issue at WSIS. So much so that, following the inability of the first session of the WSIS to make progress on Internet governance, the Secretary-General of the UN established a dedicated working group, the Working Group on Internet Governance (WGIG) on 12 November 2004 under UN General Assembly Resolution 59/220. Even defining 'Internet governance' proved vexatious. However, Kleinwaechter (a member of the WGIG) provides a helpful working definition: 'The term 'internet governance', while undefined, rather vague and partly confusing, stands mainly for the global technical management of the core resources of the internet: domain names, IP addresses, internet protocols and the root server system' (Kleinwaechter 2004: 233).

But why was Internet governance so controversial and intractable an issue at WSIS/ WGIG? The Internet is a striking global success story with connections and use of the Internet both growing rapidly. To be sure there are several unresolved governance issues, such as how users can enjoy better security and greater freedom from unwanted communications (spam); how Internet-based crime can be more effectively curtailed; how the Internet can better accommodate languages using non-ASCII scripts; and how potential threats, notably those posed by proprietary technologies and software, to the Internet's openness, easy connectivity and the established end-to-end principles, can be countervailed. But almost none of these issues came under extensive and systematic consideration (see, among others, Klein 2004). Rather the focus of controversy was an aspect of Internet governance which, in comparison to spam, security, crime and the like, works well.

The focus of controversy was the control of key elements of the Internet, now an indispensable global infrastructure, by a single country, the US, The high point of hierarchical authority for the global domain name system (DNS), that is the system for allocating names and addresses for Internet sites on which the flow of e-mail, access to web sites, etc. depends, rests with the Internet Corporation for Assigned Names and Numbers (ICANN) which is domiciled in California, established under US law and which at the time of the WSIS/ WGIG was governed by a Memorandum of Understanding (latterly known as a Joint Project Agreement) of the US Department of Commerce.[17] The exceptional importance, due to the United States' origin of ICANN, of one country in Internet governance stands in contrast to the governance of other international communications infrastructures, notably posts and telecommunications, where governance is undertaken by formally-constituted international treaty-based organizations (notably the Universal Postal Union and the International Telecommunications Union) which are part of the UN. The functional, output, legitimacy[18] of the status quo (the Internet works, traffic and connectivity increases) did not satisfy a priori expectations and stipulations that a key global communication resource should be governed under a regime formally agreed by the world's governments and that only such a regime could be legitimate.

The argument for the ICANN-based status quo was eloquently made at the WGIG on 18 April 2005 by the Internet Society (ISOC) which stated:

> The Internet Society believes that the best way to support the WSIS plan of action and the Millennium Development Goals and to extend the reach of the Internet is to build on those aspects that have worked well; namely, the long established open, distributed, and consensus-based processes and many regional forums for the development and administration of the Internet infrastructure.

In contrast, the claims of state governments for international authority over the Internet were representatively put forward by India, Syria and others at the WGIG. India said 'we are here because countries felt excluded from a system controlled by private companies operating under laws of one country'. And Syria noted: 'We cannot accept the Internet being merely an American body subject to another American body'. However, not all representatives of states concurred with the position put forward by India and Syria (or by other critical states such as Brazil, China and South Africa). Australia argued that 'if internationalization means reducing the Internet to a governance process between nations alone, then we've lost one of the very things that we've been talking so actively about for a long time; that is, the multi-stakeholder approach involving all actors'.[19]

Different non-exclusive explanations can be offered for the high profile of Internet governance issues at the WSIS. These include the institutional interest of the International Telecommunication Union (ITU), the body which organized the WSIS and WGIG, which, as telecommunications systems metamorphose from circuit switched architectures to IP-based packet switched architectures, stands to lose importance as more and more of the world's telecommunication traffic and infrastructure escapes its jurisdiction; the importance of the Internet for achievement of the goals of the UN Millennium Summit; the importance of the problems which beset the Internet such as e.g. spam, crime, viruses, the solution of which requires international coordination and so on.

But more important than these, at least in generating the intensity of the conflicts which took place at WSIS and WGIG, seems to have been issues of recognition of the kind to which Fraser referred. What seemed most important was resentment and anger about the putative offence to democracy, to the dignity of governments and the communities they represent posed by the control of an indispensable global infrastructure, the Internet, by a single country rather than by the international community.[20]

Trilateralism

However, there was also an important procedural matter at the WSIS/WGIG which provided an additional point of conflict. This concerned 'trilateralism', that is the extent to which representatives of civil society should be able to participate in the WSIS/WGIG deliberations alongside representatives of UN Member States and business.[21]

China and its allies argued particularly strongly and consistently against civil society participation in WSIS/WGIG proceedings. China's argument was consistent with its advocacy of the exclusive rights of states to undertake Internet governance (and thus against the historically-established and looser, multi-stakeholder, arrangements apparent in the ICANN regime).[22] Instead of ICANN, China proposed an intergovernmental organization under the UN framework to undertake Internet governance and made clear its position that: 'policy-making should not surpass international law and national sovereignty, as pointed out in article 49 of the Declaration of Principles. The policy authority for Internet-related public policy issues is the sovereign right of states. They have rights and responsibilities for international Internet-related public policy issues' (statement at the WGIG, Geneva 18

April 2005). Previously, at the second WGIG meeting (14 February 2005) Brazil argued that 'Governments not corporations represent the interests of their citizens' and was echoed by Syria which stated 'public policy is the business of governments'.

China demanded expulsion of civil society and business participants from small group negotiating sessions at the second, Tunis, WSIS and a member of the WGIG, William Drake (at a conference at the Oxford Internet Institute on 12 January 2004) claimed that much the same had taken place at the first, Geneva, WSIS where civil society organizations were, he said, 'kicked out' of several working groups' and where 'there was total chaos, there were no rules' (source: contemporaneous notes taken by the author). Nonetheless, despite the clear commitment of the UN, following the Cardoso Report[23] (UN 2004a), to a fuller representation of civil society in UN activities, the benefits that civil society experts are able to bring to proceedings (there is much testimony to the positive contribution which civil society made to the WGIG), the offensiveness of some attempts to exclude civil society from the WSIS/WGIG, and the contradictions and disparities in state representation in United Nations business, there were some legitimate grounds for concern about the accreditation of civil society organizations.

There is a uncertain boundary between civil society and non-governmental organizations (NGOs) to which the UN Secretary-General referred, perhaps inadvertently, in his response (UN 2004b) to the Cardoso Report where he stated that 'I welcome the emphasis placed by the Panel on all branches of the United Nations system engaging with *civil society* (my emphasis) at the country level…*NGOs* (my emphasis) now act as fully fledged partners…' (UN 2004b: 10). Moreover, the Secretary-General commented, underlining the uncertainties about the legitimacy of some civil society organizations, that 'there are currently large numbers of NGO's in consultative status with the United Nations that are not complying with the requirement to submit quadrennial reports on their activities' (UN 2004b: 9). Academic commentators, such as Benner and Witte, have noted the porous boundaries between civil society and other organizations and referred, in a pleasing neologism, to NGOs as 'gongos, bongos and dongos (NGOs organized by government, business and donors)' (Benner and Witte 2004: 40). Castells (2004b: 5) makes a similar point, proposing that 'NGOs…are…for the most part…subsidized or sponsored by some kind of public agency'.

My own participation in the WSIS/WGIG exemplifies some reasonable grounds for concern about the representativeness of civil society participation. The rules of accreditation prohibited accreditation of individuals and I applied for accreditation as a representative of a small UK university research centre and supplied to the organizers, as required, a completed hard copy application form with a copy of annual report of the research centre and its constitution. I received no acknowledgement of this request for accreditation and no response to subsequent e-mail enquiries. I asked a UK Civil Servant, known to me to be expert in the field, for advice. At his instigation, the UK Foreign and Commonwealth Office took up the matter with UN officials. I then received an e-mail from a UN organizer stating that the WSIS accreditation site had received around 8,000 spam messages and, in consequence, my e-mails had possibly been deleted. I finally secured accreditation and participated in the WSIS/WGIG as a formally-accredited civil society representative. My 'experiment' in legitimacy suggests that there are reasonable grounds for concern about the representativeness and accountability of civil society participation in the WSIS/WGIG.

Moreover, Cammaerts and Carpentier (2004: 9) state that of the 102 civil society organizations which participated in PrepCom 1 (the Summit proceedings included a number of formal preparatory meetings known as PrepComs) only about half did so in PrepCom 2 where 176 civil society organizations were represented. Of these, about 100 attended PrepCom 3. Though civil society obviously participated strongly in the first phase of the WSIS, there seems to have been some lack of continuity in participation and therefore in effective contribution to the WSIS. Only 7 per cent of active civil society organizations attended all PrepComs and the WSIS itself (Cammaerts and Carpentier 2004: 10). Cammaerts and Carpentier also noted that two civil society organizations committed to freedom of expression, Reporters without Borders and Human Rights in China, were excluded from PrepCom 3 (Cammaerts and Carpentier 2004: 17, see also O'Siochru and Girard 2002).

There is room for more than one view as to whether these processes and practices of participation and accreditation satisfied what the Cardoso Panel described as a reasonable expectation of UN Member States that 'actors engaging in their deliberative processes meet at least some basic standards of governance and demonstrate their credentials' (UN 2004a: 26). However, it seems clear that the WGIG did emphatically satisfy the Cardoso recommendation that the UN 'should emphasize the inclusion of all constituencies relevant to the issue, recognize that the key actors are different for different issues and foster multi-stakeholder partnerships to pioneer solutions and empower a range of global policy networks' (UN 2004a: 32) and exemplified what the panel later described as 'networked governance' (UN 2004a: 33). Though not, perhaps, what the panel identified as the 'concerns raised by some Member states about the number of civil society organizations seeking to take part in United Nations meetings...And the perception that some interventions by civil society organizations are offensive' (UN 2004a: 53).

Legitimacy

Though analytically distinct, the two issues of, first, the extent to which civil society should be recognized as a legitimate participant in the WSIS/WGIG and, second, how far state governments, rather than an uncertainly constituted governance network (under the formal umbrella of US law and governmental jurisdiction), should be responsible for the duties undertaken by ICANN, often ran together in exchanges at the WSIS/WGIG. They both posed questions of 'recognition'. For example, the leader of the USA delegation to the WSIS/WGIG, Richard Baird of the State Department, stated at the WGIG on 14 February 2005 that the US regarded the issue under discussion as one of 'co-ordination' (rather than governance thus implying multiple stakeholders and a decentred authority structure). 'Co-ordination' and multiple stakeholders, rhetorically at least, open the door to civil society recognition and close it to recognition of the claims for the exclusive governance prerogatives of state governments advanced by Brazil, China and other like-minded governments at the WSIS/WGIG.

Legitimacy is a key component of a recognition claim and the rival recognition claims under consideration at the WSIS/WGIG, whether of civil society, ICANN or for the sovereignty of a collectivity of state governments (rather than either a single government or a multistakeholder network) all rested on different claims for legitimacy. The claim of ICANN and the status quo rested on putative 'output' legitimacy – the Internet works, access and connectivity are growing; 'if it ain't broke don't fix it'. Civil society's recognition claim also rested on output legitimacy (the conspicuously productive contribution made by civil society experts to the WSIS and especially the WGIG) – expertise which Cardoso described as 'the original purpose' of accreditation of civil society actors for their 'expertise, competence and skills' (UN 2004a: 54). But the claims to legitimacy of civil society and also, to some extent, the status quo based on ICANN, were also claims of representativeness.

The Cardoso panel proposed that, because 'the substance of politics is fast globalizing (in the areas of trade, economics, environment, pandemics, terrorism, etc.), the process of politics is not; its principal institutions (elections, political parties and parliaments) remain firmly rooted in the national or local level' (UN 2004a: 8), new forms of political representation, notably those including civil society, should be espoused and that 'Global governance is no longer the sole domain of Governments' (UN 2004a: 3). In consequence, Cardoso recommended, among other things, fostering 'multi-stakeholder partnerships to pioneer solutions and empower a range of global policy networks…Member States… should signal their preparedness to engage other actors in deliberative processes' (UN 2004a: 32) and strongly advocated knitting civil society into UN politics and procedures because of its power 'to bring a new issue to global attention' and to ensure that action is taken through 'multi-constituency coalitions of Governments, civil society and others' (UN 2004a: 8).

Nonetheless, as my remarks above about accreditation to the WSIS suggest, the uncertain representativeness and weak accountability of civil society at the WSIS/WGIG raise questions about the legitimacy of civil society's claim for recognition. The Internet Governance Caucus' account of the process of selection of its three nominees (Vittorio Bertola, Karen Banks, Avri Doria) for membership of the WGIG makes it clear that the selection was made by five members of the Caucus: 'a rather small number of caucus members was bold enough to select Avri, Karen and Vittorio as suggested candidates of the IG caucus' (Hofmann 2004: 2). Though this account is commendably transparent (giving an account of oneself is a necessary, but not sufficient, element of accountability) there is room for more than one view as to whether such a process satisfied what the Cardoso Panel described as a reasonable expectation of UN Member States that 'actors engaging in their deliberative processes meet at least some basic standards of governance and demonstrate their credentials' (UN 2004a: 26). However, it seems clear that the WGIG did emphatically satisfy the Cardoso recommendation that the UN 'should emphasize the inclusion of all constituencies relevant to the issue, recognise that the key actors are different for different issues and foster multi-stakeholder partnerships to pioneer solutions and empower a range of global policy networks' (UN 2004a: 32). Though not, perhaps, what the panel identified as the 'concerns raised by some Member states about the number of civil society organizations seeking to take part in United Nations meetings... And the perception that some interventions by civil society organizations are offensive' (UN 2004a: 53).

The legitimacy, and thus the claims to recognition of both civil society and the governance status quo, were explicitly challenged and qualified by Lyndall Shope-Mafole (a member of the WGIG and also a representative of the government of South Africa) in the WGIG on 18 April 2005. She said:

> On the one hand, you have governments that are elected that have public accountability in their countries. You have the private sector that could be owned by one person or a number of people that is accountable to its shareholders. And you have civil society, I'm not sure what the accountability to civil society is. It depends on which part of civil society. But there are some stakeholder accountabilities there. So I think that the intergovernmental nature of whatever mechanism we would have would need to take into account, of course, this multistakeholder element. But I think that for it to be legitimate, it has to be rooted in some intergovernmental mechanism. And this is why in the input within the World Summit on the Information Society, when making the input on behalf of South Africa, we had said that the only intergovernmental mechanism or legitimate mechanism that we know that represents the will of the peoples of the world is the UN system.

Of course the principle that Shope-Mafole invoked is also open to challenge on grounds of legitimacy. Not all Governments are democratic, not all democratic governments are represented in the UN (Taiwan, for example, is excluded), and not all countries are the same size – compare the UN Member States of Niue (with, in 2005, an estimated population 2,166) and China (with, in 2005, an estimated population of 1,306,313,812).[24] Can the claims and contributions to UN proceedings of China and Niue be sensibly regarded as equivalent?

But whether or not governments are actually and effectively accountable to those whom they claim to represent, the assumed relationship between government and people is clear in a way the relationship between civil society and what Held calls 'communities of fate' (Held 2004: 20) is not. One civil society member of the WGIG, Karen Banks (at the WGIG in Geneva on 14 February 2005), asked to whom 'should these organizations [i.e. Internet governance organizations] be accountable?' She answered her question by naming 'all users of the Internet in the world and all potential users' but, as she recognized, identifying so inclusive a community of fate, in the name of whom she and those like her might speak, hardly solves the problem.

Conclusion

At the WSIS/WGIG, the linked issues of the conduct and form of Internet governance on one hand, and the extent to which non-state actors should be formally represented in both the WSIS/WGIG proceedings and also in substantive Internet governance on the other, accounted for much more of the time spent in the course of the summit and its associated activities, and stimulated a striking intensity in debates and disagreements, than did consideration of issues of resources and distribution. The 'Rawlsian' questions of redistribution (ICT4D, the Digital Solidarity Fund etc.) had a lower profile, sparked less public attention and was characterized by less indignation and outrage than were either of the 'recognition' issues of Internet governance and of 'trilateralism'.

The WSIS/WGIG, therefore, lent empirical support to Nancy Fraser's claims for the importance of 'recognition' issues in contemporary politics and contemporary political philosophy. It bears out her claim that there has been a 'relative decline in claims for egalitarian distribution' (Fraser 2000: 107). Fraser deprecates the decline in salience of redistribution issues but acknowledges the pertinence of a change in focus from a politics of redistribution to a politics of recognition at a time of 'hugely increasing transcultural interaction and communication' (Fraser 2000: 108). She argues persuasively that recognition politics and claims concern 'the status of individual group members as full partners in social interaction' and that recognition claims are directed to 'establishing the misrecognized party as a full member of society, capable of participating on a par with the rest' (Fraser 2000: 113). Fraser argues that the task of establishing a pervasive contemporary system of justice depends on progress in three distinct domains, that is:

- Redistribution
- Representation
- Recognition.

For Fraser, representational justice claims are to be realized in the political domain and redistributive claims in the economic domain and recognition claims in the cultural domain. She points to striking inequalities and inequities in representation – e.g. the disparity experienced by citizens of 'failed' states and citizens of 'predator' states. She might also have referred to the structural inequality built into the Westphalian system of representation of states in the United Nations whereby states with small populations enjoy equal status to that of states with large populations. Fraser also referred to the growth of a global civil society as a form of mitigation of the inequalities and inequities in representation deriving from the disparity in the effectiveness of different states in the established international system of representation of states.

All three of Fraser's domains were loci of conflict at the WSIS/WGIG: redistribution in the ICT4D initiative and the digital solidarity fund; representation in the substantive conflicts over the preferred institutional architecture of global Internet governance (ITU v

ICANN); and recognition in the visceral intensity of the conflicts manifested in discussion on the floor of WSIS/WGIG sessions – conflicts which involved the recognition claims *both* of states such as Brazil, China and South Africa (broadly congruent with the G21 group) *and* of civil society.

The WSIS/WGIG powerfully exemplified Fraser's contention that 'as globalisation is accelerating flows of people and communication across borders, divergent value horizons are colliding with startling results. Everyone experiences a new proximity of "the other" and a new salience of identity and difference. The effect is to fracture all self-enclosed status orders and to unleash intensified struggles for recognition' (Fraser in Fraser and Honneth 2003: 222–23). Recognition struggles certainly had a higher degree of salience than did redistribution struggles but such discussion as there was of redistribution, resulting in agreement in Clause 27 of the Tunis Agreement on several 'improvements and innovations in existing financing mechanisms', suggested that the Rawlsian difference principle can, and did (whether or not those who decided were aware of Rawls and his 'difference' principle), serve as a principle of action in real world circumstances. The capacity to improve and extend global connectivity by extending access to telecommunication infrastructures, e.g. through improved access to backbone networks via local and regional IXPs at marginal cost, neatly exemplifies a specific implementation of Rawls' model.

Although the WSIS concluded with a formal agreement, the Tunis Agenda/Agreement, which incorporated concrete proposals for addressing distributional issues, notably in respect of ICT4D, Internet governance remained an intractable and unresolved problem. The Internet governance portfolio was remitted to a new body, an Internet Governance Forum (the initial meeting of which took place in Athens from 30th October to 2nd November 2006). Remitting the unresolved issues of Internet governance from the WSIS/WGIG to the Athens Internet Governance Forum (IGF 2006a) is likely to satisfy few. The Tunis Agenda (Clause 77) provides that the IGF should have 'no oversight function and would not replace existing arrangements, mechanisms, institutions or organizations'. But although the 'constitution' of the IGF endows the IGF with only the softest of power, hardly a feather's touch, establishment of the IGF represents a partial acknowledgement of civil society's recognition claims.

Despite the IGF's absence of power, substantive issues of control (in so far as it can be controlled) of the Internet have been somewhat recontextualized by a new formal relationship between the US government and ICANN (ICANN 2006b). However, the increase in ICANN's autonomy figured by the new relationship is unlikely to satisfy either critical governments, such as China, or civil society. But the US decision to redraft the Memorandum of Understanding, on which ICANN stands, has been strongly supported by the European Union which welcomed the 'very important step towards full private-sector management of the internet, on which the EU has been working with various US administrations since 1998. We in Europe trust ICANN's expertise and the unique multi-stakeholder model of consultation it represents' (European Union 2006).

Many reasons can be identified for the inability of the World Summit on the Information Society to reach agreement on Internet governance. Clearly, influence over the Internet is an important matter of both material and political interest for many parties, whether business or governments, and these material and political interests undoubtedly strongly shaped both the course the summit took and the summit's outcome. But neither these interests nor the 'Rawlsian' matter of distributional justice can account for either, still less both, the amount of time spent in the course of the summit on Internet governance or the intensity of the exchanges on that issue.

Rather, one needs to invoke Fraser's notion of a struggle for recognition to understand why Internet governance was on the summit agenda in the first place, why it proved so intractable an issue and why it triggered so much emotional intensity in the course of the WSIS/WGIG proceedings. Certainly, distributional justice was an issue but so too were recognition politics. And recognition politics at the WSIS/WGIG took a complicated form because there was more than one recognition claim at issue. There were the recognition claims of states, (the loose association of 'Group 21' states and notably Brazil, China and South Africa), of an established multistakeholder form of quasi-network governance of the Internet centred on ICANN and, not least of all, of civil society.

Moreover, the exclusion of many substantive issues of relevance from the IGF's remit (e.g. management of the DNS and the vexed issue of 'political oversight' of Internet governance) together with the relative paucity of government contributions of papers and comments for consideration by the IGF[25] suggest that any substantive consideration of Internet governance is more likely to take place within the multistakeholder framework already established around ICANN than it is through the IGF. Although the conduct and outcomes of the IGF remain uncertain,[26] recognition issues are likely to remain prominent concerns. As Markus Kummer stated (at the Oxford Internet Institute on 31 August 2006), the challenge for the IGF is 'to make everyone equally unhappy'. His tongue in cheek comment could be re-versioned as an acknowledgement that there should be parity of recognition for everyone. And as an acknowledgement that justice, whether in distribution or recognition, may be difficult to secure when trust and respect between rival claimants (whether the distribution of recognition, rights or material goods is in question) is low or absent.

Rawls' reference, in the revised version of *A Theory of Justice,* to 'social co-operation on a footing of mutual respect' (Rawls 1999: xv) gestures towards the importance of the 'recognition' which Fraser has eloquently advocated. But it also lends support to the critique, by Honderich and others, that Rawls' doctrines are difficult to apply to real world politics. Certainly, Rawls' 'difference principle' may be said to be satisfied when access to (at least some forms) of connectivity is considered (though there may be room for debate about the pace of technological diffusion and access to different means of communication) and that, therefore, there is a real world political relevance and utility to a (the) central element of his theory of justice. But his vision of 'social co-operation on a footing of mutual respect', though comforting as a normative principle, offers scant grip on the struggles for recognition which took place at the WSIS/WGIG. For a dominant characteristic of these struggles was the desire by some claimants to recognition to deny recognition to others – far from the Rawlsian imagined state of 'social co-operation on a footing of mutual respect' and closer to Fraser's vision of the assertion of recognition claims as a matter of struggle and conflict. Equality of unhappiness, in the vein of Markus Kummer's tongue-in-cheek remark, is unlikely to provide an enduring basis for the governance of the Internet – even if equal unhappiness satisfies the difference principle.

Notes

1. A political declaration on development of a pervasive global information society linking a variety of national initiatives. For examples see: http://www.itu.int/wsis/docs2/pc2/off6.html accessed on 3.2.2006.
2. Or as Rawls put it in the first version of *A Theory of Justice*, 'Social and economic inequalities are to be arranged so that: a) they are to be of the greatest benefit to the least-advantaged members of society (the difference principle). b) offices and positions must be open to everyone under conditions of fair equality of opportunity (Rawls 1971: 303).
3. Google Scholar identified about 164,000 results for 'Digital Divide' on 25.10.2006.
4. Telephone, cellular and Internet access are among the indices used by the United Nations in monitoring the achievement of its Millennium Development Goals. See Goal 8 Target 18 'In cooperation with the private sector, make available the benefits of new technologies, especially information and communications' at http://unstats.un.org/unsd/mdg/Host.aspx?Content=Indicators/OfficialList.htm accessed on 18.10.2006.
5. The term 'digital divide' may mask as much as it reveals: the importance of factors such as literacy, access to reliable electricity supplies and so on bear differently on different digital communication technologies such as cellular telephony and Internet access and use.
6. In late 2006 the World Institute for Development Economics Research of the United Nations University published (UNU-WIDER 2006) a report on world distribution of household wealth which showed great inequalities in wealth both between states and within states. The press release launching the study was titled 'Pioneering Study Shows Richest Two Percent Own Half World Wealth' see http://www.wider.unu.edu/research/2006-2007/2006-2007-1/wider-wdhw-launch-5-12-2006/wider-wdhw-press-release-5-12-2006.pdf accessed on 5.12.2006.
7. Paltridge catalogues a heart breaking list of African countries (see OECD 2006: 36) where the power of incumbents has led to perverse underutilization of established capacity and consequentially higher prices to users – for example, he states (of the SAT-3 cable) that 'a valuable resource for Africa's development…[h]as been chronically underutilized. For the main part this has been because of monopolies charging excessive prices' (OECD 2006: 36). Similarly, Hargittai (1999) argued, using data from OECD countries, that Internet connectivity was positively related to competition in telecommunications provision.
8. GrameenPhone in Bangladesh appears to be another notable case in point (the GrameenPhone model has also been exported to Rwanda and Uganda). See http://www.grameenphone.com/index.php?id=398 accessed on 22.6.2009.
9. Mobile telephony in South Africa is not simply a device for voice communication but is a gateway to banking and other services. Phone ownership and use is high, the *Financial Times* (FT 2006), drawing on ITU data (see http://www.itu.int/ITU-D/icteye/Reporting/ShowReportFrame.aspx?

ReportName=/WTI/CellularSubscribersPublic&RP_intYear=2005&RP_intLanguageID=1 accessed on 30.11.2006), estimates that in 2005 72% of South Africans had a mobile/cell 'phone, and has far outpaced wireline provision by the former state monopoly incumbent Telkom. In this South Africa is representative of Africa where 83% of African telephone subscribers are mobile subscribers (FT 2006). Moreover 'spaza', informal, 'phone shops provide access to many unable to afford a personal cell 'phone (See Reck and Wood 2003). In comparison, the ITU (*ibid*) estimates that in 2005 the USA had a mobile penetration of only 68%.

10. Data summarized from Internet World Statistics at http://www.internetworldstats.com/stats.htm accessed on 23.10.2006. See also Cybergeography at http://www.cybergeography.org/statistics.html and the Cooperative Association for Internet Data Analysis (CAIDA) at http://www.caida.org/data/.
11. I have been unable to identify data on trends in the volume of global Internet traffic. However there seem few reasons to doubt that this continues to grow very rapidly. As Cukier (nd para 2.1) states 'Hard data on international Internet traffic volume are difficult to come by'. See OECD 2006 for an abundant collection of data and testimony to some of the problems of data collection and analysis. However, this source has much more comprehensive data for OECD member states than it does for the rest of the world – in this it is representative of other studies.
12. Paltridge also notes (OECD 2006: 13) that wholesale access process have fallen and that 'What might have cost USD 1000 per Mbps per month in 1995 may cost USD 15 per Mbps per month in 2005' and that 'transit prices well below USD 10 per Mbps were available in major cities around the world'.
13. The 40 member WGIG was constituted on 12.11.2004 with a strong civil society element (see membership of WGIG at http://www.wgig.org/members.html accessed on 2.2.2006).
14. A third issue, the 'political chapeau', was relatively uncontroversial because recognized to be a matter for individual states, rather than the Summit, to determine.
15. Paltridge (OECD 2006) suggests that Internet Exchange Points (IXP) are notably appropriate ways of facilitating Internet access in developing countries.
16. On 14.2.2005 the author interviewed the national delegate from Togo to the WSIS who emphasised the importance of access and redistribution issues and specifically mentioned the 'digital solidarity fund'.
17. The terms under which ICANN is constituted and operates changed with the expiry of the MoU between ICANN and the US Department of Commerce accessed on 30.9.2006. See: http://www.icann.org/general/agreements.htm, http://www.icann.org/general/JPA-29sep06.pdf, http://www.icann.org/general/icann-mou-25nov98.htm, http://www.icann.org/general/amend2-jpamou-07sep00.htm accessed on 20.10.2006.
18. But see criticism of ICANN on grounds of lack of functional, or output, legitimacy by Mueller who claims that 'ICANN can take anywhere from 3–5 years to come up with a policy' (Mueller 2005). Mueller has also (e.g. in an oral statement at WGIG on 14.2.2005) identified ICANN as dominated by business. See also Marlin-Bennett 2001, Mueller 1999 and 2002 and Weinberg 2000.
19. Citations from author's contemporaneous notes, documents distributed at the WGIG and from the webstream transcript corrected by reference to the author's contemporaneous notes and to eliminate obvious errors. Webstream available at http://www.wgig.org/meeting-april.html.
20. Doubtless the matter of Internet governance also provided a lightning rod on which a generalized anti-Americanism rooted in quite other matters was discharged.
21. Business has been formally recognized as a participant in UN meetings and was particularly strongly represented at the WSIS/WGIG because of the high level of business membership in

the ITU, the UN agency under whose auspices the WSIS/WGIG was organized, which has more business members than state members.

22. ICANN refers, in the statement of the operating principles of its (tellingly titled) Governmental Advisory Committee (GAC), to ICANN's purposes including 'lessening the burdens of government' see clause 3 at http://gac.icann.org/web/home/GAC_Operating_Principles.doc accessed on 24.10.2006.
23. The Cardoso report is correctly, but not usually, known as the *Report of the Panel of Eminent Persons on United Nations-Civil Society Relations* (UN 2004a). The Cardoso panel acknowledged the problems of 'loading' decision making process by Government-organized NGOs (UN 2004a: 54) and also expressed concern about the preponderance of NGO speakers who were 'male, Northern and Anglo-Saxon' (UN 2004a: 59) with 'unclear accountability to the grass roots' (UN 2004a: 65).
24. Both estimates derived from https://www.cia.gov/library/publications/the-world-factbook/rankorder/2119rank.html accessed on 22.6.2009.
25. On 26.10.2006, that is 5 days before commencement of the IGF, the only government which had contributed a paper was that of Brazil. See http://intgovforum.org/Substantive_1st_IGF/Brazilian%20Position.doc accessed on 26.10.2006.
26. One account of the IGF, Darren Waters' (BBC News website Technology editor), suggests that there were few solid outcomes from IGF discussions. Waters stated, and asked, 'The Internet Governance Forum will return in a year's time in Rio. Will the same old arguments still be traded back and forth? Quite probably'. However Waters acknowledged that, if not in substance then in process, the IGF was productive: he reported 'Overall the key success of the IGF emerging is in getting groups of people together who perhaps have never sat around a table together. To have Amnesty International talking to a Chinese government official is not something that would have happened at past meetings of this kind.' See http://news.bbc.co.uk/go/pr/fr/-/2/hi/technology/6105496.stm accessed on 2.11.2006.

Chapter 9

Trilateralism, Legitimacy and the Working Group on Internet Government

> All major communications network innovations have given rise to new enterprises, transformed economic, social and political structures, crossed borders, created international disputes, and perhaps most important, eventually led to the development of new coordination or governance frameworks. This historical pattern has been repeated with almost predictable regularity, beginning with the telegraph in the 1840s, the telephone in the 1870s, radio telegraphy or 'wireless' in the 1890s, radio broadcasting in the 1920s, television broadcasting in the 1950s, geostationary satellite communications in the 1960s, computer communications in the 1970s, optical communications in the 1980s, and the Internet and mobile communications in the 1990s. (ITU 2004: 14)[1]

Introduction

By pointing, in the quotation above (excerpted from a report on the Workshop on Internet Governance [WGIG]), to the constancy of change in the governance of media and communications, the International Telecommunication Union (ITU) suggests, implicitly, that the time is ripe for more change. And change to the governance of the Internet was the central topic of discussions at the World Summit on the Information Society (WSIS). The WSIS was notable both as the first formal UN summit on a communications issue and as the first UN summit in which civil society[2] enjoyed a formal status as participant. The WSIS addressed three chief issues[3] but the fulcrum (and still unresolved) issue was governance of the global Internet addressing system – the domain name system (DNS) – and the role of ICANN (Internet Corporation for Assigned Names and Numbers) the governing institution at the apex of the DNS.

ICANN is established under a Memorandum of Understanding with the US Department of Commerce and is thus accountable to a single government. In this respect, governance of the global Internet is different from the governance of the analogous global telephone numbering system which is coordinated by an international treaty-based organization, the ITU. The first session of the WSIS, in Geneva in 2003, was unable to make satisfactory progress on Internet governance issues and the Secretary General of the UN therefore established a dedicated working group, the Working Group on Internet Governance (WGIG) to progress these unresolved issues.

The WGIG brought together states, business and civil society in an attempt to resolve a governance conflict which exemplified several major areas of contemporary debate about global governance, notably:

- The respective roles of national governments and international organizations in global governance
- The balance to be struck between different forms of coordination and accountability and notably between hierarchical, market and network forms of governance
- The respective roles of Governments, civil society and business in global governance.

It is tempting to see both the central substantive issue of Internet governance considered at the WSIS/WGIG and the failure of WSIS/WGIG process to secure agreement on Internet governance in Held's (Held et al. 2005: 3) terms as examples of the 'erosion of the multinational order symbolized by the United Nations'. Held identified this erosion of multinational order as one of four major contemporary global challenges[4] and referred to the 'arrogance of the great powers' (Held et al. 2005: 7) as a principal cause of the weakened effectiveness and legitimacy of established institutions of international coordination and governance such as the UN. Certainly some participants in the WSIS/WGIG debate over Internet governance saw things in such terms. Syria, for example, said[5] at the Geneva WGIG meeting on 18 February 2005 that:

> the internationalization of the Internet is a natural process. We cannot accept the Internet being merely an American body subject to another American body, which I won't mention. We already said this at the summit. So the situation is clear, and our position is clear and we don't need to repeat ourselves here. The Internet today is governed by American law and managed by an American business. It's no secret. We all know it, and we cannot accept it.

In contrast to Syria's critique of different aspects of the ICANN-based status quo (notably private sector governance and the absence of formal international governance – such as the treaty-based regimes applying to posts and telecommunications), the Internet Society (ISOC), said at the Geneva WGIG meeting on 18 April 2005 that:

> many of WGIG's premises seem to start with an assumption that the Internet needs hierarchical top-down governance model implying one organization and thereby ignoring the decentralized structure on which the Internet was so successfully built. Not only does this governance hierarchy model as it was called in some of the papers prevent an accurate understanding of the internet's infrastructure and its development and forcing key organizations to be classed in prescribed categories that do not fit with the reality of their actions or their role in developing and supporting the Internet, but it also will very likely lead to conclusions that will harm the Internet's development and growth.

These statements (and similar examples put forward by different parties could have been cited) neatly contrast a top down 'command and control' hierarchical mode of governance with a looser, network, mode of governance. Syria and India argued both that hierarchical governance of the Internet actually prevails (with the US Government at the top of the hierarchy) and that hierarchical governance *should* prevail but with the UN, rather than the US, at the top of the hierarchy, whereas ISOC argued both normatively and analytically for a looser network form of governance. ISOC's institutional self-definition fills out an image of network governance as one undertaken by many organizations working through informal and often protean co-operative arrangements. ISOC states:

> Along with its natural partners – ISOC members and Chapters, the IETF, and PIR – ISOC is embedded within a fabric of Internet organisations, each with its own role to play and pursuing its own mission. ISOC collaborates with those other organisations – including ICANN, the root server operators, the NSRC, and the Regional Internet Registries (RIRs) – and with national and international government and civil society groups that share its vision, including the European Union and the Swedish International Development Cooperation Agency (Sida). Collectively, these organisations tile, or span the public policy, operations, and management space. (ISOC 2004: 8)

Political scientists have come to distinguish between three major forms of social co-ordination, or governance, that is hierarchical (command and control) governance, market (price-based) governance and network (self-regulatory) governance. These forms of governance loosely map onto three types of social and political institutions: states (for hierarchical governance), business (for market governance) and civil society (for network governance). It is a commonplace to regard the importance of network governance as growing relative to hierarchical and market systems of governance (see, among others, Thompson 2003). In the context of contemporary social and political science, the Internet is often seen both as an exemplar of a putative general shift to network governance and also as a vital enabler of network governance.

It is seldom the case in real world situations that pure forms of hierarchical, network or market governance can be found. Most governance regimes are mixed and governance of the DNS is no exception where important elements of hierarchical governance (and in some instances market governance) figures with network governance in the coordination and operation of the global Internet addressing system. However, as the citations above from India, Syria and ISOC suggest, proponents of change tended to argue for stronger hierarchical governance and for a stronger representation of states in Internet governance whereas defenders of the status quo advocated network (and market) governance and a continued predominance of business and civil society in Internet governance.

Trilateralism

Debate in the WGIG not only focused on substantive questions of DNS governance, such as whether ICANN or another body such as the ITU should 'rule the root' (Mueller 2002), but also on who legitimately could contribute to the debate and who should shape decisions. What system of governance should prevail for the global Internet and what part should the three parties to United Nations trilateralism, states, business and civil society, play in Internet governance? The question of who should decide was particularly important because WSIS was the first UN Summit formally to embody trilateralism. Civil society enjoyed a new salience following the Cardoso Panel's report on United Nations-Civil Society Relations (UN 2004a) which recommended the UN to adopt 'multi-stakeholder partnerships to pioneer solutions and empower a range of global policy networks' (UN 2004a: 32) and that 'The Secretariat should innovate with networked governance' (UN 2004a: 34). And business continued to play its long established part in UN deliberations, not least because of the high level of business membership in the ITU, the UN agency under whose auspices the WSIS/WGIG was organized (the ITU has a greater number of business members than member states).

Trilateralism on this scale was not only novel but was complicated by the different weights exerted by each group. Numerically, civil society outweighed the other two groups combined[6] but, in terms of power, states outweighed both other parties. Moreover, the legitimacy of the different parties to trilateralism was a matter of active dispute. For example, at the Geneva WGIG of 18 April 2005, one of the most actively engaged states in the WSIS/WGIG process, China, challenged trilateralism and stated[7] that:

> The policy authority for Internet-related public policy issues is the sovereign right of states. They have rights and responsibilities for international Internet-related public policy issues...The so-called trilateralism has no foundation in the report, since it deviates from the principle from Article 49, mixing the roles of all the stakeholders, denying the due responsibility and role of governments in internet policy-making. Also, trilateralism ignores the fact that the private sector and civil society between the developed and developing countries are different development levels which may aggravate the imbalance and developing and developed countries and broaden the digital divide.

China's challenge to the legitimacy of business and civil society, in favour of state-based 'unilateralism' was, not surprisingly, itself challenged within the WSIS and WGIG. Unilateralism was under challenge both because of the positive claims which business and civil society were able to make (notably on the grounds of their relevant expertise, business' control of key assets and civil society's ability to represent communities otherwise imperfectly represented) and the negative effect of some states' undemocratic practices and disrespect for human rights. Moreover, critics of unilateralism were able to point to flaws in the system of representation of the world's populations by states: notably to some gross disparities in the size of populations represented by single states and the consequential inequalities in population's voting powers (see Chapter 8).

How then was the novel practice of trilateralism implemented? The core of the WGIG – the Working Group itself – was composed in such a way that left unclear the principles underlying its composition. Some members clearly represented states, others business and other civil society. But the basis on which members were chosen and appointed in respect of each of these constituencies remains opaque. Not least because some members of the Working Group were plausibly seen as representing more than one of the three key constituencies of states, business and civil society. A source, (a member of a western national delegation interviewed by the author on 15 February 2005), stated that the few national representatives on the WGIG were 'appointed rather randomly'. The source instanced the case of Pakistan having a seat on WGIG but not India. And the account given by one important (and notably transparent – see Hofmann 2004) institutional actor, the Internet Governance Caucus, of the selection of its three nominees (Vittorio Bertola,[8] Karen Banks, and Avri Doria) for membership of the WGIG makes clear that 'a rather small number of caucus members was bold enough to select Avri, Karen and Vittorio as suggested candidates of the IG caucus' (Hofmann 2004: 2).

Civil society

The UN Charter has provided, from the UN's inception, for civil society to play a part in its activities. Article 71 states:

> The Economic and Social Council may make suitable arrangements for consultation with non-governmental organizations which are concerned with matters within its competence. Such arrangements may be made with international organizations and, where appropriate, with national organizations after consultation with the Member of the United Nations concerned.

However, latterly, civil society has played a bigger role in UN deliberations both because of its expertise and its ability to represent communities and interests that would otherwise be excluded or under-represented. Civil society's high profile in WGIG was consistent with the policies which flowed from Secretary-General of the United Nations' report on 'Strengthening of the United Nations: an agenda for further change' (UN 2002) which promised a review of the relationship between the UN and civil society. The review was undertaken by a panel of twelve 'eminent persons', including Manuel Castells,[9] chaired by the former President of Brazil, Fernando Cardoso, which reported in 2004 (UN 2004a).

The Cardoso panel (henceforth Cardoso) remarked that 'The rise of civil society is indeed one of the landmark events of our times. Global governance is no longer the sole domain of Governments' (UN 2004a: 3) and that 'A clear paradox is emerging: while the substance of politics is fast globalizing (in the areas of trade, economics, environment, pandemics, terrorism etc.), the process of politics is not; its principal institutions (elections, political parties and parliaments) remain firmly rooted in the national or local level' (UN 2004a: 8). As stated earlier, Cardoso recommended, among other things, fostering 'multi-stakeholder partnerships to pioneer solutions and empower a range of global policy networks…Member States…should signal their preparedness to engage other actors in deliberative processes' (UN 2004a: 32) and that 'The Secretariat should innovate with networked governance' (UN 2004a: 34).

In consequence, the WSIS was specifically charged (UN Resolution 56/183 clause 5) with encouraging:

> effective contributions from and the active participation of all relevant United Nations bodies, in particular the Information and Communication Technologies Task Force, and encourages other intergovernmental organizations, including international and regional institutions, non-governmental organizations, civil society and the private sector to contribute to, and actively participate in, the intergovernmental preparatory process of the Summit and the Summit itself. (WSIS 2001)

The match between the Internet and a UN with a strengthened civil society component may have seemed made in heaven, for there is a strong history of civil society involvement in network governance of the Internet. John Perry Barlow's Declaration of the Independence of Cyberspace (Barlow 1996); the Internet Engineering Task Force's (IETF) 'Tao' of 'rough consensus and running code' (see IETF 2009); and ICANN's own loose structure of organizations and advisory groups 'tiling' (ISOC's term)[10] to coordinate the operation of global Internet addressing all exemplify this civil society/network nexus and continue to inform the mentality of the individuals and institutions governing the DNS.

But what is civil society? Cardoso referred to civil society as 'associations of citizens… entered into voluntarily…it does not include profit making activity…of particular relevance…are mass organizations (such as organizations of peasants, women or retired people) trade unions, professional associations, social movements, indigenous people's organizations, religious and spiritual organizations, academe and public benefit non-governmental organizations (UN 2004a: 13). Cardoso's proposition (uncontroversial in itself) that 'Traditional democracy aggregates citizens by communities of neighbourhood… Participatory democracy citizens aggregate in communities of interest' (UN 2004a: 8) leaves open the question of how such communities of interest should organize themselves for democracy: how should they (how can they?) deliberate? How are their boundaries to be set? Who should represent them and how should representatives be accountable? And Cardoso expressed its concern about the 'unclear accountability to the grass roots' of civil society representatives (UN 2004a: 65). Kaldor et al (2005b: 12–13) make an analogous distinction by differentiating procedural democracy, characterized as territorially bound (and solidly institutionalized with constituencies, representational procedures etc.), and substantive democracy, which is not so bounded but which 'requires an active civil society, an arena where people can express themselves freely, organise associations, and try to influence decision makers'.

Neither civil society nor NGOs are easily defined and, in consequence, the theoretical possibility of some form of representational system evolving for non-territorially bound groups, what Held called communities of fate (Held 2004), remains fraught with difficulty. Civil society organizations' claims for representative legitimacy are thus likely to be weaker than are those of democratic states. Moreover, as Cardoso noted, decision making can be 'loaded' by Government-organized NGOs (UN 2004a: 54). It would take a major empirical study to establish the degree to which civil society organizations participating in the WSIS/WGIG were, or were not, linked to governments (or business). But the composition of some elements of the civil society element involved in the WSIS/WGIG seemed, prima facie, to lack a fully representative character.[11] If so, the WSIS/WGIG was not exceptional.

The legitimacy of civil society may be justified on grounds other than the representational grounds which form the principle claim to legitimacy of states. Cardoso, for example, not only argued for civil society's participation in decision making on the grounds that some communities with claims to representation were not territorially-based but also because 'the original purpose' of accrediting civil society was its endowment of 'expertise, competence and skills' UN 2004a: 54). And further principled and pragmatic grounds potentially exist for accreditation and participation.

In the WSIS/WGIG, civil society organizations made strong claims of principle (see, among others, Civil Society@WSIS 2005) but, of course, there was not always a consensus on the principles invoked or the relative importance of principled, pragmatic or representational legitimacy claims. Rival claims circulated directed towards securing either practical and pragmatic objectives (making the Internet work: 'if it ain't broke don't fix it') or more abstract goals such as freedom of expression, the right to communicate, the importance of competition. And it was not only civil society that made arguments based on principle. For example, Elizabeth Longworth, Director of the Information Society Division of UNESCO, argued (in a context which suggested support for the governance status quo rather than for the changes proposed by the speakers from Brazil and Syria who precede her) for the 'need to preserve the inherent open-ness of the Internet' (statement at WGIG 15 February 2005).

The legitimacy of civil society's participation was complicated by the remarkable lack of continuity in its presence in the WGIG/WSIS. Cammaerts and Carpentier (2004: 9) state that of the 102 civil society organizations which participated in PrepCom 1 only about half did so in PrepCom 2 (where 176 civil society organizations were represented of which about 100 attended PrepCom 3). Only 7 per cent of active civil society organizations attended all PrepComs and the WSIS itself (Cammaerts and Carpentier 2004: 10). However, they also state that two notable civil society organizations committed to freedom of expression, Reporters without Borders and Human Rights in China, were excluded from PrepCom 3 (Cammaerts and Carpentier 2004: 17).

Business

Business, the third force with states and civil society in the trilateral deliberations of WSIS and WGIG, was represented both by particular firms and by bodies which collectively put forward the business viewpoint. Chief among the collective bodies was the Coordinating Committee of Business Interlocutors (CCBI) which in turn was led by the International Chamber of Commerce (ICC) headed by Ayesha Hassan, a member of the Working Group on Internet Governance.

In contrast to both states and civil society, where cleavages within the group of states and within the civil society group were as significant as were the cleavages between the three constituent parties to WSIS/WGIG trilateralism, business put forward a coherent and focused point of view. Essentially, business argued for the status quo in Internet governance on pragmatic grounds of 'if it ain't broke don't fix it', preferring market and network governance to the prospect of hierarchy. Business at WSIS stated:

> There has been much discussion at this summit about the issue of so-called 'internet governance'. Business believes that this term is a contradiction in terms/a flawed concept/ an oxymoron. The internet is a network of networks. Its success to date – and I think we can all agree it has been spectacular – has relied on its de-centralised nature. We in business believe this is a model built on coordination and collaboration which works well. The fact that there is no real central locus is one of the internet's most important features. (Business at WSIS Press Release 12 December 2003)[12]

Ayesha Hassan herself made similar points arguing that: 'Internet governance structures and mechanisms work well today' (Hassan 2005: 127) and downplayed the importance of ICANN's coordination of the DNS by defining this as but one of several technical coordination issues all of which, whilst in varying degrees imperfect, worked well enough. As she stated: 'In general, business views the current mechanisms that handle Internet related issues to be functioning well' (Hassan 2005: 117) and, like Business at WSIS, deprecated the prospect of shifting control of the DNS from ICANN to an un-named (but obviously the ITU) intergovernmental body. She stated: 'Business and the ICC in particular do not support the transfer to an intergovernmental body of any of the functions performed by private sector led organizations, or organizations that function as a partnership between the private sector and users' (Hassan 2005: 121).

The core of business' case for the status quo was therefore an appeal to pragmatic criteria and the likelihood of continued effective operation and innovative development of the Internet being better realized through market and network governance than through hierarchy.

Legitimacy

The novel and as yet uncertain integration of civil society (and business) into a trilateral UN system, with a consequential displacement of the states which had formerly dominated proceedings, raised important issues of legitimacy. Who speaks? Who decides? What doctrines should dominate? Which view of the world has most heuristic power?

There is room for more than one view as to whether the process of appointment of WGIG members satisfied what the Cardoso Panel described as a reasonable expectation of UN Member States that 'actors engaging in their deliberative processes meet at least some basic standards of governance and demonstrate their credentials' (UN 2004a: 26). However, it seems clear that the WGIG did emphatically satisfy the Cardoso recommendation that the UN 'should emphasize the inclusion of all constituencies relevant to the issue, recognize that the key actors are different for different issues and foster multi-stakeholder partnerships to pioneer solutions and empower a range of global policy networks' (UN 2004a: 32). The formidable experience and varied Internet competencies of many representatives of business and civil society especially in the WGIG materially strengthened the capacity of the summit for informed deliberation and decision.

Nonetheless, this inclusive trilateralism did not secure the support and acceptance of all participants in the WSIS/WGIG. For example, China demanded expulsion of civil society and business participants from small group negotiating sessions at the second, Tunis, WSIS. At the second WGIG (February 2005) Brazil argued that 'Governments not corporations represent the interests of their citizens' and Syria supported Brazil and stated 'public policy is the business of governments'. A posting on the WSIS related website, hosted by the Heinrich Boell-Stiftung, stated: 'After the observers were able to participate in most of the working groups yesterday, a number of countries like China and Egypt complained that this was against the rules of procedure. They asked for the observers to be locked out of the working groups. This met fierce resistance by the EU, the US and others' (Boell-Stiftung nd).

Anecdotal evidence (interview by author with a member of a western national delegation to the Tunis WSIS on 28 November 2005) also suggests that civil society was the subject of vigorous and intrusive policing at the Tunis summit. My source stated that there was extensive photographing of participants, aggressive challenges in, and followed up outside, meetings by intimidatory groups of Tunisians, and that some civil society organizations represented at the WSIS were front organizations created by Member States. These contentions are supported by the formal complaint to the Government of Tunisia by the European Union following a number of incidents in Tunis, including police obstruction of civil society organizations from entering the Goethe Institut to plan a response to the cancellation of a previously-arranged meeting at the Summit itself. Padovani commented: 'The road to the final phase of the Summit – being held in Tunis in mid-November 2005 – is witnessing a step back in governments' commitment to participatory processes' (Padovani 2005: 21).

Civil society's association with collaborative, network, governance associated it, of necessity, with the status quo for the constitution and practice of key Internet institutions, not least ICANN, which have pronounced network governance characteristics. ICANN's MoU, for example, mandates 'bottom up' coordination; a significant number of national registries for the DNS are non-profit distributing; ICANN retains a so-called 'at large' system of representation and consultation to 'promote structured involvement and informed participation of the global individual Internet user community in ICANN' (from ICANN.org./framework); and so on.[13] Whether honoured in breach or observance, there is ample institutional testimony to the continuing presence of the distinctive, embedded, civil society involvement characteristic of the early days of the Internet in Internet governance. These legacies distinguish Internet governance from the governance of comparable systems such as circuit switched telecommunications.

Lyndall Shope-Mafole (a South African member of the WGIG)[14] eloquently put forward (WGIG plenary session 18 April 2005) the case for the superior legitimacy of states vis-à-vis business and civil society in c and of formal international governance rather than the *ad hoc* Internet status quo. She said:

> The legitimacy of things is important…in South Africa, we had structures before our democracy, we had structures that built roads, that built schools, that, you know – we had a constitution, et cetera, et cetera. But it was not legitimate. And I think this is the issue that we are addressing now…When we say the Internet community, what percentage of the population are we talking about and how representative is this Internet community?… the focus and the main reason for the establishment of this group and for asking the Secretary-General of the UN to establish this group is because the issue is not technical. I think the issue is political.

Here, Shope-Mafole implicitly equates the established order of Internet governance of US preponderance, (ICANN controlling the root zone file, much Internet traffic routed via the US and carried on US-owned infrastructures, etc.) with apartheid. She points to the exclusion of the Internet 'have nots' from decision making which, for her, includes only members of the 'Internet community' – that is the mix of business and civil society organizations operating principally through market and network governance (albeit under the 'shadow of hierarchy [Scharpf 1994] projected by the US Government). For Shope-Mafole, network governance of this kind is illegitimate. Legitimacy lies exclusively with the international state system embodied in the UN at the apex of hierarchical systems of governance rather than with other institutions or modes of governance (notably networks or markets). The principle of legitimacy to which she appeals is 'input' legitimacy – that is with legitimacy deriving from the way in which bodies charged with governance are constituted and residing particularly in their accountability to those whom they represent.

There is much to be said for Shope-Mafole's argument: markets for communication goods and services are often highly imperfect (and the ability of the world's population to enter such markets is highly unevenly distributed – see, for example, UNPEPA 2003)[15] and the representativeness and accountability of civil society participants in the WSIS/WGIG (among whom I was numbered) is highly uncertain. Interestingly, she does not refer to the role of business in UN trilateralism as controversial. This may be because business' role in the ITU (the organizer of the WSIS/WGIG)[16] is long established.[17] However, whilst correctly identifying the uncertain democratic accountability of civil society, Shope-Mafole does not acknowledge the uncertain 'input' (democratic) legitimacy of some governments. Moreover, the UN system provides an inherently unequal system of representation. Its system of parity between states makes equivalent highly unequal entities, giving rise to some striking anomalies in representation. Moreover, Shope-Mafole's argument denies validity to forms of legitimacy other than that inhering in the governments accorded recognition as UN Member States.

The problems of representativeness and accountability to which Shope-Mafole pointed are undoubtedly significant but they are perhaps more wide ranging than she acknowledged. If 'output' as well as 'input' legitimacy is considered, that is legitimacy deriving from the effectiveness of performance in securing public interest objectives, then non-state entities may well have as strong claims to legitimacy as do (some) states. A pragmatic criterion of expert competence certainly opens the door to the legitimate participation of (some) business and civil society entities and individuals. And if 'output' criteria of adherence to human rights are adduced, then states which deny their citizens access to information and to the ability to communicate freely (see UNPEPA's 2003 audit of information access for some cases in point) may be thought to have no necessarily superior claims to legitimacy than either (or both) civil society or business.

The uncertain and contested legitimacy of states, business and civil society, whereby entities in each category enjoy different levels and combinations of input (democratic representativeness and/or rights friendliness) and output (pragmatic, operational) legitimacy, contribute to the clearly evident difficulties arising from established arrangements. Whilst the formal UN system of representation by state Government is open to criticism, for the inequality of representation it affords to citizens of states of dissimilar populations and the lack of linkage between states' ability to participate in global governance and the degree to which they effectively accord rights to their citizens, it is a systematic and transparent system of representation. In this respect, its input legitimacy, though flawed, is superior to that of business and civil society. Yet the input criterion of 'rights friendliness' and 'output' criteria of competence and performance suggest that the legitimacy claims of either or both of business and civil society are not to be dismissed summarily.

In terms of 'output' legitimacy, the WGIG/WSIS saw some degree of scepticism voiced about the pragmatic competence of both the ITU and ICANN (the main rival contenders and candidates for the task of 'ruling the root') it is not necessary to take a position for or against ICANN or the ITU to see the relevance of such considerations. Legitimacy depends on more than formal political, 'input', criteria. Whilst many states do enjoy real claims to input legitimacy, on grounds both of their democratic systems of representative government and their rights friendliness, some do not. And there is room for legitimate doubt about both the extent to which all activities requiring governance should be brought under a state-based hierarchical regime, of however unimpeachable a legitimacy, and the extent to which input legitimacy 'trumps' output legitimacy. It would be a poor trade-off to substitute a poorly-working regime for one which works adequately.

Outcomes

The two main outcomes of the WSIS/WGIG, the so-called 'Chateau de Bossey' (WGIG 2004) document from the WGIG and the 'Tunis Agenda' of the WSIS (WSIS 2005a), reflected the stalemate between proponents of the status quo and those who advocated bringing Internet governance (or at least control of the DNS) under the aegis of the ITU.

The Chateau de Bossey document put forward four possible alternative courses of action for consideration at the Tunis WSIS. The main outcome of the WSIS, the 'Tunis agenda for the information society' (WSIS 2005a), which was informed by the Chateau de Bossey document, was dominated by Internet governance issues (of its 122 clauses 53 concerned Internet governance) and called on (Clause 72) the UN Secretary-General to convene 'in an open and inclusive process, to convene, by the second quarter of 2006, a meeting of the new forum for multi-stakeholder policy dialogue—called the *Internet Governance Forum* (IGF)'. The IGF would implement part, but only part, of the fourth option identified in the Chateau de Bossey document.

The call for a forum in the Tunis Agenda may be seen as advancing the cause of proponents of change, and thus erosion of ICANN's hegemony, by institutionalizing a new international body organized under UN auspices. But the IGF was explicitly defined as (at Clause 77) having no effective power: it 'would not replace existing arrangements, mechanisms, institutions or organizations, but would involve them and take advantage of their expertise. It would be constituted as a neutral, non-duplicative and non-binding process. It would have no involvement in day-to-day or technical operations of the Internet'.

However, the Tunis Agenda did assert firmly (at Clause 35a) that: 'Policy authority for Internet-related public policy issues is the sovereign right of States. They have rights and responsibilities for international Internet-related public policy issues'. It thus, rhetorically at least, de-legitimized the ICANN-based status quo. But the Tunis Agenda also recognized the role of civil society (Clause 35c) stating: 'Civil society has also played an important role on Internet matters, especially at community level, and should continue to play such a role'. The Tunis Agenda thus left open and uncertain the future role and status in deliberation and decision making of both ICANN (and other bodies in the ICANN orbit such as the Internet Society) and civil society (at best the academics and representatives of grass roots organizations and, at worst, the front organizations which spoke ventriloquistically for government and business interests).

The three parties to trilateralism, states, business and civil society, reflected differently on the outcomes of the WSIS/WGIG process. Some (but not all) important state actors were dissatisfied. China, for example, continued to assert the importance of hierarchical governance and rested its case, for 'an intergovernmental organization under the UN framework should be entrusted to make Internet resources management policies (*sic*) and authorize concrete policy implementation to various operation bodies'[18] on input legitimacy grounds stating 'We believe that the policy-making should not surpass international law and national sovereignty, as pointed out in article 49 of the Declaration of Principles' (WSIS 2003).

Civil Society, too, was less than completely satisfied but rejected the claims of proponents of stronger hierarchical governance:

> Civil Society is pleased with the decision to create an Internet Governance Forum (IGF), which it has advocated for since 2003. We also are pleased that the IGF will have sufficient scope to deal with the issues we believe must be addressed, most notably the conformity of existing arrangements with the Geneva Principles, and other cross-cutting or multidimensional issues that cannot be optimally dealt with within current arrangements. However, we reiterate our concerns that the Forum must not be anchored in any existing specialized international organization. (Civil society @ WSIS 2005: 6)

Instead, civil society affirmed the importance of 'output' legitimacy: 'Some of our greatest concerns involve what we consider to be insufficient attention or inadequate recommendations concerning people-centred issues such as the degree of attention paid to human rights and freedom of expression' (Civil Society @ WSIS 2005: 3) and network governance: 'it is very unfortunate that the Tunis Agenda suggests that governments are only willing to share this role and responsibility among themselves, in cooperation with international organisations. Civil Society remains strongly of the view that the formulation of appropriate and legitimate public policies pertaining to Internet governance requires the full and meaningful involvement of nongovernmental stakeholders' (Civil Society @ WSIS 2005: 6).

Business too affirmed the importance of network governance: 'Business sees great merit in the creation of a truly international, truly inclusive multi-stakeholder forum in which the myriad issues surrounding the Internet can be discussed', and 'the continued commitment to the private-sector led technical management of the Internet' (Business at WSIS Press Release 16 November 2005 – see note 12).

Nonetheless, in spite of its honorific mentions of civil society (e.g. in Clause 35c) the Tunis Agenda's support for a model of global coordination, discussion and decision based on state sovereignty contrasts strongly with Cardoso's powerful advocacy of civil society's interest in, and ability to contribute to, deliberation and decision on global public issues. In that respect it is the perspective advanced by China and its allies which most strongly informed the chief rhetorical outcome of the World Summit on the Information Society, the UN's first summit on communications. In terms of practical changes to Internet governance, to management of the DNS and general coordination of the large number of interdependent organizations which combine to make the global Internet function, the WSIS/WGIG changed little.

Notes

1. Also at : http://www.itu.int/osg/spu/forum/intgov04/workshop-internet-governance-chairmans-report.pdf accessed on 28.2.2006.
2. The 40 member WGIG was constituted on 12.11.2004 with a strong civil society element (see membership of WGIG at http://www.wgig.org/members.html accessed on 2.2.2006).
3. Notably, Internet governance, the 'political chapeau'/Tunis Commitment (a declaration on development of a pervasive global information society) and Information and Communication Technology for Development (ICT4D).
4. The others are failure to achieve the UN's Millennium Development Goals, the danger that trade regulation may worsen global inequality and global warming.
5. Verbatim quotations from the webstream transcript corrected by reference to the author's contemporaneous notes and to eliminate obvious errors. Webstream available at http://www.wgig.org/meeting-april.html.
6. The WSIS Executive Secretariat estimated that 175 states were represented, 481 NGOs and 98 business entities (see http://www.itu.int/wsis/geneva/newsroom/index.html accessed on 20.3.2006).
7. Referring to WSIS Declaration of Principles at: http://www.itu.int/dms_pub/itu-s/md/03/wsis/doc/S03-WSIS-DOC-0004!!MSW-E.doc accessed on 1.2.2006).
8. Bertola is also a member of ICANN's interim at large advisory committee.
9. Manuel Castells is a leading proponent of the view that network governance is both becoming normative in modern societies and that electronic communications networks are closely associated with this change (see Castells 1996).
10. The loose association between IETF, IANA and ICANN is described by ISOC as: 'Collectively, these organizations tile, or span the public policy, operations and management space' (ISOC 2004: 8).
11. Using the WGIG documentation I received I categorized accredited civil society organizations as follows:

Accredited civil society organizations	*Number*
Country with most accredited CS organizations – France	13
Tunisia	7
LDC	46
Anglophone	25
Francophone	43
Total Accredited Civil Society Organizations	94

This classification is of indicative value only because of definitional uncertainties. For example, some organizations with developed world e-mail addresses have postal addresses in less-developed countries, some organizations domiciled in the developed world have refugee and/or less-developed country orientation; countries such as India and Iran, which I categorized as less-developed countries, could plausibly be considered not to be less-developed countries (if by that we mean a country characterized by minimal industrialization, low technological development, low per capita income, and a high population growth rate). Canadian, Belgian and Swiss organizations with addresses in predominantly French-speaking areas were counted as Francophone, Arab countries with membership of La Francophonie (For an up to date list of members of La francophonie see http://www.francophonie.org/oif/membres.cfm accessed on 22.6.2009) were counted as Francophone. India, Nigeria and Pakistan were counted as Anglophone.

12. http://businessatwsis.net/newmainpages/media/press/news.php?news_id=22 accessed on 14.3.2006. This website is no longer available.
13. True, ICANN's practice has been persuasively criticized for honouring these values more in breach than observance. Verhulst conveniently represents this critique: 'The central plank of this criticism is that ICANN's organisational structures and activities do not comply with the ethos of participatory and democratic governance' (Verhulst 2001: 1) see also Mueller 2002.
14. Latterly Director-General of the South African Government's Department of Communications and formerly Chairperson of the Presidential National Commission on Information Society and Development.
15. UNPEPA study tabulates a host of indices by UN Member State to produce an e-Gov index. The indices include PCs, televisions and telephones per 100, Internet hosts per 1000 and an information access index (derived from indices developed by Transparency International and Freedom House International). The scores range from the highest of 3.11 (US) to the lowest of 0.46 (Uganda). Connectivity (fixed telephone lines) ranges from 0.13 telephone lines per 100 people in Chad to 75.97 in Luxembourg. The information access index ranges from .999 (USA + 18 other countries) to 0.001 (Saudi Arabia, Cuba, Turkmenistan) see (UNPEPA 2003: 30–33).
16. Shope-Mafole has also been strongly associated with the ITU serving as vice-chair of the 1998/99 Session of the Council of the ITU and as chair of the 1999/2000 Session of Council of the ITU and the Working Group on ITU Reform.
17. The ITU describes itself as 'unique among international organisations in that it was founded on the principle of co-operation between governments and the private sector'(at http://www.itu.int/aboutitu/overview/role-work.html accessed on 22.6.2009) and private sector organizations constitute a majority of the ITU's members (http://www.itu.int/net/about/index.aspx accessed on 22.6.2009).
18. Cited from http://www.wgig.org/April-scriptmorning.html.

Chapter 10

E-governance and the Governance of the Global Internet

Internet governance is the development and application by Governments, the private sector and civil society, in their respective roles, of shared principles, norms, rules, decision-making procedures, and programmes that shape the evolution and use of the Internet. (WGIG 2005: 4)

All major communications network innovations have given rise to new enterprises, transformed economic, social and political structures, crossed borders, created international disputes, and perhaps most important, eventually led to the development of new coordination or governance frameworks. (ITU 2004: 14)

Introduction

Much recent attention has increasingly been given to e-governance, defined by UNESCO as the 'exercise of political, economic and administrative authority' via an 'electronic medium' (UNESCO 2005), and embraced by Government bodies around the world. Dunleavy, Margetts, Bastow and Tinkler (2006: 2), for example, propose that 'digital-era governance' (DEG) represents a new norm in governance practice and theory and one which fuzzily (they write 'not in any direct technologically determined way') links 'a wide range of cognitive, behavioural, organizational, political and cultural changes' to 'information systems'. Appointment of the UK Government's e-Envoy in 1999 was but one enactment of such norms: the e-Envoy was to improve 'delivery of public services' and achieve 'long term cost savings by joining-up online government services around the needs of customers. The e-Envoy is responsible for ensuring that all government services are available electronically' (e-Envoy 2003).[1]

DEG/e-governance is often characterized as part of a bigger shift in the form of social coordination from hierarchical (command and control) and/or market (through prices) to network governance based on trust, cooperation, equality and disinterestedness (see, among others, Barabasi 2002; Barry 2001; Thompson 2003); a shift linked to the growing pervasiveness of electronic communication and connectivity (Castells 1996, Taylor 2001) and portending a new type of society – network society (Castells 1996 and 2004a).

However, neither the literature of e-governance/DEG nor contemporary social science's epochal accounts of change have given much attention to the governance of the electronic communication infrastructure which itself underpins the network society and e-governance/

DEG – that is to the Internet. This gap is surprising given the vital role such accounts attribute to the Internet,[2] a significant scholarly literature on Internet governance (see, among others, Drake 2005, Maclean 2004, Mueller 2002) and the contemporary political salience of Internet governance, (notably at the UN World Summit on the Information Society, WSIS, of 2003–5). Internet governance both shapes e-governance (because the Internet is the medium of e-governance) and provides a case study for evaluation of currently salient social scientific accounts of governance. A deservedly well-known study, *Netheads v Bellheads* (Denton 1999), casts light on these issues by contrasting distinct mentalities and practices in the governance of electronic media.

Netheads v Bellheads

Netheads v Bellheads persuasively compared the architectures, mentalities and material interests associated with, on one hand, the classic PSTN (public switched telephone network), circuit switched voice telephony system, characterized by Denton as 'Bellhead' (referring to the Bell telephone systems which long provided service to most North Americans) and, on the other hand, the packet switched, Internet-like, 'Nethead' system, latterly supplanting circuit switched systems. 'Bellhead' systems are controlled centrally enabling operators to define services, set prices and to determine standards. Whereas packet switched, Internet-like, systems are more, open permitting third parties to provide services 'at the edge of the network, without the permission, control or involvement of the network owner' (Denton 1999: 3).

The differences between 'Bellhead' and 'Nethead' networks chime with social scientists' accounts of transition from hierarchical to networked social coordination. In distinguishing between network and hierarchy I draw on Thompson's (2003) distinction between hierarchical, market or network governance or coordination. In hierarchies governance is by 'command and control', in markets by prices (through which demand and supply are balanced) and in networks through equalitarian collaboration (Thompson 2003: 112). The agents who enact these different systems of governance are, in hierarchies, a specialized body of legitimized governors (politicians, officials and managers), in markets, suppliers and consumers, and in networks, civil society.

Although it is an oversimplification to conceive of the Internet as a single 'thing' (see Collins 2006), with a single locus of control and a single form of governance, many aspects of contemporary Internet coordination continue to reflect this collaborative, network, legacy. The Internet is indeed generally permissive at the periphery and with weak central control and developed through networked informal, cooperative, working arrangements. But, in one important respect, the Internet is *more* centralized than the global PSTN. In both systems, messages have to be routed from and to particular addresses – whether between two telephones, each with a unique number, or two Internet users, each with a unique IP address.[3] But, PSTN circuit switched addressing systems are not subject to control at a single point whereas the Domain Name System (DNS), which matches Internet names and addresses, depends on a single authoritative root zone file (RZF), control of which happens, for historical reasons, to be in the US. This difference means, as an official of the International Telecommunication Union (ITU) stated (interview with author 18 April 2005), 'no-one can turn off Switzerland's 'phones' whereas, in theory at least, whoever controls the RZF can 'turn off' the Internet in Switzerland (or elsewhere). Crawford has described the Internet Corporation for Assigned Names and Numbers (ICANN), the organization controlling the RZF and administering the DNS,[4] as controlling 'a single lever by which identity on the Internet can be turned on or off. ICANN has the power to exercise the online equivalent of force' (Crawford 2004: 703).

ICANN

ICANN was set up as a not-for-profit corporation following the US Government's celebrated 'Green Paper' (NTIA 1998) in which the U.S. government resolved to 'end its role in the Internet number and name address systems' and establish a new regime characterized by 'private, bottom up co-ordination' (NTIA 1998: np) which vested control of the DNS in ICANN. ICANN, which in the words of one of its most articulate critics, 'rules the root' (Mueller 2002), thus has become the focus of intense international controversy.[5] By virtue of its control of the RZF, ICANN can determine which 'top level domains' (TLDs),[6] if any, are added to the 'root' and, in theory (though in practice such a power may be very difficult to exercise), can remove addresses from the 'root'.

ICANN is subject to criticism for its putative operational failures: notably for its stewardship of gatekeeper power over TLDs which, for some critics, creates rather than mitigates scarcity (see, among others, Komaitis and Galloway 2005); for its perceived inefficiency (Marlin-Bennett 2001; Mueller 1999 and 2002; Weinberg 2000); for its control over the root zone file and power to delegate control of country codes (ccTLD) to particular registries (which are usually, but not invariably, authorized by the government of the country concerned);[7] and for its own governance procedures which do not, in critics' eyes, sufficiently empower either national governments or Internet users, as Verhulst argues: 'The central plank of this criticism is that ICANN's organisational structures and activities do not comply with the ethos of participatory and democratic governance' (Verhulst 2001: 1; see also Mueller 2002).

ICANN's governance has come under attack both from representatives of Internet users,[8] sometimes with uncertain links to the broad constituency whom they claim to represent, who customarily advocate higher levels of ICANN accountability to, and control by, user representatives, and also from some states[9] (and allied 'Bellheads') in international fora (notably the WSIS) who advocate control of the DNS by an international treaty body rather than by ICANN and its Government Advisory Committee (GAC), which currently constitutes the sole formal institutional means through which governments can represent their concerns to ICANN.

The first, user, group of critics is a loose alliance including those who refer back to the informal, network governance, origins of the Internet and the era of John Perry Barlow's Declaration of the Independence of Cyberspace (Barlow 1996) and the Internet Engineering Task Force's (IETF) 'Tao' of 'rough consensus and running code' (IETF nd); critics of ICANN's, putatively, anti-competitive use of its monopoly power; and those who hunger for the strong representation of user representatives in ICANN governance envisaged in the NTIA Green Paper. The NTIA proposed a fifteen-member Board, consisting of three representatives of regional registries, two designated by the Internet Architecture Board (IAB), two representing domain name registries and domain name registrars, seven members representing 'at large' Internet users, and the ICANN CEO *ex officio*. In contrast, the current ICANN Board has reduced user representation.[10]

The second set of critics has argued, straightforwardly, that only duly-constituted international institutions could legitimately determine Internet policy. ICANN's 'Government Advisory Committee'[11] is perceived, as its name may suggest, to dilute unacceptably legitimate state sovereignty. For example, China, at the Geneva Working Group on Internet Governance (WGIG) of 18 April 2005, stated[12] that:

> The policy authority for Internet-related public policy issues is the sovereign right of states. They have rights and responsibilities for international Internet-related public policy issues.

ICANN's legitimacy was thus found wanting when compared to that 'Bellhead' hierarchical treaty-based governance[13] through an international body such as the International Telecommunications Union.

In attempting to reconcile the imperatives of efficiency, legitimacy and representativeness, ICANN's governance has undergone many changes. Rony and Rony (2002) observed that its Bylaws changed 11 times between 1998 and 2002. In 2002, the-then President of ICANN (March 2001 to March 2003), Stuart Lynn, argued that ICANN's governance and accountability structures were inherently unsatisfactory. He stated:

> ICANN is still not fully organized, and it is certainly not yet capable of shouldering the entire responsibility of global DNS management and coordination. ICANN has also not shown that it can be effective, nimble, and quick to react to problems. ICANN is overburdened with process, and at the same time underfunded and understaffed. For these and other more fundamental reasons, ICANN in its current form has not become the effective steward of the global Internet's naming and address allocation systems as conceived by its founders…the original concept of a purely private sector body, based on consensus and consent, has been shown to be impractical. (Lynn 2002: np)

Lynn warned against displacing network by hierarchical governance and explicitly cautioned against 'Bellhead' involvement in DNS governance:[14]

> I do not believe that there are any better alternatives than a reformed ICANN. If the ICANN experiment of private-sector self-management cannot work, the default alternative will certainly be some form of multinational governmental organization. In my view, this remains an unattractive option, for all the same reasons that were so forcefully advanced three years ago. (Lynn 2002: np)

Lynn believed ICANN's governance was flawed because a fuzzily-defined community of Internet users had too much representation and governments had too little. He proposed that five Board members be chosen by national governments, to strengthen the authority of ICANN insiders by reserving five Board places for *ex officio* nominees (namely the President of ICANN and a representative from each three new Policy Councils and a Technical Advisory Committee), and to replace the direct election of users by and from the 'at-large' constituency by a Nominating Committee's selection of the remaining five Board members. ICANN's current Bylaws (of 28 February 2006) vest authority in a fifteen-person Board of whom eight are selected by the ICANN Nominating Committee and two by each of the Address Supporting Organization, the Country-Code Names Supporting Organization, the Generic Names Supporting Organization with the ICANN President serving *ex officio.* Lynn's proposal for direct government representation was not adopted[15] though his proposal to route representation of users through a Nominating Committee was.

ICANN's formal governance arrangements remain complex, circular and open to criticism. Some members (albeit non-voting) of the Nominating Committee are appointed by the ICANN Board of Directors and others (voting) by the bodies (notably the Address Supporting Organization, the Country-Code Names Supporting Organization and the Generic Names Supporting Organization) entitled to nominate Board members directly. The Bylaws do not make clear how members of these committees come to hold office (though they do specify from where they are to be drawn).[16] The body representing the residuum or the Internet community (to which ICANN is formally accountable, albeit only through 'mechanisms that enhance ICANN's effectiveness'), the At-Large Advisory Committee (ALAC), rather than directly appointing Board members, appoints five voting delegates to the Nominating Committee, which has seventeen voting and up to six non-voting members, (and additionally one non-voting liaison member to the ICANN Board) which then selects eight Board members. However, five members of the ALAC are themselves appointed by the Nominating Committee (see ICANN Bylaws of 28.2.2006 Article XI, Section 2.4.b and e).

Network governance failure?

The Bylaws enjoin ICANN boards and committees to ensure diversity and balanced representation among office holders – paying attention to geography, competencies, range of stakeholders, etc. Provisions are also made for reconsideration of Board decisions, for an Ombudsman and for the conduct of business with appropriate openness and transparency.

But the legitimacy of the designated bodies is uncertainly grounded in established democratic principles of representation and the power distributed to different stakeholder groups remains contested. However, it is clear that the power and influence of Internet users, vis-à-vis providers, has diminished between the first and latest iteration of ICANN's bylaws – not least because of the intractable difficulties of putting bounds around the constituency to whom ICANN identifies itself as responsible, the 'Internet community' (ICANN Bylaws of 28 February 2006 Article I, Section 2.10).

Thus ICANN has yet to devise durably legitimate governance structures. The laudable intention to create an inclusive system, characterized by significant representation for the Internet community of users and open and participatory procedures, neither sufficiently represented national stakeholders nor found workable and legitimate means of representing the 'Internet community'. Successive iterations of ICANN's 'constitution' may have improved ICANN's administrative functionality and provided a solid basis for representation of key 'producer' interests associated with the DNS, but they have neither built legitimacy with ICANN's two main bodies of critics nor established clear lines of accountability. ICANN governance reflects both positive and negative aspects of network governance: attempts to balance representation of different stakeholder interests in ICANN's governance structures, ICANN's practice of publishing draft proposals and inviting public consultation and deliberation were, and are, positive characteristics of network governance and exemplify its normative attributes of trust and solidarity. However, other aspects of ICANN's governance structure, though similarly characteristic of network governance, such as its uncertain relationship to clearly defined stakeholder groups and its absence of effective mechanisms of representation and accountability when large groups of stakeholders are involved, are less positive.

ICANN's difficulties testify both to the general difficulties posed by global infrastructures, where the relevant 'communities of fate' (Held 2004: 20) are diffuse and dispersed, and to the type of failure to which network governance regimes seem to be prone. Each type of governance defined by Thompson's (2003), hierarchical, market and network, seems to be prone to a distinctive form of governance failure. Governance failure in hierarchical (e.g. ossification, elite capture) and market (e.g. exclusion of the poor, abuse of significant market power, negative externalities) systems of governance is widely recognized (see Moran 2003). But network governance failure has received less attention. Network governance failure may take the form of either domination of governance by the interests and viewpoints of those networked, (thus excluding other stakeholders) – a failure of representation, or of a failure to bind sufficiently together many stakeholder interests and viewpoints so making consensus, and thus decisions and actions, difficult to achieve – a failure of effectiveness. ICANN is, in the eyes of its two main groups of critics, subject to both types of failure.

Failure of one type of governance regime tends to lead to the regime in question being replaced by a different type of regime. For example, failure of hierarchy has led to adoption of market governance (liberalization and privatization); failure of markets to the adoption of hierarchy (regulation and state control); network failure to liberalization and/or an adoption of hierarchy. The history of Internet governance, that is governance of the DNS, seems to be a history of network governance failure (the informal early arrangements of 'rough consensus and running code' failing both to scale, as the Internet grew, and to represent adequately all stakeholders) followed by a different form of network governance in ICANN supplemented by an, as yet immature, mix of market and hierarchical governance.

It may seem incongruous to refer to Internet governance failure for, clearly, the Internet is a striking success story: it functions well, has successfully been scaled up from a geeky connection between a few US research centres to an indispensable global infrastructure, the price of communication has fallen and the accessibility of information increased dramatically. But, just as market failure in voice telephony does not mean the phones all stop working, so network governance failure does not mean the Internet goes dark. Indeed it is the very effectiveness of the Internet which, in some eyes, constitutes the greatest governance challenge. For governance is not solely a question of what sort of governance ('Nethead' or 'Bellhead', hierarchy, market or network) but also the balance between different governance regimes and the relationship of governance institutions to other centres of power and to stakeholder interests. These questions were central issues at the World Summit on the Information Society (WSIS).

Global governance and the WSIS

The United Nations convened the WSIS[17] in 2003–5 in an attempt, among other goals, to resolve the increasingly intensely contested issue of Internet governance. Both groups of ICANN's critics participated in the WSIS, and its sub-group the Working Group on Internet Governance (WGIG), where ICANN's role in governing the DNS came under continuous critical interrogation. For user representatives, ICANN's governance was too hierarchical and insufficiently represented civil society/user interests; for numerous governments, ICANN governance was insufficiently hierarchical and gave too much representation to non-governmental actors such as civil society.

WSIS was the first UN Summit on Communications[18] and provided an effective platform for a 'Bellhead' critique of 'Nethead' governance. ICANN's control of indispensable elements of the Internet, perceived to be tantamount to US Government control, was contrasted to the governance of international posts and telecommunications by the Universal Postal Union (UPU) and the ITU but the issues resonated far beyond the bounded, and somewhat arcane, issue of control and management of the DNS. The WSIS focused on three themes:

- Internet governance
- The so-called 'political chapeau'/Tunis Commitment – a political declaration on development of a pervasive global information society linking a variety of national initiatives[19]
- ICT (Information and Communication Technology) for Development (ICT4D).

Internet governance proved to be the least tractable of these issues and these difficulties led the UN Secretary-General to establish a specialist Working Group on Internet Governance (WGIG), reporting directly to him, in the hope of securing progress which had otherwise proved elusive – these hopes received scant fulfilment (see Collins 2007a and 2007b). Although the tangible outcomes of discussions in the WSIS/WGIG were hardly commensurate with the resources and efforts invested in them, they provided a kind of laboratory, or theatre, in which proponents of rival governance claims, for a network or a hierarchical principle, for ad hoc or formalized, treaty-based, international regimes, contested the basis of Internet governance.

Discussions at the Summit (and Working Group) were highly charged, for what was at stake was not just the principles and practice of management and governance of a single (albeit important) global communication infrastructure but also the Internet's impact on the PSTN, its governing institutions and the hierarchical principles on which PSTN governance has been based. There were obviously institutional interests at stake, not least that of the ITU[20] itself. Its Secretary-General, Utsumi Yoshio, staked its claim to the DNS stating that the ITU 'is now prepared to take on the coordination and management of critical Internet resources' (Yoshio 2006: 5). But the time honoured 'Bellhead' regimes of national government/telephone company dominance were also in question.

For a hundred years or so, telephony services characteristically have been provided by national monopolies – either by privately-owned and publicly-regulated shareholder companies or by state-owned corporations. Two such national companies interconnected to provide international communication, handing on traffic to each other[21] and sharing revenues under ITU norms. These arrangements have broken down. As Huston[22] claimed: 'The Internet has accelerated the pace of deregulation of the industry to an extent never thought possible…billions of dollars of telephony revenues will be diverted into the Internet market' (Huston 2002: 3). Instead of costs and revenues being divided between calling partners, as in the old telephony regime which transferred significant sums from the developed 'north' to the less-developed 'south', services increasingly are carried on dedicated leased circuits which are customarily provided by global carriers based in the north (and predominantly in the US) who retain charges.

Not only has the new regime eroded state sovereignty (in respect of the ability to set prices, control market entry and collectively make rules) but telephony can no longer provide a key source of public finance. In many developing countries, high prices for telecommunications services were, in part, paid by foreign callers, and, for countries which were unable to run efficient revenue collection services, telecommunication revenues acted, at best, as a proxy for taxation (and at worst, a source of funds for politically-appointed rent-seekers). Of course, the new 'Nethead' regime has had profoundly beneficial consequences: new services such as e-mail and web browsing are available; the price of a voice call carried over an IP network has fallen;[23] IP networks make advanced data and other services more widely available; and prices to users generally have fallen significantly. But though some benefit, others have undoubtedly lost and, crucially, the terms on which some win and others lose characteristically are set by powerful global actors rather than by, for better or worse, domestic political authorities.

What fills the gap left by the decline of 'Bellhead' institutions, such as the ITU and national telecommunication regimes, of hierarchical governance? Essentially, a series of ad hoc institutions and practices difficult to describe exhaustively and which could, in any case, only be described at tedious length. ICANN's importance inheres not only in its authority over the DNS and RZF but in its unique status as a high-profile institution of global Internet governance. In consequence, ICANN has acted as a lightning rod, through which a multitude of discontents arising from the interconnected changes, from hierarchy to networks, from 'Bellhead' to 'Nethead' networks, from national sovereignty and orderly treaty-based decision-making to global institutions and ad hoc governance, have been discharged.

Civil society

The WSIS was the first UN Summit where civil society was an official participant and it, and the WGIG in particular, drew in substantial civil society participation, significantly augmenting its competencies. Civil society's presence embodied a realization of the UN's commitment to broadening participation in its activities, and in some sense a formal opening to the network governance which it had been enjoined formally to embrace (see UN 2002 and 2004a). The WSIS and WGIG provided opportunities for civil society critics of ICANN, smarting from their reduced place in ICANN governance, to claim a bigger role in Internet governance. But civil society's assertions were matched by significant criticism from numbers of participating Member States who saw civil society's involvement as no less offensive a usurpation of the legitimate powers of governments than they perceived ICANN's administration of the DNS to be.[24] Their objections illuminated some aspects of network governance failure – notably the lack of clear criteria of inclusion within and exclusion from the governance community in question.

Just as the principles underpinning representation on ICANN's Board are uncertain so were the principles of composition of the Working Group on Internet Governance. Some participants of the WGIG clearly represented states, some business and some civil society and some could plausibly seen as representing more than one constituency. The basis of selection and appointment was opaque (a member of a western national delegation, interviewed by the author on 15 February 2005, stated that the few national representatives on the WGIG were 'appointed rather randomly'). Where procedures were transparent as, commendably, they were for the civil society Internet Governance Caucus, it is clear that few participated in selection of civil society members of the WGIG (Hofmann 2004: 2).[25] And some civil society participants, myself included, were essentially self-appointed (see Collins 2007b).

Outcome

The formal outcomes of the WSIS/WGIG are the so-called 'Chateau de Bossey' (WGIG 2005) statement of the WGIG and the 'Tunis Agenda' of the WSIS (WSIS 2005b). These documents reflect a stalemate between 'Nethead' proponents of the status quo and 'Bellheads' advocating bringing Internet governance (or at least control of the DNS) under the ITU. The Chateau de Bossey document rather lamely stated that the 'WGIG identified a vacuum within the context of existing structures, since there is no global multi-stakeholder forum to address Internet-related public policy issues. It came to the conclusion that there would be merit in creating such a space for dialogue among all stakeholders' (WGIG 2005: 10). However, the WGIG could not agree on how the vacuum should be filled and put forward four governance options to the WSIS.

Not surprisingly, the Tunis WSIS was hardly more successful than the WGIG in deciding between the alternatives identified by the WGIG but identified a way forward by calling for the UN Secretary-General to convene 'in an open and inclusive process, to convene, by the second quarter of 2006, a meeting of the new forum for multi-stakeholder policy dialogue – called the *Internet Governance Forum* (IGF)' (WSIS 2005a: Clause 72) though the IGF was explicitly defined as having no effective power: 'It would be constituted as a neutral, non-duplicative and non-binding process. It would have no involvement in day-to-day or technical operations of the Internet' (WSIS 2005a: Clause 77).

The first meeting of the IGF took place in October/November 2006; in his summing up Nitin Desai, the IGF Chair, stated: 'The essential point to realize is that this is a multistakeholder forum. It is an open-door forum. It's not a forum with a fixed membership. It is open to anybody in the stakeholder groups who has an interest and a basic bona fide competence in this area to come and enter and join the meeting. It's in that sense more like an open meeting rather than a fixed membership group. In that sense, it's not possible to speak of anything as being a product of this meeting. So it would be misleading to say that there is any such thing as an agreed conclusion or a product of this meeting in the strict sense of the term, because there is no defined meeting. The meeting is the people who are in the room' (ICANN 2006a).

Conclusion

Desai's account of the meeting can, charitably, be described as a testimony to the UN's new commitment to networked governance, to open and inclusive forms of deliberation and to creation of a global forum for the discussion, if not the formulation and implementation, of Internet governance policies. But the IGF has done nothing to resolve either the structural problems posed by network governance failure (notably delineation of clear stakeholder constituencies and the establishment of durable and legitimate mechanisms of representation and accountability) or to satisfy the 'Bellhead' critique of ICANN's role and status. The IGF does not take forward the Tunis Agenda's firm assertion that 'Policy authority for Internet-related public policy issues is the sovereign right of States' (WSIS 2005a: Clause 35a) but has been welcomed by ICANN as helping to fill the vacuum left by the absence of a global forum for Internet policy – an absence which often led to demands being projected onto ICANN because there was nowhere else to project them.

In 2002, Stuart Lynn (Lynn 2002) had stated that:

> The core ICANN mission includes no mandate to innovate new institutions of global democracy, nor to achieve mathematically equal representation of all affected individuals and organizations, nor to regulate content, nor to solve the problems of the digital divide, nor to embody some idealized (and never-before-realized) model of process or procedure.

Expectations for fulfilment of these objectives had been lodged with ICANN – there was nowhere else to lay them to rest. Now, perhaps, the IGF will fill that vacuum.

It is a truism to observe that there are more and more of what David Held has called global communities of fate (Held 2004: 20) and that these communities lack appropriate instruments and regimes of governance. Into the governance vacuum, as global relationships are created anew or supplant what were hitherto national relationships, step various ad hoc arrangements. The global Internet and ICANN represent one such ad hoc regime, others include the Basel Accords (Basel I and Basel II) governing banks' management of credit and the rules and operating procedures for financial accounting and audit of the International Federation of Accountants (see also Held and McGrew 2000). Seen thus, ICANN, and the issues of Internet governance considered at WSIS and in WGIG, are but one more example of a widespread characteristic of contemporary globalization: that is, of global relationships and practices outrunning the capacity of formally constituted political institutions to govern global interdependencies. Moreover, ICANN and the halting development of a durable regime of global Internet governance with which it is inextricably associated, provides an illuminating case study of network governance in action.

Notes

1. In 2004 the e-envoy was replaced by the Office for e-government.
2. See ITU data at http://www.itu.int/ITU-D/icteye/Indicators/Indicators.aspx# accessed on 19.12.2006 for Internet statistics.
3. An IP address is the 10 figure string, e.g. 128.240.29.3 (University of Newcastle UK) which identifies an Internet site. Because IP addresses are hard to remember they have usually been given a more easily memorable name, such as www.newcastle.ac.uk . The DNS matches IP and plain language names and addresses.
4. ICANN defines itself as: 'an internationally organized, non-profit corporation that has responsibility for Internet Protocol (IP) address space allocation, protocol identifier assignment,

generic (gTLD) and country code (ccTLD) Top-Level Domain name system management, and root server system management functions. As a private-public partnership, ICANN is dedicated to preserving the operational stability of the Internet; to promoting competition; to achieving broad representation of global Internet communities; and to developing policy appropriate to its mission through bottom-up, consensus-based processes' (at http://www.icann.org/announcements/announcement-21nov05-2.htm accessed on 3.2.2006).

5. There is an abundant literature on ICANN and associated issues of Internet governance. Mueller (2002) provides a useful, critical, orientation. See also ICANN's well documented website at http://www.icann.org/ and in particular the section on international governance arrangements at http://www.icann.org/general/fact-sheet.html (both accessed on 8.2.2006).
6. There are two types of TLD, generic top level domains, (gTLD) such as .com or .net and country code top level domains (ccTLD) such as .uk and .de.
7. Interesting case include that of Niue (cc .nu), Terres Francaises Australes (cc .tf) Cocos Islands (cc .cc), Tuvalu (cc .tv). Enic, a Verisign company, administers .cc (and .tv) .tf was formerly administered by the UK company AdamsNames (which continues to act for the ccs .tc, .vg, .ms, .gs) and, after a request by France, redelegated to AFNIC, the registry for .fr and for French overseas territories and departments.
8. See Milton Mueller (1999, 2002) see Mueller's writings at http://istweb.syr.edu/~mueller/onlinepubs.htm; Michael Froomkin (2000) see Froomkin's home page at http://www.law.tm/; Susan Crawford (2004) see Crawford's writings at http://www.scrawford.net/page.php?display=writings See also http://www.icannwatch.org/ .
9. Brazil, China, South Africa and Syria were among the critical states at the WSIS and WGIG.
10. ICANN retains a so-called 'at large' system of representation and consultation to 'promote structured involvement and informed participation of the global individual Internet user community in ICANN' (from http://alac.icann.org/framework.htm accessed on 8.2.2006).
11. ICANN's GAC Operating Principles of April 2005 provide for the GAC to 'consider and provide advice on the activities of ICANN as they relate to concerns of governments and as they may affect public policy issues'. Cl 5. at http://gac.icann.org/web/home/GAC_Operating_Principles.doc accessed on 18.12.2006. ICANN's Bylaws state that the GAC is 'open to all national governments' and 'Distinct Economies as recognised in international fora' (ICANN Bylaws Article XI 2.1.b). They define a duty on the ICANN Board to advise the GAC of any 'proposal raising public policy issues', to 'take duly into account' GAC responses and when and if the Board does not follow GAC advice it must give reasons and seek a mutually acceptable solution (ICANN Bylaws Article XI 2.1.h).
12. Referring to WSIS Declaration of Principles at: http://www.itu.int/dms_pub/itu-s/md/03/wsis/doc/S03-WSIS-DOC-0004!!MSW-E.doc accessed on 1.2.2006.
13. Postal services are also coordinated through a UN agency, the Universal Postal Union.
14. Lynn mentioned the quintessentially 'Bellhead' ITU by name: 'The United Nations, the World Trade Organization, and the International Telecommunications Union are all complex and sometimes effective organizations within their respective realms; however, each model has deep and evident shortcomings which in the Internet environment would render it a worse alternative than a reformed ICANN'. See: http://www.icann.org/general/lynn-reform-proposal-24feb02.htm accessed on 18.12.2006.
15. An ICANN source, interviewed on 20.12.2006, stated that governments did not want to implement this proposal because of the difficulty of selecting five representatives.
16. Sometimes very general – one constituency from which a voting member of the Nominating Committee is to be drawn is specified as 'An entity designated by the Board to represent academic and similar organizations' (ICANN Bylaws of 28.2.2006 Article VII, Section 2.8.g.).

17. The WSIS was proposed at the 1998 ITU Plenipotentiary Conference and was approved by the UN General Assembly in 2001 in Resolution 56/183. The first summit meeting in Geneva 10 to 12 December was preceded by 3 'prep-coms' and followed by 3 further 'prep-coms' culminating in the second summit in Tunis, 16–18 November 2005. The Working Group on Internet Governance was established on 12.11.2004 under UN General Assembly Resolution 59/220 in response to request of the WSIS to the UN Secretary General. Resolution 59/220 had endorsed the WSIS Phase 1 Principles and Plan of Action and authorized establishment of the WGIG. WGIG meetings took place on 23–25 November 2004, 14-18 February 2005, 18-20 April 2005, 14–17 June 2005. Consultations on establishment of an Internet Governance Forum, one of the WSIS recommendations, took place on 16–17 February 2006. WGIG themes were foreshadowed in the ITU Plenipotentiary Conference in 2002 which led to ITU meetings on the topic of national Internet addresses (ccTLDs), e.g. the Workshop on Member States' experiences with ccTLD Geneva 3–4 March 2003 and the Workshop on Internet Governance Geneva 26–27 February 2004. Consultations on the establishment of WGIG followed in Geneva 20–21 September 2004 (ie after the first WSIS Summit).
18. I make this claim confidently but acknowledge it may be falsified because I have not been able to identify an authoritative list of UN summits. A response (e-mail reply from Sommereyns [sommereyns@un.org]) to my enquiry (2005) to the UN suggested research using the following sources: information about current conferences and past conferences at http://www.un.org/events/index.html; Special Sessions of the General Assembly at http://www.un.org/ga/documents/lispss.htm; Emergency Sessions at http://www.un.org/ga/documents/liemsps.htm . None of these sites identify a prior summit on a communication summit but the lists at these sites are not exhaustive (for example the 2000 Millennium Summit is not listed).
19. For examples see: http://www.itu.int/wsis/docs2/pc2/off6.html on 3.2.2006.
20. The ITU was founded 1865 as the International Telegraph Union, in 1932 it was renamed as the International Telecommunication Union. In 1947 the ITU became an agency of the United Nations. In 1997 the First memorandum of Understanding to restructure the Internet was published, in 1998 the decision to hold the World Summit on the Information Society was taken and in 1999 the ITU became a member of the Protocol Supporting Organization of ICANN (ICANN PSO). ITU membership comprises 189 Member states and around 900 Private/Sector Members.
21. This simple relationship was complicated by the existence of a small number of international telecommunication enterprises such as Cable and Wireless and ITT.
22. Now Chief Scientist Telstra Internet, Secretary of the APNIC Executive Council, member of the Internet Architecture Board, and an IETF-nominated member of the ICANN Protocol Support Council. Formerly, Huston served on the International Ad-Hoc Committee (IHAC), was Chair of the Internet Society (of which he was a founding trustee) and was a member of the IANA Transition Advisors Group (ITAG).
23. To a zero incremental cost if services such as Skype (see www.skype.com) are used.
24. For example, China demanded expulsion of civil society and business participants from small group negotiating sessions at the second, Tunis, WSIS and at the second WGIG (February 2005) Brazil argued that 'Governments not corporations represent the interests of their citizens' and Syria supported Brazil and stated 'public policy is the business of governments'. A member of the WGIG, William Drake (at a conference at the Oxford Internet Institute on 12.1.2004) claimed that much the same had taken place at the Geneva Summit, civil society organizations were, he said, 'kicked out' of several working groups' and 'there was total chaos, there were no rules'. Drake's contention is congruent with that in a posting on the WSIS related website hosted by the Heinrich

Boell-Stiftung which stated 'After the observers were able to participate in most of the working groups yesterday, a number of countries like China and Egypt complained that this was against the rules of procedure. They asked for the observers to be locked out of the working groups. This met fierce resistance by the EU, the US and others' (at http://www.worldsummit2003.de/de/web/446.htm accessed on 4.2.2006).

25. The Civil Society Declaration at http://www.wsis2005.org/wsis/documents/summit/WSIS-CS-Decl-25-2-04-en.pdf accessed on 2.3.2005. was characterized by Raboy 2004: 355 as 'a political document outlining a set of principles'. See www.worldsummit2003.de/en/nav/14.htm for an extensive collection of civil society documents and postings.

References

6, Perri and Jupp, B. (2001), *Divided by information? The 'Digital Divide' and the implications of the New Meritocracy,* London: Demos.

ABC [Audit Bureau of Circulation] (2009), at http://www.abc.org.uk/. Accessed 24 June 2009.

Aitken, R. (2007), *Can we trust the BBC?* London: Continuum.

Akdeniz, Y. (1999), 'Case analysis: Laurence Godfrey v. Demon Internet Limited', *Journal of Civil Liberties,* 4(2), 260–67 (July).

Alexa Internet (nd), *Top 500 Sites,* http://www.alexa.com/site/ds/top_sites?cc=GB&ts_mode=country&lang=none. Accessed on 29 December 2008.

Anheier, H. and Isar, Y. (eds.) (2008), *The cultural economy.* London: Sage.

Assises de l'audiovisuel (1989), *Assises europeennes de l'audiovisuel. Projet Eureka audiovisual,* Paris: Ministere des Affaires Étrangères, Republique Francaise and Commission of the European Communities.

Bakhshi, H (2006) *The plateau in cinema attendances and drop in video sales in the UK: the role of digital leisure substitutes,* http://www.ukfilmcouncil.org.uk/media/word/f/q/plateau.doc. Accessed on 2 December 2008.

Bakir, V. and Barlow, D. (eds.) (2007), *Communication in the age of suspicion.* Basingstoke: Palgrave.

Barabasi, A-L. (2002), *Linked: the new science of networks.* Cambridge MA: Perseus.

BARB [Broadcasters' Audience Research Board] (2006), *Annual shares of viewing 2005,* http://www.barb.co.uk/TVFACTS.cfm?fullstory=true&includepage=share&flag=tvfacts. Accessed on 1 April 2006.

Barber, B. (2004), *Global governance: malevolent or benevolent interdependence?* in S. Stern, and E. Seligmann (eds.) (2004) *The partnership principle. New forms of governance in the 21st Century.* London: Archtype, pp. 69–76.

Barlow, J. (1996), *Declaration of the independence of cyberspace,* http://www.eff.org/~barlow/Declaration-Final.html. Accessed on 6 August 2003.

Barry, A. (2001), *Political Machines. Governing a technological society,* London: Athlone.

Barua, A., Pinnell, J. Shutter, J. and Whinstone, A. (1999), *Measuring the Internet economy: An exploratory study.* Austin, or Research in Electronic Commerce. The University of Texas at Austin. http://ai.kaist.ac.kr/~jkim/cs492a/internet_economy-UT.pdf. Accessed on 16 June 2009.

Barzanti, R. (1990), 'Audiovisual opportunities in the single market', *MEDIA* 92, Newsletter of the MEDIA 92 Programme, September (Brussels), p. 1.

BBC (2004a), *Building public value.* London: BBC.

BBC (2004b), *The BBC's contribution to informed citizenship,* http://www.bbccharterreview.org.uk/pdf_documents/BBC_submission_informed.pdf. Accessed on 16 February 2006.

BBC (2005), *Annual report and accounts.* London: BBC.

BBC (2006a), *BBC/Reuters/Media Center Poll: Trust in the media,* http://news.bbc.co.uk/1/shared/bsp/hi/pdfs/02_05_06mediatrust.pdf . Accessed on 17 June 2009.

BBC (2006b), *Reporter's log: Internet Governance Forum,* http://news.bbc.co.uk/go/pr/fr/-/2/hi/technology/6105496.stm. Accessed on 2 November 2006.

BBC (2008a), *Annual report and accounts 2007–8*, http://downloads.bbc.co.uk/annualreport/pdf/bbc_ara_2008_exec.pdf . Accessed on 2 December 2008.
BBC (2008b), *Partners to bring broadband to the TV*, http://www.bbc.co.uk/pressoffice/pressreleases/stories/2008/12_december/11/partnership2.shtml. Accessed on 27 December 2008.
BBC (2009), *Safeguarding trust*, http://www.bbc.co.uk/safeguardingtrust/interactive/index.shtml. Accessed on 11 April 2009.
Beck, U. (1992), *Risk society: Towards a new modernity*. London: Sage.
Beckett, C. (2008a), *SuperMedia: Saving journalism so it can save the world*. Oxford: Wiley.
Beckett, C. (2008b), *SuperMedia: the future as 'networked journalism'*, http://www.opendemocracy.net/article/supermedia-the-networked-journalism-future. Accessed on 11 April 2009.
Bell, D. (1973), *The Coming of the post-industrial Society*. New York: Basic Books.
Benner, T. and Witte, J.M. (2004), 'Everybody's business: Accountability, partnerships, and the future of global governance', in S. Stern, and E. Seligmann (eds.) (2004) *The partnership principle. New forms of governance in the 21st century*. London: Archtype, pp. 36–47.
Blainey, G. (1966), *The tyranny of distance*. Melbourne: Sun Books.
Bloom, M. (2003), *Key challenges in enforcing the Competition Act*, http://www.oft.gov.uk/NR/rdonlyres/eqk5haiytdrw6i4gegssbqpkanoop3qbbnf2cm2k3iag6mxbkdc5rz6lh2w2oucmdofj5bbtsh26a5u6hvklqw7e4xb/Bloom+article.pdf. Accessed on 7 January 2004.
Boell-Stiftung, Heinrich (nd), *Discussion on summit declaration is proceeding*, http://www.worldsummit2003.de/de/web/446.htm. Accessed on 4 February 2006.
Bradshaw, P. (2007), *A model for the 21st century newsroom pt2:Distributed journalism*, http://onlinejournalismblog.com/2007/10/02/a-model-for-the-21st-century-newsroom-pt2-distributed-journalism/. Accessed 23 June 2009.
Brookes, M. (2004), *Watching alone. Social capital and public service broadcasting*. London: BBC/Work Foundation. http://www.workfoundation.net/Assets/PDFs/watching_alone.pdf. Accessed on 16 June 2008.
BSkyB (2008), *Interim management statement for the three months ending September 2008*, http://corporate.sky.com/documents/pdf/latest_results/interim_results_30_september_2008. Accessed on 2 December 2008.
Byron, T (2008) *Safer children in a digital world*. London: Department for Children, Schools and Families. http://www.dcsf.gov.uk/byronreview/pdfs/Final%20Report%20Bookmarked.pdf, Accessed on 11 April 2009.
CAIDA [Cooperative Association for Internet Data Analysis] (nd) *Data collection at CAIDA*, http://www.caida.org/data/. Accessed 23 June 2009.
Calcutt, D (1993), *Review of press self-regulation. Cm 2135*, London: HMSO.
Cammaerts, B. and Carpentier, N. (2004), *The unbearable lightness of full participation in a global context. WSIS and Civil Society Participation*, http://www.oii.ox.ac.uk/collaboration/seminars/20041210_Carpentier_Cammaerts_wsis_paper.pdf. Accessed on 2 March 2005.
Canada (1991) *Broadcasting Act*, 38-39 Elizabeth II.
CAP [Committee of Advertising Practice] (nd), http://www.cap.org.uk/cap/about/. Accessed on 24 February 2006.
Castells, M. (1996 and 2000), *The Rise of the network society*. Cambridge, MA; Oxford, UK: Blackwell.
Castells, M. (2001), *The Internet galaxy*. Oxford: OUP.
Castells, M. (2004a), *Informationalism, networks, and the network society: a theoretical blueprint*, http://annenberg.usc.edu/images/faculty/facpdfs/Informationalism.pdf accessed on 29 November 2006 (also in M Castells ed *The Network Society: a cross-cultural perspective*. Northampton MA. Edward Elgar.).
Castells, M (2004b), 'Power and politics in the network society'. Ralph Miliband Memorial Lecture. London School of Economics and Political Science, http://annenberg.usc.edu/images/faculty/facpdfs/Castells-LSE-lecture.pdf. Accessed on 2 November 2006.
CEC [Commission of the European Communities] (2002) *Commission Directive 2002/77/EC of 16 September 2002 on competition in the markets for electronic communication networks and services*. OJ L 249/21 17.9.2002.

Chalaby, J. (2002), 'Transnational television in Europe. The role of Pan-European channels', *European Journal of Communication*. V 17(2) pp. 183–203.

Channel 4 News (2009), *FactCheck*, http://www.channel4.com/news/factcheck/. Accessed 23 June 2009.

CIA [Central Intelligence Agency] (nd), *The world factbook*, https://www.cia.gov/library/publications/the-world-factbook/rankorder/2119rank.html. Accessed on 22 June 2009.

Civil Society@WSIS (2005), *Much more could have been achieved. Civil Society Statement on the World Summit on the Information Society*, http://www.worldsummit2003.de/download_en/WSIS-CS-summit-statement-rev1-23-12-2005-en.pdf. Accessed on 23 March 2006.

Coase, R. (1937), 'The nature of the firm', *Economica* 4 pp. 386–405.

Collins, R. (1993), 'The internationalization of the television program market: Media imperialism or international division of labor? The case of the United Kingdom', in E. Noam and J. Millonzi (eds.), *The International Market in Film and Television Programs*. Norwood, NJ: Ablex. pp. 125–46.

Collins, R. (1990), *Television: Policy and culture*, London: Unwin Hyman.

Collins, R. (1994), *Broadcasting and Audio-Visual Policy in the European Single Market*, London: John Libbey.

Collins, R. (1999), 'Media policy, national identity and citizenry in changing democratic societies: The UK and Canada compared', in R. Boyce (ed.), *The Communications Revolution at work: Canadian and British perspectives on the practical implications of the new information and communications technology* Montreal and Kingston: McGill-Queen's University Press, pp. 181–204.

Collins, R. (2002), *Media and identity in contemporary Europe. Consequences of global convergence*. Bristol: Intellect.

Collins, R. (2005), 'From monopolies, virtual monopolies and oligopolies to … what? Media policy and convergence in South Africa and the United Kingdom', in *South African Journal of Information and Communication*. N 5: 23-39, http://link.wits.ac.za/journal/j05-collins-convergence.pdf. Accessed on 11 April 2009.

Collins, R. (2006), 'Networks, markets and hierarchies. Governance and regulation of the UK Internet'. In *Parliamentary Affairs*. 59. 2006. 314-330. Reversioned as Chapter 3 in this volume.

Collins, R. (2007a), 'Rawls, Fraser, redistribution, recognition and The World Summit on the Information Society', In *International Journal of Communication* 1. 2007, pp. 1–23, http://ijoc.org/ojs/index.php/ijoc/article/view/51/16 and Chapter 8 in this volume.

Collins, R. (2007b), 'Trilateralism, legitimacy and the Working Group on Internet Government', In *Information Polity*. v 12 1–2. 2007, pp.15–28, and Chapter 9 in this volume.

Commonwealth of Australia (1989), *National agenda for a multicultural Australia* Canberra. AGPS: Department of the Prime Minster and Cabinet Office of Multicultural Affairs.

Compaine, B. (ed.) (2001), *The digital divide: Facing a crisis or creating a myth?* Cambridge MA: MIT Press.

Council of Europe (2003), *Declaration on freedom of communication on the Internet* (Strasbourg, 28.05.2003), http://www.coe.int/t/e/communication%5fand%5fresearch/press/news/2003/20030528_declaration.asp. Accessed on 8 August 2003.

Council of the European Communities (1989), *Directive on the co-ordination of certain provisions laid down by law, regulation or administrative action in member states concerning the pursuit of television broadcasting activities*. 89/552/EEC. OJ L 298 (17 October 1989). pp. 23–30.

Crawford, S. (2004), The ICANN experiment in *Cardozo Journal of International and Company Law* 12: 701-740. At http://www.scrawford.net/display/Crawford2.pdf . Accessed on 18 December 2006.

Crystal, D. (2001), *Language and the Internet*. Cambridge: Cambridge University Press.

Cukier, K. (nd), *Bandwidth colonialism? The implications of internet infrastructure on international e-commerce*, http://www.isoc.org/inet99/proceedings/1e/1e_2.htm. Accessed on 23 October 2006.

Curran, J. (2009 2009), 'Technology foretold', in N Fenton (ed.) *New media old news: Journalism and democracy in a digital age*. London: Sage.

Curzon-Price, T. (2008), Interview with author, 2 June 2008.

Cybergeography (nd), *Internet Traffic and Demographic Statistics* http://www.cybergeography.org/statistics.html. Accessed 23 June 2009.
Davies, G. (2005), 'The BBC and Public Value', In Helm et al. *Can the market deliver? Funding public service television in the digital age*, Eastleigh: John Libbey.
Davies, G et al (1999), *The future funding of the BBC: Report of the independent review panel*, London. Department of Culture, Media and Sport.
Davies, N. (2008), *Flat earth news*, London: Chatto and Windus.
Dawson, J. (nd), *BT Yahoo! Broadband – the US model lands in Europe*, http://www.ovum.com/go/content/018869.htm. Accessed on 4.8.2003
DeLong, B and M Froomkin (1999), *Speculative microeconomics for tomorrow's economy*, http://www.j-bradford-delong.net/OpEd/virtual/technet/spmicro.doc. Accessed on 11 April 2009.
Denton [T M Denton Consultants] (1999), *Netheads v Bellheads. Research into emerging policy issues in the development and deployment of internet protocols. Study for the department of industry contract U4525-9-0038.* Ottawa, http://www.tmdenton.com/pub/bellheads.pdf. Accessed on 28 January 2006.
Devoteam (2003), *Regulatory implications of the introduction of next generation networks and other new developments in electronic communications*, http://ec.europa.eu/information_society/policy/ecomm/doc/library/ext_studies/regulatory_implications_execsum.pdf . Accessed 23 June 2009.
Drake, W. (ed.) (2005), *Reforming internet governance. Perspectives from the Working Group on Internet Governance (WGIG)*, New York: United Nations Information and Communication Technologies Task Force, http://www.wgig.org/docs/book/WGIG_book.pdf . Accessed on 14 March 2006.
DTI [Department of Trade and Industry] (1998), *Our competitive future. Building the knowledge driven economy*, http://www.dti.gov.uk/comp/competitive/main.htm. Accessed on 6 August 2003.
DTI/DCMS [Department of Trade and Industry and Department of Culture, Media and Sport], 2002. *The Draft Communications Bill. The Policy*. Cm 5508-III, Norwich: The Stationary Office.
Dunleavy, P., Margetts, H., Bastow, S, and Tinkler, J. (2006), 'New public management is dead – long live digital-era governance', in *Journal of Public Administration Research and Theory*, 16. pp. 467–94.
Dutton, W. (2007), *Through the network (of networks) – the fifth estate*, http://ssrn.com/abstract=1134502. Accessed on 11 April 2009.
Dutton, W., di Gennaro, C. and Millwood Hargrave, A. (2005), *The Internet in Britain. The Oxford Internet Survey (OxIS) May 2005*, Oxford: Oxford Internet Institute.
Dutton, W.H. and Helsper, E. (2007), *Oxford Internet survey 2007 Report: The Internet in Britain*, Oxford: Oxford Internet Institute, www.oii.ox.ac.uk/microsites/oxis/publications.cfm. Accessed on 13 October 2008.
Dyke, G. (2003), *Richard Dunn memorial lecture* at the MediaGuardian Edinburgh International Television Festival, (24.8.2003), http://www.bbc.co.uk/pressoffice/speeches/stories/dyke_richard_dunn.shtml on 25.8.2003. Accessed 23 June 2009.
Dyson, E. (2001), *Governing freedom*, http://www.opendemocracy.net/debates/article-8-10-29.jsp. Accessed on 6 August 2003.
e-Envoy (2003) *Office of the e-Envoy*, http://archive.cabinetoffice.gov.uk/e-envoy/index-content.htm. Accessed on 18 December 2006.
Elstein, D. (2004), 'Building Public Value: a new definition of public service broadcasting?' *19th IEA Current Controversies Paper*. London: Institute of Economic Affairs, http://accessible.iea.org.uk/files/upld-news217pdf?.pdf. Accessed on 28 December 2008.
Elstein, D (2008), *That elusive Rusbridger cross*, http://www.opendemocracy.net/blog/elsteindavid_aol_com. Accessed on 4 December 2008.
Eurobarometer (2008), *E-communications household survey. Special Eurobarometer 293*. Brussels, European Commission, http://ec.europa.eu/public_opinion/archives/ebs/ebs_293_full_en.pdf. Accessed on 23 December 2008.
European Parliament (2000), *European Parliament resolution on the Commission communication to the Council and the European Parliament on 'The Organisation and Management of the Internet – International*

and European Policy Issues 1998-2000' (COM(2000) 202 – C5-0263/2000 – 2000/2140(COS)), http://europa.eu.int/ISPO/eif/InternetPoliciesSite/InternetGovernance/EPResolution15March2001.html. Accessed on 6 August 2003.

European Parliament and the Council of the European Union (1995), *Directive 95/46/EC of 24 October 1995 on the protection of individuals with regard to the processing of personal data and on the free movement of such data.* OJL 281/31 of 23 November 1995.

European Parliament and the Council (1997), 'Directive 97/36/EC of the European Parliament and of the Council of 30 June 1997 amending Council Directive 89/552/EEC on the coordination of certain provisions laid down by law, regulation or administrative action in Member States concerning the pursuit of television broadcasting activities'. *Official Journal* 202, 30/07/1997 P. 0060 – 0070, http://ec.europa.eu/avpolicy/reg/tvwf/index_en.htm. Accessed 23 June 2009.

European Parliament and the Council of the European Union (2000), 'Directive 2000/31/EC of 8 June 2000 on certain legal aspects of information society services in particular electronic commerce in the Internal Market', *OJL* 178/1 of 17 July 2000.

European Parliament and the Council of the European Union (2002a), 'Directive 2002/19/EC of 7 March 2002 on access to and interconnection of electronic communications networks and associated facilities', *OJL* 108/7 of 24 April 2002.

European Parliament and the Council of the European Union (2002b), 'Directive 2002/20/EC of 7 March 2002 on the authorisation of electronic communications networks and services', *OJL* 108/21 of 24 April 2002.

European Parliament and the Council of the European Union (2002c), 'Directive 2002/21/EC of 7 March 2002 on a common regulatory framework for electronic communications networks and services', *OJL* 108/33 of 24 April 2002.

European Parliament and the Council of the European Union (2002d), 'Directive 2002/22/EC of 7 March 2002 on universal service and users' rights relating to electronic communications networks and services', *OJL* 108/51 of 24 April 2002.

European Union (2006), *Internet Governance: Commission welcomes move towards full private-sector management by 2009.* Press Release IP/06/1297 of 2.10.2006 at http://europa.eu/rapid/pressReleasesAction.do?reference=IP/06/1297&format=HTML&aged=0&language=EN&guiLanguage=en. Accessed on 25 October 2006.

Fenton, B. (2008a)*ITV set to embark on second phase of cost-cutting,* http://www.ft.com/cms/s/0/f9e687e2-bceb-11dd-af5a-0000779fd18c.html?nclick_check=1. Accessed on 28 November 2008.

Fenton, B. (2008b) *Indy gets cosy with Daily Mail to cut costs,* http://www.ft.com/cms/s/0/935765ca-bd84-11dd-bba1-0000779fd18c.html. Accessed on 30 November 2008.

Fenton, B. (2009), Papers face unpalatable prospects for survival, http://www.ft.com/cms/s/0/a7ca49b2-bdb8-11dd-bba1-0000779fd18c.html. Accessed 30 November 2008.

Fenton, N. ed (2009) *New media old news: Journalism and democracy in a digital age.* London: Sage.

Foucault, M. (2002 [1978]), 'Governmentality' in J. D. Faubion (ed.) *Essential Works of Foucault 1954–1984.* v 3 London: Penguin, pp. 201–222.

Fraser, N. (1997), *Justice interruptus,* London: Routledge.

Fraser, N. (2000), 'Rethinking recognition', *New Left Review.* 3 May/June, pp. 107–120.

Fraser, N and A Honneth (2003), *Redistribution or recognition? A Political-Philosophical Exchange.* London: Verso.

Froomkin, A. M. (2000), 'Wrong turn in cyberspace: using ICANN to route around the APA and the Constitution', *Duke Law Journal* 50: pp. 17–184, http://personal.law.miami.edu/~froomkin/articles/icann.pdf. Accessed on 18 December 2006.

FT [Financial Times] (2006) *Telecommunications. A dynamic revolution.* By D *White in FT African Infrastructure Special Report. 20.11.2006,* http://www.ft.com/cms/s/1868125e-6e5f-11db-b5c4-0000779e2340,dwp_uuid=1f2588a0-765d-11db-8284-0000779e2340.html. Accessed on 21 November 2006.

Fukuyama, F. (1995), *Trust. the social virtues and the creation of prosperity,* New York: The Free Press.

GAC [ICANN Governmental Advisory Committee] (1999), Governmental Advisory Committee operating principles, http://www.icann.org/committees/gac/operating-principles-25may99.htm. Accessed on 29 January 2006.

Geist, M. (2001), *Fair.com? An examination of the allegations of systematic unfairness in the ICANN UDRP*, http://www.udrpinfo.com/resc/fair.pdf . Accessed on 6 August2003.

Gellner, E. (1983), *Nations and nationalism,* Oxford: Blackwell.

Gellner, E. (1998), *Language and solitude,* Cambridge: Cambridge University Press.

Giddens, A. (1990), *Consequences of modernity,* Cambridge: Polity.

Giddens, A (1998) *The Third Way. The Renewal of Social Democracy*, Cambridge: Polity.

Giddens, A. (1999), 'Risk and responsibility', *Modern Law Review* 62(1): 1–10.

Gillin, P. (2009), *Guild strategy undercut globe employees,* http://www.newspaperdeathwatch.com/. Accessed on 24 June 2009.

Giovanetti, E. (2000), *Interconnection, differentiation and bottlenecks in the Internet*, http://www.econ.cam.ac.uk/dae/repec/cam/pdf/wp0011.pdf. Accessed on 15 December 2003.

Giovanetti, E and C. Ristuccia (2003), *Estimating market power in the Internet backbone using Band-X data,* http://www.econ.cam.ac.uk/dae/repec/cam/pdf/cwpe0332.pdf. Accessed on 15 December 2003.

Glasius, M. and Kaldor, M. (2002), 'The state of global Civil Society before and after September 11' in M. Glasius, M. Kaldor and H. Anheier (eds.) *Global Civil Society*, Oxford: Oxford University Press, pp. 3–33.

Globescan (2006), BBC/Reuters/Media Center poll: Trust in the media, http://www.globescan.com/news_archives/bbcreut.html. Accessed 30 June 2009.

Golding, P. and Murdock, G. (2001), 'Digital divides: Communications policy and its contradictions', *New Economy* 8 (2), pp. 110–115.

Gore, A (1994), 'Plugged into the world's knowledge', *Financial Times* 19.9.1994: 22.

Graf, P. (2004), *Report of the independent review of BBC Online*, http://www.culture.gov.uk/reference_library/publications/4591.aspx. Accessed on 31 December 2008.

Graham, A. (1999), 'Broadcasting policy in the multimedia age', in A. Graham et al. *Public purposes in broadcasting*, Luton: University of Luton Press.

Graham, A. and Davies, G. (1997), *Broadcasting, society and policy in the multimedia age,* Luton: University of Luton Press.

Greenslade, R. (2007), *Why I'm saying farewell to the NUJ,* http://blogs.guardian.co.uk/greenslade/2007/10/why_im_saying_farewell_to_the.html. Accessed on 11 April 2009.

Grefenstette, G. and Nioche, J. (2000), *Estimation of English and non-English language use on the WWW,* http://arxiv.org/ftp/cs/papers/0006/0006032.pdf. Accessed on 8 April 2009.

Guardian (2009), *The Digital Archive*, http://archive.guardian.co.uk/Default/Skins/DigitalArchive/Client.asp?Skin=DigitalArchive&enter=true&AW=1224583557035&AppName=2. Accessed 20 January 2009.

Guerra, G., Zizzo, D., Dutton, W. and Peltu, M. (2003), *Economics of trust in the information economy: Issues of identity, privacy and security.* Oxford: OII Research Report N 1, http://www.oii.ox.ac.uk/research/project.cfm?id=5. Accessed on 11 April 2009.

Hall, J. and Jarvie, I. (eds.) (1992), *Transition to modernity. Essays on power, wealth and belief,* Cambridge: Cambridge University Press.

Hansard(1982), *Satellite and cable broadcasting,* http://hansard.millbanksystems.com/commons/1982/apr/20/satellite-and-cable-broadcasting. Accessed on 7.12.2008.

Hansard (2008), *Uncorrected transcript of oral evidence to be published as HC 938 House Of Commons minutes of evidence taken before Culture, Media And Sport Committee,* http://www.publications.parliament.uk/pa/cm200708/cmselect/cmcumeds/uc938/uc93802.htm. Accessed on 17 December 2008.

Hans Bredow Institut (2006), *Final report. Study on co-regulation measures in the media sector,* http://ec.europa.eu/avpolicy/docs/library/studies/coregul/final_rep_en.pdf. Accessed on 16 June 2009.

Hargittai, E. (1999), 'Weaving the western web: Explaining differences in Internet connectivity among OECD Countries', *Telecommunications Policy.* 23. 10–11.pp. 701–18.

Hargittai, E. (nd). *The digital divide and what to do about it*, http://www.princeton.edu/~eszter/research/pubs/hargittai-digitaldivide.pdf. Accessed on 25 October 2006.
Hartz, L. (1964), *The founding of new societies: Studies in the history of the United States, Latin America, South Africa, Canada and Australia*, New York: Harcourt Brace and World.
Harvard University (nd), *Obituary: John Rawls*, http://www.policylibrary.com/rawls/. Accessed on 18 October 2006.
Hassan, A. (2005), 'Internet Governance: Strengths and Weaknesses from a Business Perspective', in W. Drake, (ed.) (2005), *Reforming Internet Governance. Perspectives from the Working Group on Internet Governance (WGIG)*, pp. 117–28.
Held, D. (2004) *Democratic accountability and political effectiveness from a cosmopolitan perspective.* Paper at the WZB/CARR Conference on Global Governance and the Role of non-State Actors. London School of Economics. 4–5 November 2004.
Held, D. and McGrew, A. (eds.) (2000), *Governing globalization: Power, authority and global governance*, Oxford: Blackwell.
Held, D. et al., (2005), *Debating globalization*, Cambridge: Polity.
Herbert, J. and Thurman, N. (2007), 'Paid content strategies for news websites. An empirical study of British newspapers' online business models', *Journalism Practice* 1.2 pp. 208–26. Also at http://www.city.ac.uk/journalism/download_files/business_models.pdf. Accessed on 5 December 2008.
Hewison, R. and Holden, J. (2004), *Challenge and change: HLF and cultural value. A report to the Heritage lottery fund*, London: Demos, http://www.hlf.org.uk/NR/rdonlyres/4A9BB4D0-CA7D-4372-92FE-38C85ED1EB20/667/DEMOS1.pdf . Accessed on 7 March 2006.
Hewson, C (2005), *Local and community television in the United Kingdom: A New beginning?* Sheffield and Lincoln: Community Media Association and University of Lincoln. Summary at http://web.archive.org/web/20051028204933/http://www.lancs.ac.uk/postgrad/hewsonc/report.pdf. Accessed on 30 June 2009.
Hilton (2007), Interview with author, 7 February 2007.
Hodgson, P. (2003), *Government, business and regulation. Has TV got news for you?* New Statesman Lecture 15.10.2003, http://www.itc.org.uk/latest_news/press_releases/release.asp?release_id=738. Accessed on 19 October 2003.
Hofmann, J. (2004), *Notes of IG caucus meeting in Geneva*, http://mailman.greennet.org.uk/public/lac/2004-September/002820.html. Accessed on 9 May 2005.
Home Office and the Scottish Executive (2005), *Consultation on the possession of extreme pornographic material.* London: Home Office, http://www.homeoffice.gov.uk/docs4/Consultation_Extreme_Pornographic_Material.pdf. Accessed on 2 September 2005.
Honderich, T. (1975), 'The Use of the basic proposition of a theory of Justice', *Mind*, vol. 84, pp. 63–78.
Honderich, T. (2001), *Philosopher. A Kind of Life*, London: Routledge.
Hooper, R. (2005), *Content regulation in the multiplatform multichannel digital age*, http://www.ofcom.org.uk/media/speeches/2005/08/hk. Accessed on 2 September 2005.
Hoskins, C. and Mirus, R. (1988), 'Reasons for the US domination of the international trade in television programmes', *Media Culture and Society*, vol. 10(4), pp. 499–516.
House of Lords (2008a) *The Ownership of the News.* Select Committee on Communications. 1st Report of Session 2007–08. Volume I: Report. HL Paper 122–I. London, TSO, http://www.publications.parliament.uk/pa/ld200708/ldselect/ldcomuni/122/122i.pdf accessed on 2.12.2008).
House of Lords (2008b), *Report of the Select Committee on Communications. The Ownership of the news.* 1st Report of Session 2007–08. HL Paper 122–II. London, TSO, http://www.publications.parliament.uk/pa/ld200708/ldselect/ldcomuni/122/12202.htm#evidence . Accessed on 26 March 2009.
Humphreys, P (2005), *The EU and audiovisual regulation: An agency for de-regulation or re-regulation - a research agenda,* Paper presented at the General Conference of the European Consortium for Political Research, Budapest, 8–10 September, 2005.
Huston, G (2002), *Telecommunications policy and the Internet*, http://www.isoc.org/oti/articles/1201/huston.html. Accessed on 29 January 2006.

Hutton, the Lord (2004), *Report of the inquiry into the circumstances surrounding the death of Dr David Kelly C.M.G.* HC 247. London, http://www.the-hutton-inquiry.org.uk/content/report/index.htm. Accessed on 29 March 2005.

IAB/PWC (2008), *UK Internet advertising expenditure grows 38% year on year to reach £2.8 billion in 2007,* http://www.iabuk.net/en/1/pwcadspendstudy080408.mxs. Accessed on 10 December 2008.

ICANN (2000), *Report on TLD Applications: Application of the August 15 criteria to each category or group,* http://www.icann.org/en/tlds/report/report-iiib1b-09nov00.htm. Accessed 11 April 2009.

ICANN (2006a), *Inaugural meeting IGF chairman's summing up,* http://www.intgovforum.org/IGF-SummingUp2-021106am.txt. Accessed on 18 December 2006.

ICANN (2006b), *New agreement means greater independence in managing the Internet's system of unique identifiers,* http://www.igfgreece2006.gr/. Accessed on 24 October 2006.

IETF [Internet Engineering Task Force] (2009), *The Tao of IETF: A novice's guide to the Internet Engineering Task Force,* http://www.ietf.org/tao.html. Accessed on 1 April 2006.

IETF [Internet Engineering Task Force] (nd), *Network working group request for comments: 3160,* http://www.ietf.org/rfc/rfc3160.txt. Accessed on 22 June 2009.

IGF [Internet Governance Forum] (2006a), *IGF Greece 2006,* http://www.igfgreece2006.gr/. Accessed on 24 October 2006.

IGF [*Internet Governance Forum*] (2006b), *Comments to the 'Programme Outline' document Brazilian position paper – 19 August 2006,* http://intgovforum.org/Substantive_1st_IGF/Brazilian%20Position.doc. Accessed on 26 October 2006.

Indymedia UK (nda), *IMC UK editorial guidelines,* http://www.indymedia.org.uk/en/static/editorial.html. Accessed 30 June 2009.

Indymedia UK (ndb), *Independent media grassroots projects,* http://www.indymedia.org.uk/en/static/about_us.html. Accessed 30 June 2009.

Internet Traffic Report (nd), http://www.internettrafficreport.com/main.htm. Accessed on 23 October 2006.

Internet World Stats (nd), *World Internet usage and population statistics,* http://www.internetworldstats.com/stats.htm. Accessed on 23 October 2006.

ISOC [Internet Society] (2004), *Annual report.* ISOC, http://www.isoc.org/isoc/reports/ar2004/ISOCar2004-08-09.pdf. Accessed on 22 March 2006.

ITN [Independent Television News] (2008), *ITN submission to Ofcom's Second PSB Review Phase 2: Preparing for the digital future,* http://www.ofcom.org.uk/consult/condocs/psb2_phase2/responses/ITN.pdf. Accessed on 16 June 2009.

ITU (nd), *Mobile cellular subscribers,* http://www.itu.int/ITU-D/icteye/Reporting/ShowReportFrame.aspx?ReportName=/WTI/CellularSubscribersPublic&RP_intYear=2005&RP_intLanguageID=1. Accessed on 30 November 2006.

ITU [International Telecommunications Union] (2004a), *Internet governance.* Geneva, ITU.

ITU (2004b), *ITU new initiatives programme 27–27 February 2004: Chairman's Report,* http://www.itu.int/osg/spu/forum/intgov04/workshop-internet-governance-chairmans-report.pdf. Accessed on 28 February 2006.

ITU (2009), *Measuring the information society.* Geneva. ITU, http://www.itu.int/ITU-D/ict/publications/idi/2009/material/IDI2009_w5.pdf . Accessed on 15 June 2009.

Jones, J. (2007), 'Branding trust: The ideology of making truth claims through interactive media', in V. Bakir and D. Barlow (eds.), *Communication in the age of suspicion,* Basingstoke: Palgrave, pp. 177–88.

Jowell, T. (2005), *Speech at the Royal Television Society 15.9.2005,* http://www.culture.gov.uk/reference_library/minister_speeches/2096.aspx. Accessed on 26 June 2009.

Kaldor, M, Anheier, H. and Glasius, M. (eds.) (2005a), *Global Civil Society 2004/5,* London: Sage.

Kaldor, M, Anheier, H. and Glasius, M. (eds.) (2005b), *Introduction* pp. 1–22 in Kaldor, M, H Anheier and M Glasius (eds) (2005), *Global Civil Society 2004/5,* London: Sage.

Kedourie, E. (1966), *Nationalism,* London: Hutchinson.

Keers, H. (2003), *BBC slated for free school software,* http://www.telegraph.co.uk/finance/2841031/BBC-slated-for-free-school-software.html. Accessed on 30 December 2008.

Keohane, R. and Nye, J. (1998), 'Power and interdependence in the information age', *Foreign Affairs* Sep/Oct. V 77 (5), pp. 81–95.

King, A. (2008), *The BBC trust impartiality report: BBC network news and current affairs coverage of the four UK Nations.* London: BBC, http://www.bbc.co.uk/bbctrust/assets/files/pdf/review_report_research/impartiality/uk_nations_impartiality.pdf. Accessed on 12 December 2008.

Kiss, J. (2007), *Web publishers are in bullish mood – but for how long?* At http://www.guardian.co.uk/media/2008/apr/07/pressandpublishing5. Accessed on 1 December 2008.

Kiss, J. (2008), *ABCe: Web traffic standards to be reviewed*, http://www.guardian.co.uk/media/2008/may/22/abcs.telegraphmediagroup. Accessed on 1 December 2008).

Kleeman, J. (2007), 'You couldn't make it up', '*times2*' on March 2nd 2007, http://women.timesonline.co.uk/tol/life_and_style/women/the_way_we_live/article1457697.ece. Accessed 7 March 2007.

Klein, H. (2004), 'Understanding WSIS: An institutional analysis of the UN World Summit on the Information Society', *Information Technologies and International Development.* V 1 N 3–4 Spring–Summer, pp. 3–13.

Kleinwaechter, W. (2004), 'Beyond ICANN v ITU?' *Gazette* 66: 3-4, pp. 233–251.

Komaitis, K. and Galloway, J. (2005), *Does the need for Internet Governance justify ICANN's Anticompetitive behaviour?* http://www.bileta.ac.uk/Document%20Library/1/Does%20the%20Need%20for%20Internet%20Governance%20Justify%20ICANN%E2%80%99s%20Anti-competitive%20Behaviour.pdf . Accessed on 3 February 2006.

KPMG (2003), *Summary of market impact assessment of BBC's online service. Final report. 24 June 2003* http://access.adobe.com/perl/convertPDF.pl?url = http://www.bbc.co.uk/info/policies/pdf/kpmg_exec_sum.pdf. Accessed on 8 December 2003.

Kymlicka, W. (1995), *Multicultural citizenship,* Oxford: Clarendon Press.

Lang, J. (1988), 'The Future of European film and television', *European Affairs,* vol. 2(1), pp. 12–20.

Lessig, L. (1999), *Code and other laws of cyberspace*, New York: Basic Books.

Lessig, L. (2001), *The future of ideas. The fate of the Commons in a Connected World*, New York: Random House.

Leyden, J. (2003), *Verisign's site finder is undead: All your typos are belong to us (Redux),* http://www.theregister.co.uk/content/6/33432.html. Accessed on 15 December 2003).

LINX (London Internet Exchange) (2003), *Memorandum of understanding. Version 7.5* 18.2.2003, London: LINX.

Lipset, S. and Schneider, W. (1983), *The confidence gap, business, labor and government in the public mind,* Baltimore: Johns Hopkins University Press.

Luhmann, N. (1979), *Trust and power,* Chichester: Wiley.

Luhmann, N. (1988), 'Familiarity, Confidence, Trust: Problems and Alternatives', in D. Gambetta (ed.), *Trust; making and breaking cooperative relations,* Oxford: Blackwell, pp. 94–107.

Lynn, S. (2002), *The case for reform,* President's report at http://www.icann.org/general/lynn-reform-proposal-24feb02.htm. Accessed 18 December 2006.

McIntosh, S. (2008), 'Collaboration, consensus and conflict', *Journalism Practice*, 2:2, pp. 197–211.

MacLean, D. (2004), *Internet governance: A grand collaboration,* New York: United Nations Department of Economic and Social Affairs, http://www.unicttaskforce.org/perl/documents.pl?id=1392. Accessed on 3 March 2005.

Maitland, D. (1984), *The missing link: Report of the Independent Commission for World-Wide Telecommunications Development*, Geneva: ITU.

Malter, R. (2001), *Global Indymedia 'Open Publishing' proposal,* cited in Platon and Deuze, (2003), http://archives.lists.indymedia.org/imc-proposals/2001-April/000003.html. Accessed on 11 April 2009.

Mansell, R. and Collins, B. (eds.) (2005), *Trust and crime in information societies,* Cheltenham: Edward Elgar.

Marlin-Bennett, R. (2001), 'ICANN and democracy: contradictions and possibilities', *Info*, 3.4 pp. 299–311.
Marquand, D. (1988), *The unprincipled society: New demands and old politics,* London: Jonathan Cape.
Marshall, C. (2008), Interview with author, 4 December 2008.
Martin, R. (1985), *Rawls and rights,* Lawrence: University of Kansas Press.
Marx, K. (1976) [1857-8] *Preface and introduction to a contribution to the critique of political economy.* Peking: Foreign Languages Press.
Meinecke, F. (1970) [1907]), *Cosmopolitanism and the national state,* Princeton, NJ: Princeton University Press.
Miller, D. (1989), *Market, state and community: The foundations of market socialism,* Oxford: Clarendon Press.
Miller, D. (1995), *On nationality,* Oxford: Clarendon Press.
Moeglin, P. (1991), 'Television et Europe', *Communication* vol. 12(2), pp. 13–51.
Moore, M. (2005), *Creating public value. Strategic management in government*, Cambridge MA: Harvard University Press.
Moran, M. (2003), *The British regulatory state. High modernism and hyper-innovation,* Oxford: OUP.
Morphett, T. (1989), *Television program standard 14: Australian content on commercial television*, Australian Broadcasting Tribunal IP/86/11A, November, North Sydney: Australian Broadcasting Tribunal.
Mueller, M. (1999), 'ICANN and Internet governance. Sorting through the debris of "self-regulation"', *Info* 1.6, pp. 497–520.
Mueller, M. (2002), *Ruling the root*, Cambridge, MA: MIT Press.
Mueller, M. (2005), *Comments of Dr. Milton Mueller, Professor, Syracuse University School of Information Studies, Principal, Internet Governance Project, and Chair, ICANN Noncommercial Users Constituency. RE: Domain Names Management (Cluster One B2 Assessment Report),* http://www.wgig.org/docs/Comments-Mueller-April.pdf . Accessed on 23 October 2006.
Nature (2005),'*Nature*'s comparative evaluation of the accuracy of Wikipedia and the '*Encyclopaedia Britannica*', *Nature* 438: 900–90.
Negroponte, N. (1995), *Being digital,* London: Hodder and Stoughton.
Nelson, P. (1970), 'Information and consumer behavior', *Journal of Political Economy* 78(2), pp. 311–29.
Newton, K. (1995), 'The mass media: fourth estate or fifth column?' in R. Pyper and L. Robins (eds.), *Governing the UK in the 1990s*, London: Macmillan, pp. 155–76.
Newton, K. (1999), 'Social and political trust in established democracies', in P. Norris (ed.), *Critical Citizens,* Oxford: Oxford University Press, pp. 169–87.
Nominet (nd), http://www.nominet.org.uk/. Accessed 23 June 2009.
Norris, P. (1996), 'Did television erode social capital? A reply to Putnam', *Political Science and Politics.* XXIX, 3, pp. 474–80.
Norris, P. Ed. (1999), *Critical citizens. Global support for democratic government,* Oxford: Oxford University Press.
Norris, P. (2001), *Digital divide: Civic engagement, information poverty, and the Internet worldwide,* Cambridge: Cambridge University Press.
Norris, P. (2002), 'Social capital and the news media', *The Harvard International Journal of Press/Politics.* 7, 1, pp. 3-8. And at http://ksghome.harvard.edu/~pnorris/Acrobat/Social%20capital%20&%20the%20news%20media.pdf . Accessed on 16 June 2008.
Nozick, R. (1974), *Anarchy, state and utopia,* New York: Basic Books.
NTIA [National Telecommunications and Information Administration] (1998), *Improvement of technical management of internet names and addresses.* Docket Number: 980212036-8146-02. Washington DC, United States Department of Commerce, http://www.ntia.doc.gov/ntiahome/domainname/022098fedreg.htm. Accessed on 19 December 2006.
O'Hara, K. and Shadbolt, N. (2005), 'Knowledge technologies and the semantic web', in R. Mansell and B. Collins (eds.), *Trust and Crime in Information Societies,* pp. 113–64.

O'Neill, O. (2002a), *A question of trust. The Reith Lectures 2002,* http://www.bbc.co.uk/radio4/reith2002/lectures.shtml. Accessed on 19 June 2007.

O' Neill, O. (2002b), *Autonomy and trust in bioethics*, Cambridge: Cambridge University Press.

O'Neill, O (2002c), *A question of trust. The BBC Reith Lectures 2002,* Cambridge: Cambridge University Press.

O' Neill, O. (2004a), 'Accuracy, independence and trust', in W. Runciman, (ed.), *Hutton and Butler in lifting the lid on the workings of power,* Oxford: Oxford University Press, pp. 89–109.

O'Neill, O. (2004b), *Rethinking freedom of the press,* Royal Irish Academy, Dublin (text provided to the author as personal communication).

O'Neill, O. (2005), 'Gerechtigkeit, Vertrauen und Zurechenbarkeit', in O. Neumaier, C. Sedmak and M. Zichy, (eds.) *Gerechtigkeit:Auf der Suche nach einem Gleichgewicht,* Frankfurt: Ontos Verlag, pp. 33–55.

O'Reilly, T. (2006), *Web 2.0 compact definition: Trying again,* http://radar.oreilly.com/archives/2006/12/web_20_compact.html. Accessed on 6 March 2007.

O'Siochru, S. and Girard, B, (2002), *Civil society participation in the World Summit on the Information Society; Issues and Principles,* Mimeo.

OECD [Organisation for Economic Co-operation and Development] (2001), *Report on OECD Workshop on Internet Traffic Exchange 2001,* http://www.oecd.org/dataoecd/43/55/1894684.pdf. Accessed on 15 December 2003.

OECD (2006), *Internet traffic exchange: Market developments and measurement of growth.* DSTI/ICCP/TISP(2005)11/FINAL 05 April 2006, http://www.oecd.org/dataoecd/25/54/36462170.pdf. Accessed on 23 October 2006.

Ofcom (nd) *The Ofcom broadcasting code,* http://www.ofcom.org.uk/tv/ifi/codes/bcode/bcode.pdf. Accessed on 16 June 2009.

Ofcom (2004), *Annual report 2003-04,* London: Ofcom.

Ofcom (2005), *News release of 23.6.2005,* http://www.ofcom.org.uk/media/news/2005/06/nr_20050623. Accessed on 5 September 2005.

Ofcom (2006), *Digital LOCAL – options for the future of local video content and interactive services,* London: Ofcom, http://www.ofcom.org.uk/tv/psb_review/digital_local/. Accessed on 28 February 2006.

Ofcom (2007), *New News, Future News:The challenges for television news after digital switch-over,* http://www.ofcom.org.uk/research/tv/reports/newnews/. Accessed on 26 November 2008.

Ofcom (2008a), *International market report,* London: Ofcom, http://www.ofcom.org.uk/research/cm/icmr08/. Accessed on 2 January 2009.

Ofcom (2008b), *Ofcom's second public service broadcasting review – Phase 2: preparing for the digital future,* http://www.ofcom.org.uk/consult/condocs/psb2_phase2/psb2_phase2.pdf. Accessed on 26 March 2009.

Ofcom (2008c), *Communications market report 2007,* London: Ofcom, http://www.ofcom.org.uk/research/cm/cmr07/ccm/ . Accessed on 2 December 2008.

Ofcom (2008d), *Ofcom fines the BBC for unfair conduct of viewer and listener competitions,* http://www.ofcom.org.uk/media/news/2008/07/nr_20080730. Accessed on 11 April 2009).

OFT [Office of Fair Trading] (2003), *Nominet UK and Scotnom Limited,* http://www.oft.gov.uk/shared_oft/ca98_case_closures/2003.pdf. Accessed on 26 June 2009.

Oftel (2001), *Effective competition review of Internet connectivity,* http://www.ofcom.org.uk/static/archive/Oftel/publications/internet/icmr0801.pdf. Accessed on 26.6.2009.

Oftel (2003a) *The UK Telecommunications Industry. Market Information 2001/2.* Formerly at http://www.oftel.gov.uk/publications/market_info/2003/ami0303.pdf. Accessed on 15.12.2003 [This text appears to be no longer available at the Ofcom Legacy Regulators website but is available at: http://web.archive.org/web/20030628095319/http://www.oftel.gov.uk/publications/market_info/2003/ami0303.pdf. Accessed on 26 June 2009]

Oftel (2003b), *Wholesale unmetered narrowband Internet termination services – UK excluding Hull area market,* http://www.ofcom.org.uk/legacy_regulators/oftel/narrowband_mkt_rvw/internet_term_uk_ex_hull.pdf . Accessed on 7 January 2004. [This text appears to be no longer available and appears not to be at the Ofcom Legacy Regulators website but is available at: http://web.archive.org/web/20040613110708/http://www.ofcom.org.uk/legacy_regulators/oftel/narrowband_mkt_rvw/internet_term_uk_ex_hull.pdf accessed on 26 June 2009].

Oftel (2003c), *Wholesale unmetered narrowband Internet termination services – Hull area market,* http://www.ofcom.org.uk/legacy_regulators/oftel/narrowband_mkt_rvw/internet_termin_hull_area.pdf. Accessed on 7 January 2004. [This text appears to be no longer available at the Ofcom Legacy Regulators website but is available at: http://web.archive.org/web/20040613085309/http://www.ofcom.org.uk/legacy_regulators/oftel/narrowband_mkt_rvw/internet_termin_hull_area.pdf accessed on 26 June 2009].

Oftel (2003d), *Review of the fixed narrowband wholesale exchange line, call origination, conveyance and transit markets, consultation – 17 March 2003,* http://www.oftel.gov.uk/publications/eu_directives/2003/eu_narrow/narrow2.htm#7. Accessed on 15 December 2003[This text appears to be no longer available and appears not to be at the Ofcom Legacy Regulators website but is available at: http://web.archive.org/web/20030408135232/http://www.oftel.gov.uk/publications/eu_directives/2003/eu_narrow/narrow2.htm accessed on 26 June 2009].

Oftel (2003e), *Oftel's Internet and broadband brief 10.12.2003,* http://www.ofcom.org.uk/legacy_regulators/oftel/oftel_internet_broadband_brief/?a=87101. Accessed on 7 January 2004. [This text appears to be no longer available and appears not to be at the Ofcom Legacy Regulators website but is available at: http://web.archive.org/web/20040612212055/http://www.ofcom.org.uk/legacy_regulators/oftel/oftel_internet_broadband_brief/?a=87101 accessed on 26 June 2009].

Oftel (2003f), *Internet and broadband brief* of September 2003, http://www.ofcom.org.uk/static/archive/oftel/publications/internet/internet_brief/broad1003.pdf . Accessed on 17 June 2009).

OII (Oxford Internet Institute (nd), *Internet governance for development,* at http://webcast.oii.ox.ac.uk/?view=Webcast&ID=20060831_157. Accessed on 25 October 2006.

Olivier, L. (2009), *NUJ plans 'concerted campaign' against Johnston press cuts,* http://blogs.journalism.co.uk/editors/2008/08/13/nuj-plans-concerted-campaign-against-johnston-press-cuts/. Accessed 23 June 2009.

ONS [Office of National Statistics] (2005), *An aging and more diverse society.* News Release 22.3.2005, http://www.statistics.gov.uk/pdfdir/sot0305.pdf. Accessed on 2 September 2005.

ONS (2006) *Social trends 35.* Basingstoke: Palgrave Macmillan, http://www.statistics.gov.uk/downloads/theme_social/Social_Trends36/Social_Trends_36.pdf. Accessed on 20 December 2006.

OPSI [Office of Public Service Administration] (2000), *Postal Services Act 2000 Chapter 26,* http://www.opsi.gov.uk/acts/acts2000/20000026.htm. Accessed on 24 February 2006).

OPSI (2003), *Communications Act 2003 Chapter 21,* http://www.opsi.gov.uk/acts/acts2003/20030021.htm. Aaccessed on 24.2.2006).

Osborne, D. and Gaebler, T. (1992), *Reinventing Government,* Reading, MA: Addison Wesley.

OxIS [Oxford Internet Survey] (2007), *The Internet in Britain 2007,* Oxford: Oxford Internet Institute, www.oii.ox.ac.uk/research/oxis/OxIS2007_Report.pdf. Accessed on 11 April 2009.

Padovani, C. (2005), 'Thinking beyond Tunis: A multi-stakeholder monitoring initiative', *IAMCR Newsletter* 15.2 November, pp. 21–22.

Paltridge, S. (1998), *Internet traffic exchange: Developments and policy,* DSTI/ ICCP/TISP(98)1, Paris: OECD.

Parliament (2003), *Communications Act 2003,* Chapter 21.

Paterson, C. (2005), *News Agency Dominance in International News on the Internet,* http://ics.leeds.ac.uk/papers/cicr/exhibits/42/cicrpaterson.pdf. Accessed on 23 June 2009.

PCMLP [Programme in Comparative Media Law and Policy] (2004), *Self-regulation of digital media converging on the Internet: Industry Codes of Conduct in Sectoral Analysis. 30 April 2004.* http://pcmlp.socleg.ox.ac.uk/sites/pcmlp.socleg.ox.ac.uk/files/IAPCODEfinal.pdf. Accessed on 26 June 2009.

Peacock, A. (1986), *Report of the Committee on Financing the BBC*, [The Peacock Report], Cmnd 9824, London: HMSO.
Peneneberg, A. (2005), *Whither The Wall Street Journal?* http://www.wired.com/print/culture/lifestyle/news/2005/02/66697. Accessed on 12 May 2008.
Picard, R. (2003), 'Cash cows or entrecôte: Publishing companies and disruptive technologies', in *Trends In Communication* 11(2), pp. 127–36.
Plato (360 B.C.), *The seventh letter*, translated by J. Harward, http://classics.mit.edu/Plato/seventh_letter.html. Accessed 10 April 2009
Platon, S and Deuze, M. (2003), 'Indymedia journalism. A radical way of making, selecting and sharing news?' *Journalism*, 4(3) pp. 336–55
POLISMedia (2009), *The future of news seminars: Property and profit: independent online journalism*, http://www.polismedia.org/futureofnews.aspx. Accessed on 20 January 2009.
Ponsford, D. (2009), *Journalists in strike ballot over Trinity Mirror Midlands job cuts*, http://www.pressgazette.co.uk/story.asp?storycode=41972. Accessed on 30 September 2008
Porat, M. (1977), *The information economy: Definition & measurement*, Washington: US Dept. of Commerce Publication, 77-12(1).
Power, M. (1997), *The audit society: Rituals of verification*, Oxford: Oxford University Press.
Putnam, R. (1993), *Making democracy work: Civic traditions in modern Italy*, Princeton: Princeton University Press.
Putnam, R. (2000), *Bowling alone: The collapse and revival of American community*, New York: Simon & Schuster.
Raboy, M. (2004), 'The WSIS as a political space in global media governance', *Continuum* v 18. N 3 September, pp. 347–61.
RAJAR [Radio Joint Audience Research Limited] (2006), *Data release – quarter 3, 2006*, http://www.rajar.co.uk/content.php?page=news_data_release_2006_Q3. Accessed 30 June 2009.
Rawls, J. (1980), 'Kantian Constructivism in Moral Theory', *Journal of Philosophy*, vol. 77/9, pp. 515–72.
Rawls, J. (1999 [1971]), *A theory of justice* Oxford: Oxford University Press.
Reck, J. and Wood, B. (2003), *What Works: Vodacom's Community Services Phone Shops*, http://www.digitaldividend.org/pdf/vodacom.pdf. Accessed on 8 November 2006.
Reeskens, T. and Hooghe, M. (2008), 'Cross-cultural measurement equivalence of generalized trust. Evidence from the European Social Survey (2002 and 2004)', *Social Indicators Research* 85 pp. 515–32.
Riles, A. (2001), *The network inside out*, Ann Arbor: University of Michigan Press.
Rony, E. and Rony, P. (2002), *ICANN By-laws, then and now*, http://www.domainhandbook.com/archives/comp-icannbylaws.html. Accessed on 8 February 2006.
Rose, A. (2008), Interview in *EBU Technical Review 2008-Q4 p 4-17*, http://tech.ebu.ch/docs/techreview/trev_2008-Q4.pdf. Accessed on 31 December 2008.
Rousseau, J-J. (1953) *Political writings*, trans. and ed. F. Watkins, Edinburgh: Nelson.
Sabbagh, D. (2008), *Telegraph braced for 5 per cent job cuts*, November 24 2008, Times Online, http://business.timesonline.co.uk/tol/business/industry_sectors/media/article5225401.ece. Accessed on 26 November 2008.
SACOT [Scottish Advisory Committee on Telecommunications] (2003), *Promoting effective self-regulation. Criteria for transferring functions to co-regulatory bodies. Comments by the Scottish Advisory Committee on Telecommunications*, November, Edinburgh: SACOT.
Sandel, M. (1982 and 1997), *Liberalism and the limits of justice*, Cambridge: Cambridge University Press.
Sandel, M. (2005), *Public philosophy. Essays on morality and politics*, Cambridge MA: Harvard UP.
Scharpf, F.W. (1994), 'Games Real actors could play: Positive and negative co-ordination in embedded negotiations', *Journal of Theoretical Politics*, 6 (1), pp. 27–53.
Schiller, H. (1989), *Culture Inc: The corporate takeover of public expression*, New York: Oxford University Press.

Schonfeld, E. (2008), *Newspaper death spiral continues: Industry advertising contracts $5 bn so far this year*, http://www.techcrunch.com/2008/11/27/newspaper-death-spiral-continues-industry-advertising-contracts-5-billion-so-far-this-year/. Accessed on 3 December 2008.

Schulz, W. and Held, T. (eds.) (2008), *Mehr vertrauen in inhalte*, Berlin: Vistas, pp. 59–90.

Scotsman Archive (nd), http://archive.scotsman.com. Accessed on 20 January 2009.

Sennett, R. (1998), *The corrosion of character*, New York: Norton.

Shafer, J. (2006), *Chronicle of the Newspaper Death Foretold. The newspaper industry knew it was doomed 30 years ago*, http://www.slate.com/id/2154678/. Accessed on 26 November 2008.

Shaw, D. (1976), 'Newspapers challenged as never before', *Los Angeles Times* Nov. 26, 1976, p. 1.

Slashdot (nd), *How does moderation work?* http://slashdot.org/faq/com-mod.shtml#cm600. Accessed 23 June 2009.

Smith, A. (1776), *An inquiry into the nature and causes of the wealth of nations*, http://www.econlib.org/library/Smith/smWN1.html. Accessed on 5 February 2004.

Smith, A. (1980), *Goodbye Gutenberg. The newspaper revolution of the 1980s*, New York: Oxford University Press.

Smith, A. (1991), *National identity*, London: Penguin.

Smith, A. (1995), *Nations and nationalism in a global era*, Cambridge: Polity.

Starr, S (2003), *Responsible' regulation*, http://www.spiked-online.com/Articles/00000006DE74.htm. Accessed on 8.8.2003.

Starr, S (2005), *Indecent proposals*, http://www.spiked-online.com/index.php?/site/article/730/. Accessed on 27 October 2006.

Stolle, D. (1998), 'Bowling together, bowling alone. The development of generalized trust in voluntary associations', *Political Psychology*, 19(3), pp. 497–526.

Stolle, D. and Hooghe, M. (2005), 'Inaccurate, exceptional, one-sided or irrelevant? The debate about the alleged decline of social capital and civic engagement in western societies', *British Journal of Political Science*, 35(1), pp. 149–68.

Strategy Unit (2002), *Electronic networks. Challenges for the next decade*, http://www.cabinetoffice.gov.uk/media/cabinetoffice/strategy/assets/su_electronic.pdf. Accessed on 26 June 2009.

Swift, J. (1704), *A tale of a tub*, http://www.lehigh.edu/~amsp/tubb9.html. Accessed on 11 November 2005.

Taylor, C. (1993), *Reconciling the solitudes. Essays on Canadian federalism and nationalism*, Montreal and Kingston: McGill-Queen's University Press.

Taylor, C. (1994), 'The politics of recognition' in A. Gutmann (ed.), *Multiculturalism. examining the politics of recognition*, Princeton, NJ: Princeton University Press, pp. 25–74.

Taylor, M. (2001), *The moment of complexity*, Chicago: University of Chicago Press.

Tessier, M. (2007), *La presse au défi du numérique*, Paris, Ministre de la Culture et de la Communication, www.culture.gouv.fr/culture/actualites/rapports/tessier/rapport-fev2007.pdf . Accessed on 2 June 2008.

Thompson, G. (2003), *Between hierarchies and markets. The logic and limits of network forms of organization*, Oxford: Oxford University Press.

Thompson, K. and Tunstall, J. (eds.) (1971), *Sociological perspectives*, Harmondsworth: Penguin.

TNO (forthcoming), *Evaluatie stimuleringsregeling bladen voor etnische en culturele minderheden en journalistieke internet informatieproducten*, Delft: TNO.

Trudeau, P. (1968), *Federalism and the French Canadians*, New York: St Martin's Press.

UK Film Council (2008), *Statistical yearbook*, London: UK Film Council, http://rsu.ukfilmcouncil.org.uk/. Accessed on 2 December 2008.

UN [United Nations] (2002), *Strengthening of the United Nations: an agenda for further change, Report of the Secretary-General General Assembly A/57/387*, New York: United Nations.

UN (2004a), *We the peoples: civil society, the United Nations and global governance. Report of the Panel of Eminent Persons on United Nations-Civil Society Relations. General Assembly. With note by the Secretary General and transmittal letter by the Chair.* A/58/817, New York: United Nations, http://www.wtis.org/DOCS/CardosoPanel2004.pdf. Accessed on 26.7.2009.

UN (2004b), *Report of the Secretary-General in response to the report of the Panel of Eminent Persons on United Nations-Civil Society Relations.* General Assembly A/59/354, New York: United Nations.

UN (2008), *Millenium development goals indicators*, http://unstats.un.org/unsd/mdg/Host.aspx?Content=Indicators/OfficialList.htm. Accessed on 18.10.2006.

UNCTAD [United Nations Conference on Trade and Development] (2008), *Creative Economy Report.* Geneva and New York: United Nations, www.unctad.org/en/docs/ditc20082cer_en.pdf. Accessed on 26 November 2008.

UNESCO (1998), *World Communication Report. The challenge of the new technologies,* Paris: UNESCO, http://unesdoc.unesco.org/images/0011/001112/111240e.pdf. Accessed on 26 November 2008.

UNESCO (1999), *World Communication and Information Report 1999-20,* Paris: http://unesdoc.unesco.org/images/0011/001112/111240e.pdf. Accessed on 26 November 2008, and UNESCO *List of boxes,* http://www.unesco.org/webworld/wcir/en/boxes.html. Accessed on 26 November 2008.

UNESCO (2005), *Defining E-Governance,* http://portal.unesco.org/ci/en/ev.php-URL_ID=4404&URL_DO=DO_TOPIC&URL_SECTION=201.html. Accessed on 29 November 2006.

UNPEPA [United Nations Division for Public Economics and Public Administration] (2003), *Benchmarking e-Government a perspective. Assessing the UN Member States,* New York: United Nations Division for Public Economics and Public Administration, http://unpan1.un.org/intradoc/groups/public/documents/UN/UNPAN021547.pdf. Accessed on 28.1.2006.

UNU-WIDER [The World Institute for Development Economics Research of the United Nations University] (2006), *The world distribution of household wealth.* http://www.wider.unu.edu/research/2006-2007/2006-2007-1/wider-wdhw-launch-5-12-2006/wider-wdhw-report-5-12-2006.pdf. Accessed on 5 December 2006.

USGAO [United States General Accounting Office] (2002), *Report Department of Commerce: Relationship with the Internet Corporation for Assigned Names and Numbers OGC-00-33R July 7 2000,* http://www.gao.gov/archive/2000/og00033r.pdf . Accessed on 13 October 2004.

Uslaner, E. (2002a), *The moral foundations of trust,* New York: Cambridge University Press.

Uslaner, E. (2002b), *The moral foundations of trust,* http://papers.ssrn.com/sol3/papers.cfm?abstract_id=824504#PaperDownload. Accessed on 16 June 2008.

Verhulst, S. (2001), *Public legitimacy. ICANN at the crossroads,* http://www.opendemocracy.net/media-internetgovernance/article_35.jsp. Accessed on 29 January 2006.

Vixie, P. (2003), *Internet governance,* http://www.caida.org/outreach/presentations/2003/lisa03/internet_governance.2003.pdf . Accessed on 14 Dcember 2003.

WAN [World Association of Newspapers] (2008), *World press trends,* http://www.wan-press.org/worldpresstrends/articles.php?id=18. Accessed on 26 November 2008).

Warnock, M. (1974), 'Accountability, responsibility – or both?' *Independent Broadcasting 2.* November, pp. 2–3.

Weber, M. (1964 [1922]), *The theory of social and economic organization,* New York: The Free Press.

Weigel, G. and Waldburger, D. (2004), *ICT4D – Connecting people for a better world,* Berne: Swiss Agency for Development and Cooperation (SDC).

Weinberg, J. (2000), 'ICANN and the problem of legitimacy', *Duke Law Journal* 50, pp. 187–260.

Werbach, K. (1997), *Digital tornado: The Internet and telecommunications policy,* Washington DC: FCC, http://www.fcc.gov/Bureaus/OPP/working_papers/oppwp29.pdf. Accessed on 11 April 2009.

WGIG [Working Group on Internet Governance] (2005), *Report of the Working Group on Internet Governance. Château de Bossey,* http://www.wgig.org/docs/WGIGREPORT.doc. Accessed on 8.2.2006.

WGIG (nd), *The Working group,* http://www.wgig.org/members.html. Accessed on 2 February 2006.

Wikipedia (nd), *Statistics,* http://en.wikipedia.org/wiki/Wikipedia:Statistics accessed on 8 April 2009.

Williamson, O. and Winter, S, (eds.) (1991), *The nature of the firm,* New York: Oxford University Press.

Wilson, E. (2005), 'What is Internet Governance and where does it come from?' the *Journal of Public Policy,* 2005. 25, pp. 29–50.

Wolff, M. (1998), *Burn rate*, New York: Touchstone.

WSIS [World Summit on the Information Society] (2001), *Resolution adopted by the general assembly 2001*, http://www.itu.int/wsis/docs/background/resolutions/56_183_unga_2002.pdf. Accessed on 2 March 2005.

WSIS (2003), *Declaration of principles*, http://www.itu.int/dms_pub/itu-s/md/03/wsis/doc/S03-WSIS-DOC-0004!!MSW-E.doc. Accessed on 1 February 2006.

WSIS (2004), *The Report of the task force on financial mechanisms for ICT for Development*, http://www.itu.int/wsis/tffm/final-report.pdf on 26.6.2009.

WSIS (2005a), *The Tunis agenda*, http://www.itu.int/wsis/docs2/tunis/off/6rev1.html. Accessed 26 June 2009.

WSIS (2005b), *Preliminary report on the WSIS stocktaking*, http://www.itu.int/wsis/docs2/pc2/off6.html. Accessed on 3 February 2006.

WSIS (nd), *Summit newsroom*, http://www.itu.int/wsis/geneva/newsroom/index.html. Accessed on 20.3.2006.

YouGov (nd), http://www.yougov.com/uk/ accessed on 11.6.2008.

Yoshio, U. (2006), 'Toward a bright future', *New Breeze Quarterly of the ITU Association of Japan*. V 18 N1 Winter, pp. 4–6.

Zakon, R. (2003), *Hobbes' Internet timeline v6.0*, www.zakon.org/robert/internet/timeline. Accessed on 7 August 2003.

Zhang, W. and Chia, S. (2006), 'The effects of mass media use and social capital on civic and political participation', *Communication Studies*, 57, 3, pp. 277–97.

Additional website references

http://about.reuters.com/aboutus/editorial/independence.asp

http://alac.icann.org/framework.htm

http://www.ard-zdf-onlinestudie.de http://www.asa.org.uk/ASA_2004_rebuild/ASAAppBase/AnnualReport2004/cap_introreview.shtml

http://www.asa.org.uk/asa/adjudications/Public/TF_ADJ_45583.htm

http://www.bbc.co.uk/a-z/

http://www.bbc.co.uk/bbctrust/news/press_releases/2007/ofcom_blue_peter.html

http://www.bbc.co.uk/bbctrust/framework/public_value_test/decisions.html

http://news.bbc.co.uk/1/hi/technology/6379621.stm

http://www.bbc.co.uk/bbctrust/news/press_releases/2008/local_video_prov.html

http://www.bbc.co.uk/bbctrust/assets/files/pdf/consult/decisions/on_demand/decision.pdf

http://www.bbc.co.uk/blogs/bbcinternet/2007/12/brandons_history_of_bbc_on_the_2.html

http://blogs.guardian.co.uk/greenslade

http://blogs.zdnet.com/Ou/?p=152

http://www.caida.org/data/

http://www.channel4.com/about4/pdf/c4response_cbb_review.pdf

http://www.channel4.com/news/articles/arts_entertainment/books/why+flat+earth+news+falls+flat/2038147

https://www.cia.gov/library/publications/the-world-factbook/rankorder/2119rank.html

http://www.competition-commission.org.uk/inquiries/ref2008/kangaroo/pdf/notice_provisional_findings.pdf

http://www.contractoruk.com/004150.html

http://www.concurringopinions.com/archives/2006/01/wikipeding_cong.html

http://www.cybergeography.org/statistics.html

http://www.cyber-rights.org

http://en.wikipedia.org/wiki/Web_2

http://en.wikipedia.org/wiki/Klingon_language

http://ec.europa.eu/community_law/state_aids/comp-2003/n037-03.pdf
http://ec.europa.eu/information_society/media_taskforce/pluralism/study/index_en.htm
http://ec.europa.eu/avpolicy/reg/avms/index_en.htm
http://ec.europa.eu/information_society/media_taskforce/doc/pluralism/pfr_report.pdf
http://ec.europa.eu/information_society/eeurope/i2010/docs/studies/interactive_content_ec2006_final_report.pdf
http://www.francophonie.org/oif/membres.cfm
http://gac.icann.org/web/home/GAC_Operating_Principles.doc
http://www.ifra.com
http://www.grameenphone.com/index.php?id=398
http://www.guardian.co.uk/media/table/2008/nov/07/abcs-pressandpublishing
http://www.guardian.co.uk/media/2008/may/22/abcs.telegraphmediagroup
http://hansard.millbanksystems.com/commons/1982/apr/20/satellite-and-cable-broadcasting
http://www.icann.org/
http://www.icann.org/general/fact-sheet.html
http://www.icann.org/announcements/announcement-21nov05-2.htm
http://www.icann.org/general/JPA-29sep06.pdf
http://www.icann.org/general/icann-mou-25nov98.htm
http://www.icann.org/general/amend2-jpamou-07sep00.htm
http://www.icra.org
http://www.indymedia.org.uk/en/static/mission.html
http://www.indymedia.org.uk/en/static/editorial.html
http://www.indymedia.org.uk/en/static/about_us.html
http://www.indymedia.org.uk/en/static/mission.html
http://intgovforum.org/Substantive_1st_IGF/Brazilian%20Position.doc
http://www.internetworldstats.com/stats1.htm
http://www.internetworldstats.com/stats.htm
http://www.icann.org/general/lynn-reform-proposal-24feb02.htm
http://www.interworldradio.net/about/mission.asp
http://www.itu.int/net/about/index.aspx
http://www.itu.int/wsis/docs2/pc2/off6.html
http://www.itu.int/wsis/geneva/newsroom/index.html
http://www.itu.int/dms_pub/itu-s/md/03/wsis/doc/S03-WSIS-DOC-0004!!MSW-E.doc
http://www.itu.int/aboutitu/overview/role-work.html
http://www.itu.int/ITU-D/icteye/Indicators/Indicators.aspx# accessed on 19.12.2006
http://www.itu.int/dms_pub/itu-s/md/03/wsis/doc/S03-WSIS-DOC-0004!!MSW-E.doc
http://www.itu.int/osg/spu/forum/intgov04/workshop-internet-governance-chairmans-report.pdf
http://www.iwf.org.uk/public/page.114.htm
http://www.iwf.org.uk/about/annual_report/annual2002.htm
http://www.iwf.org.uk/public/page.114.htm
http://www.journalism.co.uk/2/articles/531560.php
http://www.law.tm/
http://www.latimes.com/business/la-fi-tribune9-2008dec09,0,5273854.story
http://www.lse.ac.uk/collections/EUKidsOnline/Reports/WP2Germany.pdf
http://www.lse.ac.uk collections/EUKidsOnline/repository.htm
http://maps.google.co.uk/maps?ie=UTF-8&oe=UTF-8&hl=en&tab=wl&q=http://www.mediacenter.org/pages/mc/trust_in_media
http://www.mayorwatch.co.uk
http://www.nature.com/nature/journal/v438/n7070/full/438900a.html

http://www.newsombudsmen.org/what.htm
http://news.bbc.co.uk/go/pr/fr/-/2/hi/technology/6105496.stm
http://news.bbc.co.uk/1/hi/technology/6379621.stm
http://www.ofcom.org.uk/tv/obb/prog_cb/obb124/issue124.pdf
http://www.ofcom.org.uk/media/news/2008/05/nr_20080508
http://www.ofcom.org.uk/media/news/2008/07/nr_20080730
http://www.ofcom.org.uk/static/tvlicensing/cs/main.htm
http://www.ofcomwatch.co.uk
http://www.seomoz.org/dp/page-strength-faq
http://www.scrawford.net/page.php?display=writings See also http://www.icannwatch.org/ .
http://www.statistics.gov.uk/pdfdir/int0903.pdf
http://www.statistics.gov.uk/STATBASE/Expodata/Spreadsheets/D7678.xls
http://www.tno.nl/content.cfm?context=markten&content=publicatie&laag1=182&laag2=1&item_id=57
http://www.tvlicensing.co.uk/information/conditions.jsp
http://www.ukaop.org.uk
http://uk.reuters.com/article/tnBasicIndustries-SP/idUKLH33688320081017
https://rni.nic.in/
http://www.un.org/ga/documents/liemsps.htm
http://www.un.org/ga/documents/lispss.htm
http://www.un.org/events/index.html
http://unstats.un.org/unsd/mdg/Host.aspx?Content=Indicators/OfficialList.htm
http://www.yougov.com/archives/pdf/OMI050101003_2.pdf
http://webcast.oii.ox.ac.uk/?view=Webcast&ID=20060831_157
http://www.wgig.org/members.html
http://www.wgig.org/members.html
http://www.wgig.org/meeting-april.html
http://www.wgig.org/April-scriptmorning.html
http://www.wgig.org/meeting-april.html
http://www.wider.unu.edu/research/2006-2007/2006-2007-1/wider-wdhw-launch-5-12-2006/wider-wdhw-press-release-5-12-2006.pdf
http://www.wikipedia.org/
http://www.worldsummit2003.de/en/nav/14.htm
http://www.worldsummit2003.de/de/web/446.htm

Index